Which way is up?

R.W. CONNELL

Which way is up?

Essays on sex, class and culture

GEORGE ALLEN & UNWIN   SYDNEY LONDON BOSTON

© R.W. Connell 1983
This book is copyright under the Berne Convention. No
reproduction without permission. All rights reserved.

First published in 1983 by
George Allen & Unwin Australia Pty Ltd
8 Napier Street, North Sydney, NSW 2060 Australia

George Allen & Unwin (Publishers) Ltd
Park Lane, Hemel Hempstead, Herts HP2 4TE England

Allen & Unwin Inc.
9 Winchester Terrace, Winchester, Mass 01890 USA

National Library of Australia
Cataloguing-in-Publication entry:
Connell, R.W. (Robert William).
    Which way is up? Essays on sex, class and culture.

    Bibliography.
    Includes index.
    ISBN 0 86861 366 5.
    ISBN 0 86861 374 6 (pbk.).

    1. Social classes. I. Title.

305. 5'01
Library of Congress Catalog Card Number: 83-70678

Printed in Australia by Globe Press Pty Ltd

Contents

Preface

This is a book of essays about social theory. More exactly, it is an attempt to unravel some troublesome issues that have come up in recent attempts to understand class, patriarchy and culture. If the kind of approach suggested here is sound, the book may help people engaged in quite a range of political and intellectual struggles to develop a better analysis of structures of power and the process of liberation.

The title is not facetious, though I will admit it first occurred to me as a one–line review of a particularly obscure (though extremely distinguished) theorist, and has come to mind quite often while reading his successors. Social theory itself has to be about such questions.

The business of theory is to help us think clearly, and see what is difficult to see. In social analysis, the forces and relationships we are trying to understand themselves create systematic obstacles to understanding. Governments and companies lie and suppress information as a matter of course; information, when let out, is often distorted and sometimes invented; dominant groups shape the words we have to talk with, the concepts we have to think with. Our mass media are a sea of manipulative fantasy and half–truths. Such basic facts as unemployment statistics are currently among the chief works of imaginative fiction in the western world.

To establish the most elementary truths about social life, then, is no elementary business. It often involves a deliberate and sustained effort of criticism and synthesis. This is what social science should be helping people to do.

But social science doesn't provide an easy solution. Its authors are not exactly immune from their environment. Here too are histories, pressures and interests that produce mystification, dogmatism, and the defence of privilege. Social theory itself has to be taken critically, tested, and where necessary re–worked. That is the main business of the essays in this book.

They do not grow from a single starting–point, or from a well–defined system. Most of them began when I came across some body of writing about a problem I was concerned with, found it persuasive or at least interesting, but gradually came to see difficulties, and tried to sort them out. Working through and beyond them has been a slow business, often erratic. What is offered here is theory–making in process, more emphatically than most books of theory are, or at least claim to be. I don't hope to have the right answers. I do hope to have identified some of the right directions to move, and hope to get feedback from other people concerned with the same issues.

For all this, the essays have a common approach, a concern with practice as a way to the understanding of power and liberation; and in bringing them together I am trying to make propaganda for this conception of good theory. I am also hoping to reticulate ideas. Debate about a particular problem often stays in a restricted circuit simply because the channels to other audiences are closed, even though it may have important news for them. That is often not a matter of deliberate censorship—simply the sense that editors, conference organisers and other gatekeepers have of what's appropriate to say to a given audience and who's appropriate to say it. It would be nice if this book helped some fences to sag.

Each essay has an introductory note sketching its context and occasion. There are three parts, loosely defined by the themes of sex, class, and culture; loosely, because there is a lot of crossing and re–crossing, and three essays are explicitly about the relations between them. Within each section the essays are arranged in chronological order. (There is no need whatever to read them in that order.) In some cases, because they were addressed to different audiences, there was overlap. I have re–written to reduce this, to clarify and simplify the expression, and to take account of helpful criticisms of earlier versions.

About half have previously appeared as journal articles. I am grateful for permission to reprint:

- 'Doctor Freud and the course of history' *Arena* 47–8, 1977, pp.120–32.
  'Class, patriarchy, and Sartre's theory of practice' *Theory and Society* 11, 3, 1982, pp. 305-20.
  'Logic and politics in theories of class' *Australian and New Zealand Journal of Sociology* 13, 3, 1977, pp.203–11.
  'Complexities of fury leave ... A critique of the Althusserian approach to class' *Theory and Society* 8, 3, 1979, pp.303–45.
- 'On the wings of history' *Arena* 55, 1980, pp.32–55.
- 'The concept of role and what to do with it' *Australian and New Zealand Journal of Sociology* 15, 3, 1979, pp.7–17.
  'The glory of God and the permissible delectation of the spirit' *Bulletin of the Department of Organ and Church Music,* NSW State Conservatorium of Music, 3, 1977, pp.5–18.

Over the last decade I have been involved in several programmes of research, whose results are reported in *Ruling Class, Ruling Culture; Class Structure in Australian History; Making the Difference*, and *Ockers and Disco-maniacs*. To a considerable extent the papers in this book grapple with theoretical problems those projects raised; and the people with whom I worked, Terry Irving, Sandra Kessler, Gary Dowsett and Dean Ashenden, have had a large influence on their argument. A number of the papers, in their earlier lives, were discussed in conferences, seminars or classes, which are acknowledged in the relevant introductory notes. I have talked about these questions to a great many people in the course of the thirteen years they have been in gestation, and it would be impossible to recall everyone who helped. I have specific debts for ideas, criticisms and encouragement to Gill Bottomley, Teresa Brennan, Clare Burton, John Iremonger, Rosemary Pringle, Elizabeth Reid, Tim Rowse, David Rumsey and Peter van Sommers. Heather Williams has done the main work of design, typing, and circulation of these papers, as well as the typing of the book.

The editorial work was done by Pam Benton. That was only the final stage of an involvement with this work that goes back to its beginning. What is here, both in shape and substance, is the product of her patient conceptual criticism, impatient demand for realism, and acute sense of audience and style.

PART ONE

1
Dr Freud and the course of history

Every social scientist has an essay on Freud concealed somewhere about the person; this is mine. I first heard of Freud while I was at high school. I began to read some translations that were in my father's library, couldn't make them out, and asked him to explain. I have a vivid memory of him carefully expounding the id, the ego and the super-ego as we drove one rainy night along a street in North Sydney. With that beginning I could hardly go wrong! But after studying Freud's theories of development for a year or two as a psychology student, which got me interested in the case histories; and reading a swag of psychoanalytic interpretations of politics (ghastly stuff for the most part) while working on my Ph D; and browsing through Marcuse, as all good lefties did in the late 1960s, I had nothing much more to do with it until I was teaching sociology in the mid 1970s.

Two things brought an interest in psychoanalysis to a focus at that time. The women's movement and gay liberation had put questions of sexuality back on the political agenda. And my own attempts to reckon with the problem of hegemony in Australian life, the main product of which was *Ruling Class, Ruling Culture*, also led me to think about the ways sexuality was connected with power. About this time, as the essay itself explains, there was something of a revival of interest in Freud among radical intellectuals. But what had been brought back from the dead was a mummy rather than the flesh and blood analyst: a peculiarly angular and dessicated Freud, refracted through Lacan and Althusser, stripped of his dynamics and insight—in short, made into part of the machinery of a mechanical social theory. I thought this was missing the point rather badly. Freud, taken critically, *is* important to social analysis, but it is a rather different Freud that we have to look for.

I had several goes at formulating these ideas about sexuality and social structure; this essay finally took shape in March 1977.

Every so often there is a Freud revival. We are having one now, and in rather unexpected quarters—among two groups that have been generally hostile to psychoanalysis in the past, the women's movement and marxist intellectuals. In the course of this revival there has been a notable insistence on going back to the texts of the master. I think the revival is entirely justified, and if anything has not yet fully realised the strength of Freud's analyses as a basis for a theory of oppression. And I agree it is necessary to go back to the original; not for the joy of archaeologising, but because—as Marcuse and Mitchell have both remarked in different contexts—it has typically been the most radical of Freud's insights that have been lost in the process of incorporating his work into mainstream psychology and sociology.

For reasons that will become evident, it is desirable to sketch some features of Freud's life and the development of his psychological work before turning to his own attempts at social analysis. The 'standard' life, by Ernest Jones, is particularly good on the interrelation of Freud's life with the development of his theory. Further useful background is provided by Mitchell's (1975) sketch of the Viennese cultural and intellectual milieu of Freud's time.

Freud was born in 1856, moved as a child to Vienna, and grew up in a liberal Jewish environment in the Hapsburg metropolis. He studied medicine at the University of Vienna, graduating in 1881 after delays partly caused by an involvement in biological research that brought him under the influence of the positivist movement in natural science. He entered private practice as a doctor, and after some struggles became known as a specialist in neurology, with a practice among the wealthier inhabitants that continued for most of his life. In the 1890s he focussed on the 'psycho–neuroses' and formulated a thesis of their sexual origins; then as a result of his self-analysis recognised the 'oedipus complex', and in 1899 in *The Interpretation of Dreams* published the early and decisive elements of psychoanalysis.

His theories of unconscious mental processes and the importance of sexual motivation were first received with indifference, then abuse; but a group of supporters gathered, congresses were held from 1909 on, and an international psychoanalytic association formed (1910).

Variant psychoanalytic theories rapidly sprang up (at this stage notably Jung's and Adler's), and a series of dissensions developed in the movement, which badly shook Freud. War and a severe cancer followed. After the war he was famous, though never completely accepted. He developed a structural theory of personality (the id, ego, and superego), and turned to what he called 'metapsychology', developing a dual theory of the instincts (erotic and destructive) and engaging in cultural, historical, biological and religious speculations. He lived through the rise of Austrian fascism, though when Hitler captured Austria he agreed to leave Vienna, and died in London in 1939.

Freud was a doctor, and constantly thought in terms of 'illness', 'symptom' and 'treatment'. In the realm of interpersonal relations this can obviously be repressive—psychoanalysis *can* be a technique of social control. Therefore one of the constant difficulties is disentangling his critical ideas from the language in which they were expressed. Though he distinguished psychology as a science from medicine as a practice, and saw most of his writings as scientific, his analyses are deeply rooted in the practice which gave him his material, i.e. his sustained analytic arguments with his patients. This gives a peculiar concreteness to even his most grandiose speculations—they always refer back to a mass of clinical experiences—and gives a sharp edge to his methods of dissecting minds and analysing motives. This is in striking contrast to the treatment of such matters in the sociology and academic psychology of the time.

But if psychoanalytic practice was a strong lever to shift reality, it also placed limits on the type of reality that was shifted, and which became the basis of his theorising. I am thinking not so much of the limits of class, place and time implied by his Vienna practice. This has been much criticised, but was a point of which Freud was aware and which he rectified as far as he could by gathering comparative material. The important thing, rather, is that this imposed a perspective in which the individual person's transactions had to be the analytic focus and the source of concepts. His famous case history of 'Dora' (*Fragment of an Analysis of a Case of Hysteria*, 1905) is by any standards a brilliant reconstruction of hidden motives, a classic piece of psychological detective work; but I have to agree with Rieff:

> His entire interpretation of the case—and also his efforts to reindoctrinate Dora in more tolerable attitudes toward her own sex life—depends upon his limiting the case to Dora when, in fact, from the evidence he himself presents, it is the milieu in which she is constrained to live that is ill. (1963: 10)

This does not, as some critics have suggested, *prevent* Freud from

making social analyses; but it gives them a peculiar character, to
which I shall come back.

The basic concepts of classical psychoanalysis, which came out of
(and fed back into) this therapeutic practice, are well-known. I won't
try to expound them, merely mention those that are crucial to the
social analysis. Freud's own basic statements are *The Interpretation of
Dreams* (1899), *Three Essays on the Theory of Sexuality* (1905), and
the 'papers on metapsychology' of 1912–1915. An excellent summary
of his concepts, and the shifting usages of his technical terms, is now
available in a dictionary compiled by Laplanche and Pontalis (1973).

The central concept is that of the *dynamic unconscious*, a 'system of
mental activity' of which the person is unaware but which yet exerts a
powerful influence on her life. Intimately connected with this is the
concept of *repression*, the forcing of an impulse (or more exactly its
mental representations) into unconsciousness; this is central to
Freud's account of psychological development and his later structural
theory of personality. A number of concepts, such as symptom
formation, the dream–work, and parapraxis, refer to ways in which
unconscious impulses escape or evade repression. The *oedipus
complex* refers to the situation that develops at the end of early
childhood, where the child, whose sexuality is now becoming genital,
faces a crisis in emotional relations with its parents and has to shift or
transform the previous attachments to the parents and repress their
powerful sexual component. (It is notorious that 'his' is the
appropriate word, i.e. the theory of psychosexual development is
more fully worked out for boys, and Freud struggles to give an
adequate account of the matter for girls; nonetheless he seeks the key
in an analogous though differently–structured crisis in both sexes.)

This oedipal crisis is thought by Freud to be the node of all
psychosexual development, and difficulties in its resolution the roots
of later neuroses. In this the concept of *cathexis*, the attaching of an
impulse or its energy to a particular 'object', is essential. The impulses
are analysed as *instincts* (*'Trieb'* in German, ambiguously translated
as 'instinct', but also with the sense of 'drive', 'urge', 'growth',
'motive power'). Freud revised his theory of instincts several times,
but always held to the notion of their being mental forces with some
(as yet obscure) biological bases, and always insisted on the extreme
importance of sexual (interpreted broadly) instincts in mental life.

The development of these concepts, and their application to the
neuroses in clinical work, took something like twenty years, the
immensely creative middle period of Freud's life. He was into his
fifties before he turned, with this armamentarium, to any serious
social analysis. Even then, it seems to have been accidental—in part a
response to the developing splits in the psychoanalytic movement and

particularly Jung's heretical excursions into cultural analysis, in part a response to other psychological theories (e.g. Wundt's excursion into social psychology). This probably is the main reason for the oblique way he came at it, and the difficulty of many of the texts produced, which are often repetitive and scrappy. In general, the social was distinctly derivative in the structure of his thought; though towards the end he gave some hints of what can now be seen as a radical sociologising of psychoanalytic concepts.

There were, in Freud's own writings, two main streams of thought relating his psychoanalytic discoveries to social structure and history. The first, and much the better known, is represented by *Totem and Taboo* (1913), *Group Psychology and the Analysis of the Ego* (1921), and *The Future of an Illusion* (1927). I regard this work as fairly superficial and misleading, and will sketch it only briefly. The second, much more difficult, is a line of thought that appears in some papers of 1908 and 1915 and was never fully developed, though Freud worked at it in *Civilization and its Discontents* (1930) and in his fragmentary writings on the psychology of women. It springs from a deeper level in his psychoanalytic thinking and is, I think, incomparably more important in its sociological implications, however incompletely Freud himself saw them.

The works of the first group are based on analogies Freud thought he saw between situations and symbolic processes with which he was familiar in the analysis of neurotic patients, and a series of more or less unreliable observations in anthropology, social psychology, and comparative religion. The approach is clearly indicated in the sub-title of *Totem and Taboo*: 'Some Points of Agreement between the Mental Lives of Savages and Neurotics'. Once Freud gets on this track the analogies flow thick and fast. In that book he discovers similarities between the 'taboo' in non–western societies and the structure of obsessional neurosis; between animism in primitive religion and the mechanism of phobia (no doubt encouraged by having recently analysed animal phobias in the famous cases of 'Little Hans' and the 'Rat Man'); and between totemism and childhood identifications. The line of thought is summed up in the famous 'scientific myth' of the Primal Horde which draws together exogamy, totemism, the oedipus complex, and repression in a spectacular flight of fancy, whose verve has to be admired but which is theoretically worthless—perhaps worse than that, as it gives some credence to a notion of racial inheritance of the content of the unconscious. In *Group Psychology and the Analysis of the Ego*, which must rank among the worst of Freud's writings, the primal horde rides again and takes over social psychology via the supposed ubiquity of leaders.

The approach here is completely reductionist, and the reduction is uncontrolled by the self–criticism and weighing of clinical evidence which give force to Freud's equally daring speculations on other topics. It gave licence to his followers in no uncertain way, and in subsequent decades there was a rash of psychoanalysing of literature, history, politics, and other spheres of life which has given a deservedly bad name to psychoanalytic social theory. I need only mention the literature which attempted to explain fascism as essentially the product of a search for a father-figure. Still, this does some injustice to Freud himself—even in the grip of analogy, he was able to produce some acute observations, such as his notes on ambivalence in taboos.

The second line of thought, as I suggested, starts from a deeper level of psychoanalytic theory, from the concept of repression itself. Freud developed it in what may now appear a peculiar way, in a series of discussions of the problem of happiness and why it seems unattainable. Perhaps that was not surprising for a man who spent most of his time in psychiatric practice (he once gloomily remarked that the goal of his treatment was to allow patients to replace hysterical misery with common unhappiness), and who experienced war, dissension, and serious illness in the later part of his life. In the paper where he came closest to commentary on current politics ('Thoughts for the Times on War and Death', 1915) he remarked on 'our present sense of estrangement in this once lovely and congenial world', and there is definitely a darkening of outlook in the works that culminate in *Civilization and its Discontents*. (Again, the nuances are not quite given by the usual translation: Freud's title is *Das Unbehagen in der Kultur*—more literally, 'the malaise (or disquiet, discomfort) in civilisation'.)

In these works Freud comes to the view (which indeed was latent in the concept of repression from the start) that the barrier to happiness lies in civilisation itself—the social structure in which escape from natural misfortunes was sought. As he put it in the 1915 paper:

> Civilized society, which demands good conduct and does not trouble itself about the instinctual basis of this conduct, has thus won over to obedience a great many people who are not in this following their own natures. Encouraged by this process, society has allowed itself to be misled into tightening the moral standard to the greatest possible degree, and it has thus forced its members into a yet greater estrangement from their instinctual disposition. They are consequently subject to an unceasing suppression of instinct, and the resulting tension betrays itself in the most remarkable phenomena of reaction and compensation. In the domain of sexuality, where such suppression is most difficult to carry out, the result is seen in the reactive phenomena of neurotic disorders. (1915b: 284)

There are many implications in this deceptively straightforward passage. The very way the issue is posed betrays the deeply–buried libertarianism which made Freud an obscure ally of those groups which in his lifetime were most bitterly opposed to the bourgeois society he lived in and treated, the anarchists. Though ultra-respectable in his personal life, he was in a basic sense a partisan of the instincts. This can be seen in the analysis of Dora, in his barely–concealed suggestion that she should have given way to Herr K's seduction. And we have the parallel evidence of another famous patient, the 'Wolf Man', who appears to have trusted Freud because he was the only doctor who did not oppose his socially–unsuitable affair with a nurse he had met at a sanatorium (Gardiner, 1971). In the 1908 paper 'Civilized sexual morality and modern nervous illness' this spirit leads him to a remarkable psychological critique of marriage—another point of contact with the left—and to his first systematic formulation of the opposition of civilisation and the instincts, the 'piece of unconquerable nature', as he later put it, that lies at the root of the trouble.

A conflict between civilisation and nature is of course a traditional theme of western social thought—one recalls Rousseau and Burke, to take only two who happened to espouse opposite sides. Anthropologists have been able to find the same kind of antinomy between 'nature' and 'culture' in the thought of a range of non–western societies also. But Freud is not merely doing the rounds of antique philosophy. The clinical tools of psychoanalysis, especially the concept of repression, enable him to formulate the issue in a much more precise and complex way. In *Civilization and its Discontents* he argues a similarity 'between the process of civilization and the libidinal development of the individual', which is not just an analogy but a relation: 'civilization is built up upon a renunciation of instinct'. The 'renunciation' is not projected into a mythical past or a philosophical heaven, as in Rousseau's *The Social Contract* (and indeed *Totem and Taboo*); it is something which operates in every person's life in the process of psycho–sexual development, and takes effect at the level of the individual unconscious, through the mechanism of repression. Neurosis is a material, not a metaphorical, consequence of the social pressures on the person required by the advance of civilisation. The structure of the adult personality—naively presupposed in most libertarian thought—is *formed* by this pressure, principally by the way it is experienced by the young child in the family. The formation of the superego as a part of the psychic constitution of the person is itself a social mechanism. In Freud's striking simile:

> Civilization, therefore, obtains mastery over the individual's dangerous desire for aggression by weakening and disarming it and by setting up an agency within him to watch over it, like a garrison in a conquered city. (1930: 123-4)

But if 'nature' is thereby rendered partly social, so, conversely, the social is brought within the sphere of nature. Civilisation is not seen as something *external* to the events and processes of psychic life: it is seen as a product and extension of them. Its achievements represent a sublimation of the impulses that would, but for repression, find expression in a more raw and bloody fashion. In these later and more complex formulations Freud has shifted from a position that makes civilisation the *cause* of neurosis, to one—admittedly not clearly stated, but certainly implied—that sees civilisation as *continuous* with neurosis, as part of the same structure. And at this point, he expounds the important concept of a historical dynamic in repression:

> This conflict [of Eros and Thanatos] is set going as soon as men are faced with the task of living together. So long as the community assumes no other form than that of the family, the conflict is bound to express itself in the Oedipus complex, to establish the conscience and to create the first sense of guilt. When an attempt is made to widen the community, the same conflict is continued in forms which are dependent on the past; and it is strengthened and results in a further intensification of the sense of guilt... If civilization is a necessary course of development from the family to humanity as a whole, then ... there is inextricably bound up with it an increase of the sense of guilt, which will perhaps reach heights that the individual finds hard to tolerate. (1930: 132-3)

Which brings back the problem of unhappiness, and closes the circle, for him; but is precisely the point of departure, for others.

By the use of the technical concepts of psychoanalysis, Freud thus decomposed the age–old antinomy of nature and culture. He replaced it, most unexpectedly—it is certain that he did not himself see the theoretical significance of this—by the concept of a historical process. This process operates simultaneously at the macro–social and the individual level, in which human personalities and their troubles, as well as collective social achievements, are integrally produced.

There are two striking consequences of this. One is the possibility of a fundamental sociologising of psychoanalytic concepts (taking sociology to be continuous with history). The Oedipus complex can be seen as a product of a definite historical type of the family; repression itself as no abstract consequence of human relation in general, but taking definite form and intensity in specifiable historical contexts. This does not reduce psychoanalysis to sociology, any more than Freud's followers succeeded in the opposite attempt. But it does offer the possibility of a synthesis of a much more powerful kind than those theories which, for instance, have simply tacked a few psychodynamic notions such as 'identification' on to a sociology of social control. It makes possible a socially critical use of psychoanalysis, which is no longer the theory of an eternal contest between instinct and reality.

The second consequence, then, is disconcerting: we have at the same time lost the ground which the earlier theorising seemed to provide for a critique of civilisation. Once the partisan of the instincts, Freud now seems to have become, at least to an extent, a partisan of repression. He does make some metaphorical gestures towards civilisation as a process in the service of Eros, but these are feeble in comparison with the sharpness of his earlier formulations of the opposition between civilisation and impulse. (In fact I think he has, by a bit of fast footwork, come to think of socially–based repression as acting only against aggressive drives, which is plainly impossible given his analysis of the Oedipus complex.) When he remarks that 'the evolution of civilization may therefore be simply described as the struggle for life of the human species' (1930: 12) he is obviously writing in the spirit of Kropotkin's *Mutual Aid*, but he has also reached a position which offers no resistance to fascism. (It's all a matter of who defines 'civilisation'.) Marcuse, who was the first to see the full importance of Freud's sociologising of his concepts, tries to stop the rot at this point by reasserting the biological basis of the instincts, to find a standpoint outside history for the critique of historically–developed societies. But that is hardly adequate even to Freud's own conceptualisation.

There is a political problem with this step in Freud, because here the audacious development of his theorising has come into conflict with its roots. As I remarked earlier, Freud's concepts arose from a practice which made the individual person the subject of analysis and the effective actor. When he took these concepts into social analysis he applied them directly to the most general level, with no intermediate source of concepts, and thus set up theoretical relations between the individual and society (or civilisation) *as a whole*. Freud, above all other psychologists, saw the individual as a differentiated unit, internally divided, racked by ambivalence, packed to the ears with contradiction and strife. He utterly failed to see society in the same light. Like most other psychologists who have attempted to generalise their concepts into a social theory (G.H. Mead being a distinguished example), he operated with a consensual model of society, and saw repression as emanating from society as such. It appeared to him then that whatever level of repression existed, was necessary for that level of civilisation. Hence the melancholy 'no consolation' of the conclusion of *Civilization and its Discontents*.

In *Eros and Civilization* Marcuse offered an alternative to this pessimism from the viewpoint of philosophical marxism. He pointed out that Freud failed to distinguish the level of repression needed to sustain human society *per se*, from the level needed to sustain a system of social domination where one class controls and exploits another. This difference could, however, be analysed. Marcuse dubbed it 'surplus–repression', and held that it bore down mainly on the non–genital aspects of sexuality, narrowing spontaneous eroticism sharply to those bits of sex which were necessary to reproduce the workforce, or which could be repressively organised via commercial exploitation. Along these lines Freud's concepts can be developed, with remarkably little alteration, to deal with the psycho–sexual consequences of class exploitation, and even to formulate some of the reasons why it should be overthrown.

A very similar issue arises from Freud's arguments about the psychology of women; though, interestingly, neither he nor Marcuse attempted to relate this question to the macro–social analysis of repression. In *Psychoanalysis and Feminism* Mitchell has gathered, with exemplary patience, the many fragments in which Freud worked at this question, and has shown that they issue in a theory which is far from being the crude biologism sometimes attributed to him. I won't go over this theory in any detail, as Mitchell has done the job so well, but want to bring out the parallel with the problem stated by Marcuse. Here also, in a more specific case, Freud was dealing with the process of production of a psychic structure (i.e. 'femininity') as a series of contradictions between instinctual impulse and social barriers in the growth of the child. The barriers, as Freud saw them, were given within the family, notably in the marital relationship of the parents which the child had no real means of breaking into. This was true both for boys and for girls, though Freud gradually came to see the structure of the Oedipal crisis as differing for the two sexes.

What is striking is that here too, when formulating the social source of a pattern of repression, Freud adopted what amounted to a consensual social theory. As I have already remarked he was relatively libertarian in his attitude to sex, and in a number of his writings, such as the 1908 paper on 'civilized' sexual morality, he was sharply critical of the oppression of women in marriage and the oppressiveness of their upbringing for it. But this attitude did not enter his *theorising* of the production of women and men. In developing this argument he took for granted the conventional division of labour and the power structure of the patriarchal family. Thus a potentially very radical critique of patriarchy was aborted just as it was conceived.

There is a remarkable illustration in the case of Dora, one of Freud's most formidable opponents. In a striking passage—concealed in a footnote—Freud summarises the course of her life:

> Her declaration that she had been able to keep abreast with her brother up to the time of her first illness, but that after that she had fallen behind him in her studies, was in a certain sense also a 'screen–memory'. It was as though she had been a boy up till that moment, and had then become girlish for the first time. She had in truth been a wild creature; but after the

'asthma' she became quiet and well–behaved. That illness formed the boundary between two phases of her sexual life, of which the first was masculine in character, and the second feminine. (1905a: 82)

In short, Freud is saying that Dora became a woman, and a neurotic, at the same time. What he nearly says, but doesn't quite, is that they were the same thing. He gets even closer to this view in 'Some general remarks on hysterical attacks': 'In a whole number of cases the hysterical neurosis at puberty merely represents an excessive accentuation of the typical wave of repression which, by doing away with her masculine sexuality, allows the woman to emerge' (1909a: 234). And in *Three Essays on the Theory of Sexuality*, he connected this wave of repression with the 'greater proneness of women to neurosis and especially to hysteria' (1905b: 221). Regarding Dora it is hardly a speculation, given the material of his case report, to say that the neurosis was the means by which Dora lived the experience of becoming a woman in a profoundly sexist and oppressive environment. Even, to some extent, the means by which she resisted it—being successively betrayed, in her character as a woman, by the three people to whom she was most deeply attached. But Freud is firm on the necessity of the sexual division of labour and a corresponding object–choice and character formation, and his theoretical analysis breaks off. So did the case, since Dora walked out.

In several ways, then, the political meaning of Freud's analyses is vitiated by a failure to extend the same kind of thinking to the larger social structure that he applied to the psyche. No doubt one could find good reasons for this in Freud's own social position, as a man and a member of the professional bourgeoisie. But the important thing is that this potential is still present in psychoanalysis. Its concepts are inherently critical and subversive, and that is why they keep coming back despite all the efforts of what Marcuse (1955) called 'Freudian revisionism'. I would like to illustrate one of the lines along which its critical content can be developed, before returning to the general character of Freud's thought and its significance as method.

Presumably one reason why Dora broke off her analysis (since there was no overt conflict) was her sense that Freud was systematically subverting her own understanding of herself and her environment. Classical psychoanalysis, as a sample of transactions between people, is the most complete exercise imaginable in what Laing was later to call 'transpersonal invalidation'—a systematic course of argument by one person that what another person says about herself isn't really so. This was both a fundamental principle of method with Freud, and one of his important theoretical claims (for it is of course bound up with the concept of the dynamic unconscious). Far more radically than Descartes, Freud proceeded from a principle of universal doubt and distrust. Nothing that a patient said or did was to be taken at face value; everything was scrutinised for hidden meanings, and the hidden meanings themselves scrutinised for even more deeply hidden ones. Again a formulation from the case study of Dora:

> He that has eyes to see and ears to hear may convince himself that no mortal can keep a secret. If his lips are silent, he chatters with his fingertips; betrayal oozes out of him at every pore. And thus the task of making conscious the most hidden recesses of the mind is one which it is quite possible to accomplish (1905a: 77-8).

On the positive side, this led to an understanding of the phenomena in which Freud was interested as complex structures of meaning. Dreams and symptoms said one thing and meant another (more exactly, many other things). The process of psychoanalysis was in large part a process of exegesis. Freud's theories of dream and symptom formation can be interpreted as the grammar of a strange language, which may be applied in decoding 'communications' from patients.

This possibility was taken up by a number of psychiatric theorists in the 1950s and 1960s. Szasz's (1961) account of 'iconic communication' in hysterical symptom–formation, and more generally, Lacan's reinterpretation of Freud (Wilden, 1968), are two well–known examples. There is, however, a danger. If this hermeneutic element in Freud is divorced from the theory of motivation and the dialectic of instinct and social barrier, the concept of repression, and with it the critical force of the theory, are lost. This has happened, I think, in the 'linguistic' version of critical theory due to Habermas (1976: 95).

Given some theory about typical underlying motives—which Freud always had, though he changed it from time to time—the 'grammar' can obviously be extended much more widely. Freud duly extended it to the 'psychopathology of everyday life', slips of the tongue, small lapses of memory; and, in a number of essays, to art and literature. Here, unquestionably, the method of analogy had another field day, and Freud was quite capable of falling on his face—his well–known analysis of Leonardo is partly built on speculations about a document that happened to be wrongly translated. But there was rather more substance to this work than to his cross–cultural analogies; and anyway the significance of this line of thought can be based on the concept of the symptom alone.

The point is that we have here a way of showing how it is possible to live in a conflict–ridden and oppressive situation by a falsification of its meaning, the falsification becoming the 'reality' of conscious life. At the level of psychology, this is closely parallel to critical analyses that had been developed at the social level from quite different points of departure. The most important of these was the marxist analysis of ideology, which showed how the most respectably 'scientific' ideas about the economic life of European society, which had become the commonsense reality of much of the population, were in fact distortions which served to conceal exploitation. Like the symptom they could be decoded ('unmasked' was the more usual term) with the aid of theory to reveal the forces (here class interest) which produced them. The Freudian theory of the symptom and the dream thus flowed into a more general movement of thought, providing a wealth of detail, an intimate precision, to which the theory of ideology could not by itself aspire. The relations between them have occupied a number of theorists, and though I don't think they have been worked out very satisfactorily, the attempt is plainly important for an account of the working of oppression and the experience of the oppressed.

In trying to relate the psychological and social analyses of oppression, and especially the stabilisation of oppressive societies, there is a constant danger of falling into a position which supposes total oppression and total control. In psychological argument this is usually represented by some form of trait psychology, where an account is given of the formation of dominant, fixed character traits (e.g. 'passivity', 'authoritarianism') which are supposed to account for the quiescence of the oppressed. This must be avoided, both because it is a grossly inadequate account of the person, and because it obliterates in theory the sources of resistance. Oppression is *never* totally internalised. It always implies an expenditure of energy, a struggle.

And here the most general features of Freud's way of thinking about people become critically important. His theory is—as Osborn (1937) noted long ago in what is still one of the most impressive attempts to marry Freud and Marx—fundamentally dialectical, a theory of contradiction and transcendence. It is a psychology of impossible situations, where irresistible forces of lust and rage meet immovable obstacles of social relations and culture, and produce our lives as a result. It is a theory, in fact the only theory, that begins to account for the way oppressive situations are *lived* by the people in them, the way consciousness itself is distorted by psychological *force majeure*.

To come back to symptoms—I seem to have an obsession about them—I am impressed, in Freud's most persuasive analyses, both by the deviousness of their contradictory derivations, and by their extraordinary force, once established; by the solidity and constraining power of the mad internal world constructed by (and for) his patients. That is the kind of analysis we need also to give an account of the experienced solidity and constraining power of the most irrational, oppressive and dangerous social relations. And that is the basic political point of Freud. Not that we live in a world wholly composed of neurotic fantasies. We live in something much worse.

2
Men's bodies

This was written in London in September 1979, and shows some local influences, ranging from the English books I was then reading to the esoteric lore about canals. But its origins go further back, to some years of wrestling—in practice and in theory—with the implications of feminism for men. I have discussed the more practical side of this in 'Men and socialism' (in Evans and Reeves, 1982). It was clear there were also theoretical tasks: obviously one of the things men had to do was make a critical analysis of masculinity. But in doing that, one constantly came across the belief that masculinity was unproblematic because it was all settled by the constitution of the male body. Hence the subject of this essay.

It wasn't the first thing I had written about masculinity, just the first that has got to a shape where it could be given a public airing. The essay draws on two main sources of data. One is my own memories. The other is the life–histories of teenage boys I was writing at that time, with Dean Ashenden, Sandra Kessler, and Gary Dowsett, for the 'School, Home and Work' project, the results of which are now published in *Making the Difference* and *Ockers and Disco-maniacs*. To some extent the paper bounces off the 1970s literature about men, notably Tolson's *Limits of Masculinity*, by far the best of its genre; but its main theoretical point of departure (and criticism) is psychoanalysis.

The physical sense of maleness

In *Ways of Seeing* (1972) Berger remarks that the social presences of a woman and a man are different in kind. While women conventionally

have an image of attractiveness, men conventionally have a presence
dependent on the promise of power they embody. Berger treats this
essentially as a question of wealth and social prestige. But it is also,
quite literally, *embodiment*. In fact it only becomes an element of
masculinity, embedded in character, motive and sexuality, through
becoming an aspect of men's relationships with their bodies, and an
organising principle in social practices that crucially concern the body.

The significance of the body in the formation of masculinity has
mainly been discussed, under Freud's influence, as a question of the
psychological and symbolic importance of the penis. The key motive
involving the body's integrity, castration anxiety, is thought to
precipitate the oedipal crisis out of which the psychic structure of
masculinity emerges. I will come back to this, but I would like first to
take up the story at a later point, adolescence, and with something
more immediately obvious, the importance of sport.

Sport is, all considered, astonishingly important. It is the central
experience of the school years for many boys, and something which
even the most determined swots have to work out their attitude to.
What is learned by constant informal practice, and taught by formal
coaching, is for each sport a specific combination of force and skill.
Force, meaning the irresistible occupation of space; skill, meaning the
ability to operate on space or the objects in it (including other bodies).

The combination of the two is a power—meeting Weber's definition, the capacity to achieve ends even if opposed by others.
And at the same time it is a sensuous experience. I am not very good
at cricket, so it doesn't happen very often, but I am enormously exhilarated when I happen to hit a ball hard and with good timing,
even if it is caught. I can remember such shots years afterwards,
notably a hook that went over the boundary on the first bounce; the
recollection is no doubt reinforced by the fact that the ball ran up a
drain and stopped the game. I am almost equally exhilarated when,
bowling, a faster ball swings or cuts and beats the groping bat,
whether or not it takes a wicket (usually not).

Plainly this pleasure is also competitive: that magical ball has
overcome an opponent's skill. But that fact is more a way of
confirming that I have got it right, than skill at the technique is a
means for putting some unfortunate down. So the desire for force and
skill can be strong even when a person isn't much of a competitor,
which is probably true of most boys. At school matches it is
commonly the parents and teachers, yelling from the sidelines, who
insist on the element of competition, on the importance of winning;
thereby jacking up the level of anxiety about the whole performance.

This, of course, happens much more at football, where the issue is
explicitly a violent confrontation with another body. This is clear in

the reactions of Australian Rules crowds at league games in
Melbourne. A deft bit of passing, an accurate kick, is cheered by that
side's supporters; but the jarring collision of two ruckmen at speed
draws gasps and roars from the whole crowd. Among adolescent
football players, pure brawn is respected, but not wholly admired.
On the other hand pure cleverness is admired, but slightly con-
descendingly (a 'tricky winger', etc.), in much the same way as
the joker in a group of male friends. So one wants to be big, or at least
strong, as well as fast and adept. Players develop an accurate and
detailed knowledge of their own bodies' capacities, and their exact
suitability for different positions in the team.

A teenage boy who is under-sized for his age is likely to be worried
about it, sometimes desperately so. He knows that growth is under
way but might stop abruptly, leaving him a runt. I wasn't exactly
small as a teenager, but I certainly wasn't anything like the size of my
father and my uncles, and I can remember being very relieved when a
late growth spurt put on several inches and I got to be nearly six feet
(duly checking from time to time with a tape measure to see if I had
made that mark).

To be an adult male is distinctly to occupy space, to have a physical
presence in the world. Walking down the street, I square my shoulders
and covertly measure myself against other men. Walking past a group
of punk youths late at night, I wonder if I look formidable enough. At
a demonstration I size up the policemen and wonder if I am bigger and
stronger than them if it comes to the crunch—a ludicrous
consideration, given the actual techniques of mass action and crowd
control, but an automatic reaction nevertheless. (Some of the early
American women's liberation literature has nice descriptions of
machismo among male lefties, their competition to take most risks in
a confrontation with police. Admittedly the police in places like
Chicago are a pretty frightening lot.)

That these are reasonably common concerns is shown by the many
cults of male physicality. Following football is one; and as the English
experience shows, for groups of young male supporters that can be the
usual occasion for actually practising the physical skills and attitudes
that the rest of the spectators merely celebrate on the field. Kung-fu,
and the incredible proliferation of specialised 'martial arts' cults, is
another. Martial arts magazines are full of fantasies about street-
fighting as the justification for being skilful at mayhem, so perhaps
feeling physically rivalrous in the street is a common imagination.

The surfing cult gives it a more aesthetic twist, but still centres on
strength and skill, the peak experience being the conquest of the
dangerously big wave. I remember reading in a surfing magazine a
rhapsody about surfing gigantic waves at a spot in Hawaii that has no

beach. The waves run in on a cliff, so the idea was to lift the surfers in and out by helicopter!

Body-building is some kind of logical extreme, and it is interesting that this more than the others is popularly seen as slightly ludicrous. I think this is for two reasons. Though it is flesh developed, it is flesh unused, unskilful. And it is a rather too naked revelation of the narcissism in men's preoccupation with their bodies, which contradicts other elements in the hegemonic ideal of masculinity (suppression of affect, doing rather than being).

It isn't only size which provokes anxieties about the body among teenage boys. There is the question of shape. Pubescent, I was quite convinced I was brutally ugly, that my ears stuck out, my face was misshapen, that other people could hardly bear to look at me. There is also the question of clumsiness, a particularly sticky one because teenagers usually are, for a time, really clumsy. Those hideous ballroom dancing classes made one sure of it; teenagers now have sensibly taken to a style of dancing that minimises the barriers to entry. One of the great joys of Jaques Tati films is the sense of an eternal adolescence—the hero is amazingly clumsy, but clumsy with grace, and manages to come out of it both triumphant and unaware.

But more important, these anxieties have a great deal to do with the physical definition of oneself as male. The cults of physicality, and especially of sport—the cult which is not only allowed to schoolboys but positively encouraged by their elders—give clear ideal definitions of how a male body should look and work. The point is not just that most boys never will look and function like a first-grade forward. It is more that this feeds in to the adolescent boy's usual struggle with his own femininity.

There are many ways in which a boy may find part of himself to be feminine. There is often a continuing identification with mother, with an older sister, or some other member of the close circle, by no means obliterated by the passage through the oedipal period. There are often interests, tastes, emotions, responses which (in a patriarchal environment) are recognisably 'feminine'. There are erotic responses to other boys and to men. The adolescent boy may be trying himself out covertly as a woman just as he is trying himself out all-too-publicly as a man.

Either the physiological upheavals of puberty, such as swelling of the breasts, incomprehensible emotional ups and downs, even delay in the onset of puberty, or the social relations of adolescence (such as a crush on an older boy or young man), may push these contradictions to the point of an emotional crisis about masculinity. And in some cases they do get resolved by the formation of a sexuality and sense of self quite different from hegemonic masculinity. This may be in any of several forms: homosexual preference; a suppressed but determinant female identification; or, in flagrant contradiction of the body, transvestism and transsexuality.

Though the main concern in this paper is with hegemonic masculinity, it is worth considering the involvement of the body in such other patterns of sexuality. Pure auto-eroticism, when it is the established way in which a person's sexuality is organised and not just a last resort, seems on the face of it to separate sexuality entirely from social practice, whether supportive or rejecting. But this isn't so. Auto-eroticism builds up the narcissism implicit in the ordinary masculine cult of physicality, making one's own body the object of skill and an object of admiration. Nor is that body a-social or pre-social. As any reflection on masturbation fantasies will show, the body is still invested with a heavy load of social meanings; and the rituals of masturbation are the practices of the minimal society, transactions between the self and the self. They can, after all, go wrong.

Transvestism and transsexuality involve rejection of the relationship to one's body that is implicit in hegemonic masculinity, by dint of seizing the main alternative model. But the identification as female, because it has to cut right across the landscape of the body, is likely to be partial, ambivalent, or heavily stressed. One common outcome of this is an exaggeration of the trivia of feminine dress and manners, such as one sees in the conservative transvestite clubs. More seriously, it can focus a lot of emotional energy on acquiring the more obvious secondary sexual characteristics of women, such as artificial breasts, and eliminating the physical stigmata of maleness, by surgical castration and remodelling of the genitals.

Homosexual masculinity seems to me to involve another order of argument. As a form of sexuality it covers the same range of relationships as heterosexuality; here too there is a main pattern of genitally organised coupling, with a penumbra of the same kind of variations as heterosexuality: transvestite, sadistic, pederastic, and so forth. The striking implication about the body is the cathexis of the category to which one belongs onself, the repression of the desire for women rather than of the desire for men. This clearly enough implies a different process of construction, though how far back in the story the divergence must go is not clear; there is nothing *a priori* unlikely about a resolution in either a heterosexual or a homosexual direction being characteristic of adolescence. At all events, it is a serious error to equate homosexuality with a feminisation of the body or the body-image. Like hegemonic heterosexuality, it involves a distinct relation to one's body, not a distinct form of the body.

There is, nevertheless, heavy pressure from outside for the

possibilities of youth to be resolved by the formation of a conventionally masculine character and sexuality. And that is also how most boys mostly want to be, as they lay claim to the place of power in a man's world. Firestone (1972) acutely observed the role of this claim to power in the formation of masculinity and repudiation of femininity; but it is really to adolescence, not the oedipal period, that the point applies.

It would be wrong to presume, just because there are acute anxieties involved in the formation of hegemonic masculinity, that they persist unchanged as a permanent insecurity within masculinity. This seems to be what Tolson (1977) thinks; and it is important for the critique of masculinity as a restriction on men's capacity for experience, which was a common theme in the 1970s literature on men. I disagree profoundly with the idea that masculinity is an impoverished character structure. It is a richness, a plenitude. The trouble is that the specific richness of hegemonic masculinity is oppressive, being founded on, and enforcing, the subordination of women. Most men do become secure in their physical masculinity. It isn't just a matter of the end of puberty, the first 'nocturnal pollution' (carefully recorded in the diary), the breaking of the voice, and the pleasure of having to shave. It is, crucially, a *social* process, a matter of the social practices that lead boys into adulthood.

The body in adult practices

Some, of course, continue with the practices that spelt maleness in childhood, such as playing football and cricket; but only a minority of men keep up team sports after leaving school—usually those who were rather good at them, and probably found this an important way of defining themselves. Most men find other ways, other practices. Three among them seem to implicate the body in particularly important ways.

Work. The way that certain kinds of manual work are seen as properly masculine, and being able to do them as confirming masculinity, have been well mapped out by Tolson and by Willis (1977). Being tough, able to keep up heavy labour over a long period or to exert sudden force in lifting or shifting, is essential in labouring jobs and is obviously closely linked to the sense of bodily force in masculinity. Of course pure labouring has drastically declined with the advance of mechanisation; but then mastering a trade (with one or two exceptions), and especially being good with machinery, is also felt to be masculine. The protection of male claims to physical strength and machine-related physical skills has obviously been one motive in the long resistance to women's entry into apprenticeships and heavy industry generally, by male workers and their unions as well as training authorities and employers. Wartime experience in the economically advanced countries, and women's agricultural labour in peasant economies, had long ago made nonsense of the idea that there was any difference in real physical capacities that was important to production.

Given the decline of pure labour, the relation of masculinity to machinery is particularly important and interesting. The English canal system was created by masses of men with spades (incidentally the origin of the term 'navvies', from 'navigators'), but the equivalent work now is done by the drivers of bulldozers, scrapers, front-end loaders and dump-trucks. The 'maleness' of such work is maintained by a network of social practices, in which teenage boys' involvement with motorbikes and cars is an important transitional form. Here, the desire for skill and force of the body is translated into a preoccupation with technology and speed, institutionalised in 'motor sport', a revealing term.

It is interesting that manufacturers often don't want to be involved in this 'sport', for reasons of cost and risk. But the connection with masculinity is so important in the marketing of motor products that the industry is drawn into it willy-nilly. When General Motors-Holden wanted to get out of racing, the banner was taken up by a 'Holden Dealer Team' on the Australian circuit. Cars and bikes give an amplified way of occupying space and putting one's impress upon it. The pleasure is doubled on an open vehicle that brings the controller in direct contact with the space that is being subdued, but is fast enough to get you away from the irate bushwalkers and picnickers who are also being subdued. Bikies especially descant on the theme so neatly offered them, their riding leathers insisting almost obsessively on the masculinity implied in being master of a big machine, on the themes of danger, strength, recklessness, speed and skill.

For large parts of the male workforce, of course, the daily round means neither sweat nor grease. For office workers nothing whatever about the physical process of work either tests or signifies masculinity. It is doubtless no accident, then, that this vastly expanded part of the male workforce has provided a mass market for new forms of commercialised masculinity fantasies, notably *Playboy* magazine and its imitators. And it is notable that the social customs of the male-controlled office heavily stress the femininity of the women workers there. This goes as far as the technically farcical inclusion of instruction on grooming, deportment and dress in the training of secretarial workers.

And for office workers as well as manual workers, the physical

definition of masculinity is sustained in the typical division of labour
in the home. Men are held properly responsible for jobs such as
building and building repairs, digging and constructing the garden,
maintaining cars and other household machinery—jobs, in short, that
are seen as requiring strength, skill with tools, exposure to the
elements, toughness. It is nicely summed up in the Staffordshire
village studied by Hunt (1978): women are responsible for cleaning the
inside of windows, men the outside. Typically, the skill involved in
work such as cooking is devalued; though there are some households
where men appropriate this too, becoming the 'fancy cooks' for big
occasions while their wives do the everyday plain cooking, the
husband thus getting the accolade from visiting friends.

Sexuality. The insistence by many employers on secretaries wearing
skirts and make-up is only one of a number of ways in which sex is
marked out in the workplace. Many male workplaces are decorated
with pin-ups, emphasising the langour, decorativeness, and
uselessness of a woman's body in tacit but effective contrast to the
toughness and purposefulness of the male inhabitants. One classic
example I have seen, pinned up in a garage, was a calendar put out by
a motor parts company that showed a naked model wearing the
manufacturer's shiny clutch and transmission parts as jewellery.
Constant stylised humour about women drivers, The Wife's
hopelessness with tools, and conversations on such topics as the size
and wetness of the cunts of women in the neighbourhood, are also
familiar practices confirming the sense of physical maleness.

The more important practice, however, is the construction of adult
sexual relationships themselves. These can, and often do, settle into a
pattern in which the man's arousal and control of movement is
central. Not that it is biologically decreed, by the architecture of the
genitals, that Man must thrust and Woman lie still. (Though that is a
belief on which a great tower of sub-freudian bullshit has been
erected, even by otherwise perceptive psychoanalysts.) This too is
constructed, as a relation, in a practice of sexual encounter that begins
with erection and ends with ejaculation, and in which the woman's
pleasure is marginal to what the man does, or is assumed to be
guaranteed by powerful ejaculation. In eroticism focussed on the
penis and on penetration, passive or gentle contact is likely to be
dispensed with or hurried through, for fear of losing the erection,
failing; and the man may be quite unable to come to climax except
when moving, thrusting.

This pattern is the normal assumption in 'straight' pornography.
Erections are always huge and hard, and mighty ejaculation routinely
follows a vigorous occupation of the woman's well-lubricated inner
space. By contrast, Sade's heroes of libertinage often suffer from
failure of erection—one of the few touches of realism in his fucking

scenes—which drives them on to worse and worse atrocities in the attempt to become hard. Other ways of stimulating the erectile tissues have to be relied on by mere mortals; their effectiveness varies. The tragi-comedy of erectile impotence is thus scripted within this pattern of sexuality.

Sadistic and masochistic sexuality, that is, the practice of a relationship organised around the eroticism of pain, tends to de-emphasise genitality. Rather, it makes the whole body the object of erotic penetration through pain or bondage. Skill modulates as mastery, and force becomes the technique of arousal.

By contrast rape—assuming it to involve a specific organisation of sexuality—is the extreme of phallocentrism. Force without skill, rape is the attempt to imprint one's presence not just in space, but in the most protected space by an irresistible penetration. The analogy with football is irresistible, as is the thought that a common slang term among young men for what Greer (1971) calls 'petty rape' is 'scoring'. Full-scale rape magnifies the conventional put-down of women into full-scale hostility—sometimes also, as we see in Cleaver's *Soul On Ice*, revenge on other men.

As Freud argued in the *Three Essays*, there is nothing automatically given about the dominant pattern of sexuality. It is constructed out of much the same raw materials as these and other non-hegemonic forms. Where we can go beyond Freud now is in insisting that the hegemonic pattern is dominant because it is socially-sustained. The *collective* practices of men—except in a few very well defined milieux like gay bars and the Beaumont Society—almost always reinforce the hegemonic pattern. The intimidation of women in public by groups of men, and the aggressive occupation of streets at night by groups of teenage boys, which can make even outer suburbs places where women are afraid to walk out, are familiar examples.

Fatherhood. The social definitions of man as worker and as controller of sexuality come together in the moment when the courses towards adulthood decisively end. The action of the body is now extended not just in space but also in generational time; signifying that the moment is not far off when one will have to start dealing with a decline of one's own physical powers, while those of the body's offspring grow. Commonly enough this is the moment when the wife stops working and the husband becomes unequivocally the 'breadwinner'. The ribald jokes that greet a new father (not, be it noted, the mother) mark this too as an occasion when the body is socially confirmed in its masculinity. Retrospectively, the privatised sexual practice within the marriage is collectively certified and endorsed. It is ironic that this is also the moment in many marriages when sexual interest begins seriously to decay.

Men's involvement in upbringing is, typically, restricted in scope and stylised in content. It seems more governed by considerations of the sexual division of labour than by any close involvement of their physical masculinity—except, perhaps, for physical punishment of the children, and that much less than a generation ago. The parents' concern is much more focussed on the correct development of masculinity in their sons. This involves teaching them to be active, to be tough, to control their emotions, and to be good at football. But that was where we came in.

Psychological and social dynamics of masculinity

How to make sense of all this theoretically? What are the dynamics, the key moments, if any, and the points of change?

In Freud, the fantasy-amplified fear of castration is important not because of its own piquancy, but because of its role in precipitating the crisis of emotions that leads to identification with the father and eventual substitution of other women for the little boy's attachment to his mother. What is important for this account is not the penis as such, but whatever will precipitate that crisis. Stoller, however noxious in other ways, is surely right in arguing that the key point is not the fear of a particular mutilation, but the threat of the loss of sexual identity. This of course implies that some such thing has already been formed. In Stoller's case histories of transsexuals, boys who had not formed a masculine gender identity didn't have an oedipal crisis.

We do know that, under adult pressure, the social differentiation of boys and girls is accomplished astonishingly early. And there are indications enough that it becomes emotionally important to the children. This can happen even where parents attempt to rear them in non-sexist ways.

In an issue of *Humpty Dumpty* on child-care, a feminist mother tells a story about her young son which brilliantly illustrates the play of emotions involved:

> When D was about 3 he decided one morning to wear a woman's smock (the same one I mentioned before) he loved to 'dress-up' in. He put it on, but when his father realised D wanted to wear it to walk (with me) to the CCC [child care centre], he became furious and yelled that D was not to go out with a dress on. He refused to explain why he was so violently opposed to this. I was very upset but told D that he could wear the dress if he wanted, comforted him, and we left. When we arrived at the CCC a male visitor greeted us and said to me "Is she your child? What's her name?" (D also

had, at the time, long blonde curly hair which both I and his father loved). I retorted that my child was a boy called D but D turned to me, gripped me intensely and whispered "take off the dress, take off the dress". No amount of comforting could persuade him to change his mind. He has never worn a dress since.

D was obviously upset by both men's reactions. How he interpreted them in relation to the dress is hard to say, although he must have understood that the dress was a symbol of sex-identity which he could not bear to have threatened; but then, it would seem, nor could his father. My own 'blankness' vis-a-vis some of D's games, coupled with my feeling of 'resonance' when playing with the doll, are on the same dimension as D's father's reaction to his son wearing a dress 'outside'. Such is the extent to which we are bound by our own experience, our own unconscious. ('Cheshire Cat', 1978: 21-3)

I can't help thinking, then, that a lot of recent discussion, under the influence of Lacan, has vastly exaggerated the symbolic significance of the Phallus. There is a whole range of ways in which the body can be defined, perceived, cathected and symbolised as masculine; and a whole range of ways in which, and ages at which, that bodily masculinity can be called traumatically into question. Only in a limited number of them will the course of events resemble that described in the theory of the oedipus complex.

And there are other difficulties with that model. It offers little grip, for instance, on what must be one of the most striking features of hegemonic masculinity as an organisation of emotions, the fact that it allows the cathexis only of women, but of almost any member of that category. Freud talks vaguely in the *Three Essays* (1905b: 222-230) of a transfer of desire for the mother into desire for other women, but treats it teleologically, as a goal that normal development has to reach by hook or by crook. It is not in itself a matter to be puzzled about. The abstractness of the cathexis of women, what we might call the fetishistic character of male desire—massively evidenced by the social institutions of prostitution and pornography as well as knowledge of individuals—is left unaccounted for.

In linking the construction of masculinity with the social power structure of patriarchy, I think we have to take much more seriously the combination that comes up repeatedly in schoolboy sport, in physical labour, in the cult fantasies of bodily perfection: the combination of strength and skill. It is important here that these are attributes of the body as a whole; they are not focussed, even symbolically, on a particular part of it. What it means to be masculine is, quite literally, to embody force, to embody competence. Genital potency is a specific organisation *within* this pattern, and one that in a good many patterns of development fails to get organised, not because of trauma but simply because events took another turn.

Force and competence are, obviously enough, translations into the language of the body of the social relations which define men as holders of power, women as subordinate. They become statements embedded in the body, not just in a mental body-image but in the very feel and texture of the body, its attitudes, its muscular tensions, its surfaces. There is a material source for this in the practices that actually shape one's physique, such as boys' constant exercising and the usual constraints on girls', or the stress on attractiveness that directs teenage girls' attention to slimness and diet. This is important as it is one of the main ways in which the superiority of men becomes 'naturalised', i.e. seen as part of the order of nature, an amazingly tenacious belief. And it is especially important in allowing this belief and the attendant practices to be sustained by men who in other social relations (notably class relations in employment) are personally powerless, who cannot sustain any claim to social potency. Thus a particular form of masculinity becomes hegemonic, in the strict sense of the term.

It is notable that this normally develops, through the course of childhood, without the boy actually exercising power over females. The characteristic and necessary relations a boy has with females are being under the control and direction of various adult women, and interacting, usually with a fluctuating mixture of friendliness and antagonism, with girls of about his own age, at school and in the neighbourhood. It is evidently more remote features of social structure, not the immediate experience of relations between the sexes, that translate into the bodily sense of masculinity. (*Through* immediate relationships, needless to say, but not *as* the structure of those relationships.)

It seems to me that this might be very significant indeed in understanding the constitution of hegemonic masculinity. The boy's struggle to establish distance from the mother and negate his own femininity, and the man's need to enforce the subordination of women as the condition of sustaining his own masculinity, have to be seen in the double context of immediate and more remote relationships. The tension that is so marked in the formation of masculinity, and the continuing mobilisation that is part of the hegemonic pattern, is in part traceable to the contradictions between the emotional implications of immediate social relations and the powerful but indirect effects of the larger structure of patriarchal power. This puts it abstractly, but the immediate forms of contradiction are familiar: family quarrels about 'over-protective' mothers making sissies of their sons, boys oscillating between affection and anxious withdrawal from their mothers, intermittent hostility towards girls, and so on.

None of this implies that the bodily embedding of masculinity must be complete or totally effective; it never is. No man is a hero to his valet. The argument now perhaps gives some grip on why the imperfections, the moments when the body lets the developing male down, are so emotionally fraught. He is, in effect, carrying the can for the patriarchal system in a context of personal relations that are often abrasive, if not actually hostile, towards his pretensions to masculine force and competence, as long as he is a child. These range from put-downs by agemates, to assertions of control by parents, to intimidation by teachers. My most vivid school memory is of being bashed against a wall by a teacher who claimed I had knocked against him while hurrying up the stairs (I was late for a chemistry class), and the memory is of terrible, impotent, physical rage.

It is no wonder, then, that boys grasp with considerable fervour the social practices that confirm physical masculinity, even when, as is particularly true for working-class boys, these attract a good deal of hostile pressure from adults. Teenage peer groups, collectively distancing themselves from the adults who exert these pressures (parents, teachers, police) are in no sense distancing themselves from *adulthood*, the error in much discussion of 'youth culture'. The points on which the issue of control is fought out, smoking, drinking, driving, fucking, foul language, and physical aggression, are an inextricable mixture of claims to adulthood and claims to masculinity. Their barrenness reflects the very limited claims that can be made by people who, because of the age and class structure, have very few resources.

I have already noted the fetishistic structure of hegemonic male sexuality, and the difficulty classical psychoanalysis has in accounting for it. It is neither a natural fact—*Higamus hogamus, woman's monogamous, Hogamus higamus, man is polygamous*—nor a generalisation of repressed desire for Mum. We can still get some grip on the reasons for it. Despite the practice of monogamy, the structural tension within hegemonic masculinity is dificult to resolve into the emotional pattern of an exclusive attachment. Especially as that would be to concede a good deal of interpersonal power to the woman concerned, by the mere fact of her uniqueness. The pattern is copiously acknowledged in popular humour about married men chafing at the matrimonial bit. The intimate physical sense of masculinity has been constructed not just through the structure of immediate personal relationships, but also through more abstract determinations in which the social categories of male and female are directly at issue. The categories come themselves to be emotionally laden.

For male sexual response to be aroused by any member of a large category of women does not require free-floating affect, i.e. a quantum of lust roaming around looking for an object, so much as a capacity for ready physical response coupled with a massive blocking out of men as emotional objects. These two features may develop separately, giving the appearance of a 'phase' of homosexual attraction, in middle adolescence for instance, before being synthesised, under heavy pressure, into hegemonic masculinity. The skein is also tangled by the thread of hostility to women.

This probably has no single source. The struggle to deny one's own femininity, resentment against the women who held power in one's childhood, jealousy of the power to bear children, bad faith about the oppression of women, rivalry with other men, may all feed in. In a context of heavy emotional repression this may crystallise as misogyny, as fixation on particularly unthreatening women (e.g. girls), or as classic object-fetishism. The last two were fused in the striking case of the artist L.S. Lowry, as can be seen in Rohde's biography (1979). More generally it feeds the objectification of women, the sexual metonymy of tits and bums; and the practices, already discussed, that give an aggressive rather than paternalistic colouring to men's use of their social and physical power. In the intimate politics of a particular relationship men can easily find themselves insisting, in words or deeds, on the abstractness of their own desire, on men's capacity for other involvements and encounters, as a way of ventilating the hostility generated within that relationship.

What does all this tell us about the social dynamics of masculinity, its points of pressure and change, its involvement in the historical processes that make up patriarchy? Any reference to the body is liable to be taken, one way or another, as reference to a fixed point, a biological given, which must act as a drag on the change of social relations whenever it is implicated in them. I hope to have shown that isn't so; that the embedding of masculinity in the body is very much a social process, full of tension and contradiction; that even physical masculinity is a historical, rather than a biological, fact. That is to say it is constantly in process, constantly being constituted in actions and relations, constantly implicated in historical change.

That, however, is only an abstract truth. For any practical reckoning with social dynamics we need to know about the points where change becomes mutation, where the possibilities of qualitative difference, of transcendence, arise. The argument so far suggests both the contradictory process of formation, and the incoherent structure formed.

The most striking single fact about the construction of hegemonic masculinity is the length and complexity of the process. If the arguments of this essay are anywhere near the mark, it is not achieved in early childhood, nor in the oedipal period, nor even by the end of schooling, but over a span, usually, of twenty years or more. There is a complex relationship, within the life history, of the events at different stages: earlier patterns are used, expanded, negated and transformed in later ones. As a working hypothesis, I would suggest that three moments in this succession might be particularly important as points where paths might diverge, and structural change enter:

1 The moment when the determination of physical masculinity by the social definitions of gender first seriously comes into contradiction with the emotional implications of intimate relationships. One form of this is the oedipal crisis. (Which cannot be theorised as the form of the entry of the child into culture, as in Mitchell's reworking of the myth of the Phallus in *Psychoanalysis and Feminism*, if only because as crisis it presupposes the possession, and cathexis, of a cultural definition of masculinity.) Any variation in the pattern of parenting is liable to change the form of this contradiction, and its consequences.

2 The moment when physical maturation both offers adult sexual powers and (very often) stages a physiological upheaval that calls masculinity into question, in a context where adult controls are often suddenly increased and at the same time become more impersonal and difficult to negotiate. This is liable to happen in the transition to high school, about the time of puberty and the upsurge of parents' anxiety about the child's sexuality.

3 The entry into economic adulthood, which usually means an end of adult surveillance of the boy's sexuality, and of childhood involvement in public sport as the main practice confirming masculinity. For the vast majority this also means the beginning of the life-long wrestling match with the experience of wage labour.

Though I have suggested most adult men are more or less secure in their physical masculinity, that is not to say it is coherent, perfect and incorruptible like the crystalline spheres. A number of points of incoherence and vulnerability are evident. The technical and economic changes that have replaced bodily force and skill by mechanisation, and are sweeping on to replace mechanisation by cybernation wherever it is profitable to do so, continue with the dynamic of profit itself. And though physical masculinity has been reasonably successfully integrated with machinery, it certainly hasn't been with computers. The genteel oppressions that sustain the sense of masculinity in the expanding world of office work are vulnerable to any attack on their patent irrationality, including of course the specific resistance of the women concerned. Korda's *Male Chauvinism* perceptively demonstrates this.

The construction of sexual practices in marriage that reinforce hegemonic masculinity are vulnerable to demands by women for full sexual gratification, even without change in the organisation of households. They are much more shatteringly contested when, as now happens in a restricted group, particularly the younger intelligentsia, the nuclear household and privatised monogamy are called into question. The confirmation of masculinity in fatherhood seems at the moment the most secure part of the whole pattern. But even this has greatly changed in form in the last generation, as women have gained significant control of contraception. Even more dramatic are the implications of techniques such as A.I.D. (artificial insemination by donor) where the physical attendance of a male is not required for the conception of a child. With surrogate mothering also a possibility, the link between biological parenthood and social identity is being levered apart.

It would be ludicrous to suggest that any general crisis of masculinity had emerged from all this. But the conditions are certainly there for a good many local crises of varying forms. Their variety is no doubt one reason for the difficulty of organising any coherent counter-sexist practice among men, which would turn undirected contradiction into a conscious politics directed to the overthrow of patriarchy. I think that would be ultimately to the advantage of men as well as women. But it is clear that it involves a painful transformation in men's relation to their own bodies as well as their relation to women. The early stages of that transformation are as likely to provoke bitter resistance as any determination to press on into the flames.

3
Crisis tendencies in patriarchy and capitalism

The first version of this essay was a rather rambling paper I gave at the 'sex and class' workshop of the Conference of Socialist Economists (CSE) in England in July 1979. Like a good many other socialist intellectuals (if not economists), I had followed the development of socialist–feminist theory through the 1970s with a good deal of excitement. Here, it seemed, were ideas that were not only sharply relevant to current political practice, but also called into question the basic concepts of socialist theory. But by the end of the decade the theoretical movement had got badly bogged. It seemed to me that was partly because it had accepted structuralist notions of class, culture and patriarchy, and consequently was stuck with static and abstracted notions of the relations among them.

This piece was an attempt to show what the problems might look like if they were shifted back towards questions of dynamics. I had been reading Habermas' *Legitimation Crisis* with an honours class, and it seemed that a free adaptation of some of his ideas might be helpful, and should be compatible with a practice–based notion of structure.

The paper went down, if not quite like a lead balloon, then at least like a wounded jellyfish. It was trying to do too much, and not getting enough of it right. Later in the year, with the aid of Sibelius and Wagner, I condensed and reworked it. I offered the product to the CSE's journal *Capital and Class*, who after long thought rejected it, saying that they might be interested in a literature review instead...

Analyses of the patriarchy/capitalism relationship

Socialism and the new feminism have been eyeing each other warily for about ten years now. The caution is justified, if only because union is bound to be painful. The persistence is also justified. For, in talking about the relation between socialism and feminism, we are talking about nothing less than the linking of the resistances to the two main structures of power and oppression in human history.

If this is agreed, the issues now mainly debated in a specialised literature on 'patriarchy–and–capitalism' can in no sense be treated as marginal. They are root questions of theory and practice. They affect the socialist project trunk and branch, from the most universal formulations of class analysis and strategy to the most mundane details of the monthly branch meeting.

And it becomes very important *how* we understand the relation between class exploitation and sexual oppression. It is not just that stances on this question have become badges of political factions. The theoretical problem bears directly on the practical question—to which we still lack any real answer—of how the potential for a new structure of gender relations, that is presently a gleam in the eye and a knot in the lives of a rather small number of intellectuals and activists, can become a mass practice actually capable of transforming structures.

About the least helpful thing to do is get entangled in arguments about priority: whether gender divisions or class divisions came first, whether one arose from the other. Fantasies about origins have infested discussions of both class and gender for the past few hundred years. In the actual historical record both patterns can be traced back, faintly, to the Palaeolithic. There is no possibility of establishing priority between them. Both become more clearly defined in the historical record as we move forward towards Sumer and Old Kingdom Egypt. (For examples of the fragmentary evidence on which a realistic discussion of origins would rely, see the papers on the upper Palaeolithic by Klima (1962) and Pericot (1962); and for a dose of patriarchal ideology from Sumer, complete with hypermasculine heroes, sorrowing wives and mothers, and polluting whores, see any edition of the *Epic of Gilgamesh*.)

Both gender and class divisions can be traced through a complete evolution and interaction since that time. It is this evolution and interaction that is the object of real historical knowledge. What concerns us is the dynamic, not its largely unknowable point of departure. Only myth, not history, makes determinations out of origins.

In the theoretical work of the last decade this debate has mercifully been superseded, mainly by adaptations of marxist structuralism. Capitalism and patriarchy have been approached as logically distinct, though practically interconnected, structures of relationship. Each is seen as defining a system of places into which people are inserted; and which, as systems, can be seen to use and modify each other. The focus has shifted from origins to practical interdependencies.

This perspective has yielded a deal of useful detailed research, and two main lines of theoretical argument. One, starting from the feminist critique of the family, has concentrated on the economic significance of housework, specifically the contribution it makes to capitalist exploitation by affecting overall wage levels and labour market segmentation, or by reproducing labour-power. The other, taking off from the feminist critique of patriarchal culture and the Althusserian theory of ideology, has concerned itself with the role of patriarchy in securing the reproduction of the whole system of social relations that makes up capitalist society.

As this literature has recently been summarised in several places (by Molyneux, 1979, Hartmann, 1979, Gimenez, 1978, Barrett, 1980, and the theoretical papers in books edited by Kuhn and Wolpe, 1978, Eisenstein, 1979, and the Women's Studies Group of the Centre for Contemporary Cultural Studies, 1978), I won't dwell on the details. But I do want to raise several problems about the general approach to understanding capitalism and patriarchy that underlies much of this theoretical argument.

The first point is wittily made by Hartmann: in this literature, 'marxism and feminism are one, and that one is marxism'. This is not just a matter of patriarchal attitudes on the left. It is implicit in the way the whole analysis has been set up. Even while rejecting the 'class comes first' mutterings of unreconstructed leftism, doctrines can still be taken for granted that have many of the same consequences. Not only is the sphere of production given 'analytic primacy', as McDonough and Harrison (1979) put it. In most of this literature, production of any kind is analysed by means of categories—those of the received marxist conception of 'mode of production'—which derive exclusively from a periodisation of the history of *class* relations. The usual effect is to give unchallenged logical primacy to a structuralist model of capitalist production relations as the context within which sexual social relations are examined. For some theorists, the effect is virtually to identify production relations with capitalism and confine 'patriarchy' to the sphere of culture or social reproduction. Even those who insist on the importance and difference of housework are often so mesmerised by the mode–of–production model that they attempt to stuff housework into the same kind of bag (the 'domestic MOP', the 'family MOP', etc.). They then must analyse its relations with capitalism as a formal, external connection between two modes of production.

The problem here is not just the conceptual tangles to which a misplaced materialism and a dogmatic method lead. It is more substantial. Such an approach obliterates in advance the most important prospects opened up by feminist insights into history. Research on patriarchy points towards a theory of total social production which might alter the received periodisation and conceptualisation of material production in quite fundamental ways. But this can only be realised if exchange and labour *in the money economy* cease to be theorised in advance of all other kinds of exchange and labour. They must be placed from the start in the full context of the housework, child–rearing, education, household maintenance, building and gardening, informal neighbourhood exchange of services, etc., that in fact make up the greater part of *total social labour* even in advanced capitalist societies. As Stretton (1976) argues, the failure to realise this has been a basic weakness of economics generally, not just the political economy of the left.

A second problem arises in the attempt to theorise cultural processes as social reproduction. It is difficult for discussions of the reproduction needs of an *a priori*–defined structure to come up with explanations that are anything other than functionalist. This is a chronic problem in structuralist marxism's accounts of class, ideology and the state, as will be argued in Chapter 7. Functionalist arguments pepper the literature on patriarchy and capitalism almost as thickly. We find them at every level from the most general formulations about the sphere of reproduction, to specific arguments about economic exchanges. Thus, in the domestic labour debate, it is argued that women's domestic oppression is functional for capital because it holds down the price of labour–power. Similarly, Campioni (1976) among others argues that hierarchy in the home prepares future workers for insertion into hierarchical relations of production.

While such arguments often sound plausible at first, like most functionalism they have a nasty habit of dissolving as soon as a critical attempt is made to pin them down. Molyneux has forcefully shown this for the presumed functionality of domestic labour. More generally, they exaggerate the smooth integration of capitalism in itself. This directs attention away from the incoherencies, contradictions, and historical mutations where strategies of resistance might gain leverage.

A third problem has to do with the way structure is understood. There is a strong tendency to treat capitalism and patriarchy as systems of abstract relations defining categories into which people may be sorted, or inserted. While the categories can be refined and subdivided, they remain essentially a logical grid, constructed prior to the analysis of actual events. Cross–classification of the two grids of capitalism and patriarchy yields a more complex system of categories, without changing their formal character.

It has been argued by critics of structuralism in class analysis that this approach results in a radically impoverished, abstracted understanding of class. The same arguments surely apply in the case of patriarchy. Just this kind of criticism has been made, for instance, by Barrett and McIntosh (1979) in reflecting on the categorisation in Delphy's (1977) account of the sexes. Most importantly, the logical multiplication of conceptual grids is no way of theorising the interaction of the very historical processes in which the categories themselves are constructed and reconstructed. Some of the most interesting contributions to recent theory are precisely those which point to ways in which the analysis of patriarchy obliges us to modify conceptions of class. Some bear on general conceptions of class, such as the essays by Ehrenreich (1977) and Hartsock (1979). Others bear on particular cases: a good example is West's (1978) observation on how theories of the 'new middle class' based on discussions of clerical labour are inadequate until full account is taken of the specific position of the women who predominate in office work.

The general way these difficulties may be overcome is clear enough. It is a matter of taking seriously what is already perfectly well known, the historical character of social structures. Class and gender categories have to be treated as emergent in social practices by which groups are constituted and by which they constitute themselves.

To think this way is not to retreat from the idea of capitalism and patriarchy as tough and resistant systems of domination and exploitation. Nor need it imply that either dissolves into the other, or is truncated. Both class relations and sexual power relations embrace all the people. Both simultaneously invest every kind of human activity, from spreading dung on the farm to admiring the Matisse in the salon. They are of course very different forms of structure, involving markedly different kinds of control and exploitation, giving rise to different kinds of groups and different kinds of resistance. But they are both fully historical. They are extended, and undergo transformation, in time. They show intelligible, if complex, dynamics. And they are capable of being abolished.

This has been harder to accept in the case of sexual power relations, since a number of cultural habits converge to define their subject matter as being outside history. It is a familiar assumption about sexuality:

> Eternity is passion, girl or boy
> Cry at the onset of their sexual joy

'For ever and for ever'; then awake
Ignorant of what Dramatis Personae spake
Yeats, 'Whence Had They Come?'

And birth, housework, and the unconscious are often enough regarded the same way.

But this is no more tenable scientifically than the once equally popular belief that the House of Lords is a consequence of the order of nature. No form of social power is written in the genes, or in the fact of culture. The shapes of desire, the bodily senses of masculinity and femininity, the sexual division of labour, are all historically constructed. There are social struggles to control conception, birth, and child care, which result in historical change. 'Woman' and 'man' are social categories as complex, and historically specific, as 'ruling class' and 'working class'.

If we follow this approach, an understanding of the relation between class structure and sexual power structure must focus on historical change. It is a question of the interplay between the generative processes that produce capitalism and patriarchy, their processes of transformation, and their tendencies toward crisis.

The concept of crisis is, as Habermas notes in *Legitimation Crisis*, decidedly slippery, and not at all easy to distinguish from system adaptation or social change at large. It has become a thoroughly debased term in journalism, where any significant changes (and some imaginary ones) become 'the crisis of the family', 'the economic crisis', and so on. Habermas attempts to pin the idea down by means of an evolutionary scheme of the 'principles of organisation' of societies. These serve as a framework upon which the social analyst, like a surveyor, can triangulate the pressures for change.

There are two difficulties with this. In the first place, like the scheme of 'modes of production' from which it derives, Habermas' scheme is ultimately based on a class periodisation of history. Sex appears as a 'principle of organisation' of pre–class societies only. The objections already raised to the mode–of–production model apply equally forcefully here. For all its sophistication, Habermas' concept of crisis is still that of a pre–feminist historical materialism. (The same must be said for the treatment of crisis in most socialist discussions of the economic upheavals of the 1970s.)

Secondly, the arguments rest on what amounts to an essentialist notion of structure. It is assumed that there is something at the core of a given society (e.g. the capital/wage–labour relation) which defines the fundamental character of the society. This something defines 'crisis' when it fails to be reproduced, or 'crisis tendencies' when its reproduction comes into question. The objection to this (applied to reproduction analysis in more detail in chapter 8) is that it requires us to *postulate* the unity or systematicity of a set of social relations, when that should be seen as historically produced and historically variable.

But without some such notion of an inner core, a defining essence, can there be a concept of crisis in either capitalism or patriarchy at all? Short of a treatise on method, it is impossible to answer this adequately. But I can perhaps gesture towards a solution, adapting some ideas from Giddens' (1976) account of social structure.

All discussion of structure is concerned with the constraints and possibilities that are the conditions for practices. (Socialism and feminism are specifically concerned with the conditions for liberating practices.) We talk about a system in a given field of social practices when the constraints and possibilities governing each of those practices substantially involve properties of the whole field. (Thus we speak of capitalism and patriarchy as systems, meaning the inter-connected sets of constraints and possibilities operating in the labour market, gender relations, etc.) This is always to argue that the field in question is not simply an agglomeration of discrete elements. How then are we to understand 'properties of the whole field'? Essentialist treatments of structure assume there must be an underlying uniformity, seeing this as the only alternative to the notion of a shapeless agglomeration.

The nub of the argument is that there is another way of understanding properties of a field of practice—as *effects of composition*. I mean 'composition' as in music: a tangible, active, and often difficult process of bringing elements into connection with each other and thrashing out their relationships. It is a matter of the real historical process of interaction and group formation. The practices that comprise class struggles are the most familiar example.

The notion of 'crisis' then refers to developments in practice—not logically of a different order from any others—that as a matter of fact alter the conditions of many particular practices by bringing about alterations in the properties of the whole field. The notion of a 'mutation' of the conditions of practice may be a useful label for this.

Since it is deciphered at the level of practice, the concept of crisis does not require an *a priori* characterisation of the field (as is the case with Habermas' approach to the problem). But it does refer to large-scale structures, and assumes that we can give a practical account of the ways they are formed and transformed.

Structure and contradiction in patriarchy

Crisis tendencies thus have to be understood as located in the same generative processes by which structure is created. In the analysis of patriarchy, we seem to be concerned with four main kinds of structuring, of division and relation:

1 the organisation of power—both the direct and indirect ways in which people are controlled by, or in the interests of, others;
2 the division of labour—meaning 'mental' work as well as physical, unpaid as well as paid;
3 the organisation of character and personality—the relation between conscious and unconscious processes, the dominance of particular motives;
4 the pattern of cathexis—who and what you get stuck on.

(This characterisation of the sub–structures of patriarchy is meant as a first approximation rather than a settled theory. It differs from what in other respects still seems to me the best treatment of the issue, that in Mitchell's *Woman's Estate*, a book unaccountably neglected in recent discussion. Mitchell's four 'structures'—production, reproduction of children, sexuality, and socialisation of children—are not so much structures as types of practice; within which, I think, these sub–structures will be found.)

These types of structuring are both the conditions and the consequences of the continuing ordinary activities of life: work, biological reproduction, rearing children, sexual pleasure, and so on. In some circumstances they take definite institutional form, as in the family, the labour market, the cultural subordination of wives to husbands. Through the social struggles that form institutions and arise out of them, these patterns are composed into a global pattern, an overall social definition of gender and power relation between women and men. In turn this global pattern reacts back upon its parts, becoming part of the conditions of its own constitutive practices. (Sometimes this happens in a way that reinforces itself, the case extensively discussed in the literature on 'sex role socialisation'. And sometimes in ways that disrupt or transform the global pattern, as is clearly seen in the sexual politics of the last decade.)

Practices related to sex and gender can certainly be composed into other patterns than the one we are most familiar with. Anthropologists report sexual power structures and forms of sexism which, if not unambiguously matriarchal, are also not simply patriarchal. The term 'patriarchy' might best be kept for situations where predominant power is unequivocally held by adult men—which certainly includes most of Western history.

Such patterns do not fall from the sky. They are generated in history, as aspects of oppressions that are established, enforced, and sometimes overthrown, by social struggle. There is no convenient term for this process which is analogous to the term 'class formation'. 'Gender formation' sounds silly, 'sex-class formation' tendentious. But it is important to bear in mind, as with the processes of class formation, that there is a constant construction and reconstruction of groups, boundaries and relations. At times when structural mutation is particularly clear, we talk more easily of formation or creation. A notable example is the formation of the social category of the homosexual man in late nineteenth century Europe, described by Weeks (1977). But in less dramatic ways, the same kind of thing goes on all the time.

In the course of this, a complex of relations and groupings is produced *within* the major categories, the genders. Men do not all occupy the same position of superordination, nor women of subordination; and, contrary to some radical-feminist views, not all men oppress all women. Let us consider briefly the internal structure of one case, the category 'adult man' as we find it in the contemporary capitalist world.

There is a hegemonic form of masculinity, to which most feminist criticism is addressed, but which is by no means evenly spread among men. The celebration and enforcement of this hegemonic form creates a complex penumbra of repression and subordination. It defines by exclusion groups of men who are systematically oppressed: gays and effeminates, notably. Partly this is a result of the work of other men who are engaged in maintaining the sexual faith, without necessarily being the direct beneficiaries of it, such as male priests. (A measure of the significance of this task is the importance of sexuality in both Hildebrandine and Lutheran reformations.) All other men are devalued by the splendidly hypermasculine; though except where it is commercialised, as in football and films, hyper-masculinity is not necessarily cashable as power. There are large numbers of men who do not themselves instance hegemonic masculinity very well—'I was a 90-pound weakling'—but whose formation has left levels of anxiety about masculinity that can be mobilised in its defence. Perhaps the key form of this is the anti-homosexual scare, such as the classic 'Boys from Boise' case of manipulated hysteria described by Tripp (1977). And there are some situations where the hegemonic pattern has visibly come unstuck without any alternative integration having taken its place.

This is very schematic, but is perhaps enough to indicate that the generative processes in patriarchy work not only to mark out gender boundaries (some males are excluded; some—transsexuals—exclude themselves) but also to produce differentiation and domination *within* them.

The point of this argument is not to arrive at a graduated scale of sex–power, as seems to be implied in some sociological discussions of 'sexual stratification' (bearded Marlboro advertising executives with 100, pregnant teenage lesbians with 0?). Rather, it is to stress that the gender categories, in social interaction as well as ideology, are composite, constructed. They, and the relation between them, reflect the balance of forces in a complex generative process that is rich in possibilities of dislocation, contradiction, and crisis. Let us consider some cases in point.

The social category of 'housewife' is, as we know, a fairly recent construction. It is a specific integration of hegemonic femininity with a social division of labour that only became possible in industrial capitalism, and after the struggles that produced a 'family wage' for significant parts of the workforce. The changes in family size, reducing child–bearing and early child–rearing to a fraction of the adult life of most women, plus the partial mechanisation of domestic work with fridges, hoovers and washing machines that followed within a couple of generations, made this division of labour increasingly obsolete. But the global effects of a patriarchal structure which now incorporated this category—and which included the work of ideologues from *Married Love* (Marie Stopes) to Mills and Boon—did not allow it to be easily abandoned. Rather, as Game and Pringle (1979) argue, they threw heavier stress onto the reciprocal cathexis of husband and wife, their exclusive love, to provide an emotional basis for this organisation of domestic life, the famous 'nuclear family'.

But this was based on a linking of eroticism and reproduction that defined the other parent of your children as sole emotional object. And this has been undercut by the same complex of developments, including the spread of contraceptive knowledge, that is reflected in the reduction of family size. Even the imperfect and sometimes dangerous contraceptive techniques now in use have allowed, for widening groups, an almost complete divorce of love–making from child–bearing. This potentially wipes out the greatest single difference between men's sexual life and women's, creating possibilities of eroticism as pure play that could eliminate the dimension of power from its most intimate embedding.

But if adult women's sexuality could increasingly be freed from control by husbands, there was not automatically a corresponding change of emotions. For the lifelong effects of character formation that organised emotions around fertility, child–rearing, and homemaking were supported by the ideological pressures exerted by men. The general consequence has been a dislocation between the changing structure of power and labour, and the organisation of character and consciousness. This created the tensions within hegemonic femininity picked up by Friedan in *The Feminine Mystique*. They have obviously been experienced very unevenly, but still count among the most painful and difficult transitions now being undergone on a large scale.

The issue of control here is only one moment of a much longer dialogue between cathexis and power. Socialists in the nineteenth century were not alone in perceiving a breakdown in the regulation of sexuality by marriage and kinship; some even saw a dissolution of the working–class family. (Engels' gentle alternative program in *The Origin of the Family*, 'individual sex–love', is a touching transitional product between the traditional regulation and total dissolution of families.) As Foreman (1977) has noted, this perception was one of the reasons for the socialists' inability to develop an analysis of working–class sexism, despite their belief in the emancipation of women. They had indeed little sense of the complexities of mire and blood to come.

The most striking, in terms of the relationship of sexuality and power, was fascism. In one important respect fascism is a violent attempt to reimpose hegemonic sexuality and male domination by means of state power, gained through a mass mobilisation based in a group that had been through a particularly bloody test of masculinity, the front line soldiers of World War I. Macciocchi (1979) has raised the question of the role of female sexuality in fascism. It implicates the tensions of masculinity in no less striking ways. For the unrelieved exaltation of toughness and violence, the attempt to impose hegemonic masculinity as a template across the whole society, can both fascinate and undermine the very large numbers of men who cannot really match up to this standard of brutality. And it creates a violent contradiction in the position of the homosexual men involved in the fascist mobilisations–which of course many of the storm troopers, including their leadership, were—who became the agents of oppression in the most direct and physical of ways. One of the most dramatic moments in the history of sexual politics must be the murder and denunciation of the homosexual Roehm by the practically sexless Hitler in June 1934.

Contradictions between the structures of cathexis and power are, arguably, peculiarly important and explosive, as they touch on a fundamental way in which subversive energies are bound and may be released. It is hardly an accident that Sade's nightmare vision of patriarchy as a system of erotic violence, one of the most remarkable moments in the understanding of sexual power structure, came from a man whose sexuality was so far in contradiction with kinship and the state that he spent half of his adult life behind bars. (See Sade, 1966. I agree with Carter's (1979) estimate of his significance, though I think she has missed the element of satire against patriarchy that defines him as a sexual radical, not just a libertine.)

In such examples we can trace dislocations, contradictions and changes. But more is implied in the conception of crisis: properties of the whole that enter the conditions of practice. To go back to an earlier point, though not all men oppress all women, it is still true that there is a general oppression of women by men. This is precisely the defining point of patriarchy. All women live and act in conditions shaped by the structural fact of men's supremacy, even those women, the Thatchers and Gandhis, who are very powerful indeed. It is only when that global relationship and its effects are brought into question that it is possible to speak of crisis tendencies. Gandhi and Thatcher can advance to supreme power without improving the conditions of practice for the mass of other women. Indeed in the latter case the effect seems to be entirely the opposite.

Clearly, not all the contradictions that can be traced in the history of the four structures listed at the start of this section, lead towards liberation. Some have led to new forms of subordination, such as the creation of the housewife; towards more horrific forms of oppression, such as fascism; or into the praxis traps discovered in turn by several generations, starting with the 'new women' of the 1910s, who escaped from the home into clerical work and found there an increasingly routinised and regimented—and patriarchal—work life. But others have indeed called the global relationship into question. The contradictions surrounding the later development of the situation of housewives provided the basis for the mobilisation, limited as it may be, represented by Friedan's kind of feminism. In other milieux, mainly among the younger intelligentsia, the contradictions experienced in a period of political radicalisation and cultural struggle precipitated the far more radical mobilisation represented by Women's Liberation and Gay Liberation.

There is a crucial relationship between crisis tendencies and mobilisation. To say a tendency 'calls into question' the global relationship is mere metaphor unless it really is being called into question by word and deed. For crisis to be 'deciphered at the level of practice', it must be discoverable there in actual practices. Further, the dynamics of a complex and uneven structure—and one of the main structures of power and oppression in history is bound to be that—are extremely unlikely to produce neat little tendencies that unambiguously lead in only one direction. The 'calling into question', then, can only be a matter of the appearance of possibilities for mobilisations which can seize the time, and shape the complexities and contradictions into transforming practices.

The sexual liberation movements then, practices whose

subject–matter is the crisis tendencies in patriarchy, are not riding a wave of transformation whose direction is automatically set towards a liberated future. Socialism got its fingers badly burned with that kind of assumption. For what emerged from the capitalist crises of the twentieth century was not the confidently expected transition to socialism, but bureaucratic dictatorships and a revived imperialism. The movement has still not recovered, in its relationship with the Western working class, from that reversal.

Yet it is still enormously important that the opposition to patriarchy is not only critical of patriarchal culture but is also the bearer of an alternative, that it actually embodies other values and ways of life. These too will be transformed, in ways we cannot yet know. In the meantime the image of an alternative must serve as the source of ideas for the responses that a transforming practice constantly has to improvise in the evolving situation it confronts. Nothing is more disastrous for the project of liberation than a liberation movement that is organised in repressive ways.

Joint dynamic and crisis

I suggested in the first section that the relationship of capitalism and patriarchy is not just a matter of the diplomatic relations between two sovereign structures. It is much more intimate, with sexuality and gender relations entering into the very constitution of classes. If this is true of structure it must also be true of dynamics. We should find the dialectic of capitalism and patriarchy operating in capitalist crises, and in the convulsions of practice—strikes and lockouts, depressions and political breakdowns—in which crisis tendencies issue.

Certainly the balance of class forces in an industrial confrontation is affected by this relation. Employers' attempts to mobilise strikers' wives as strike–breakers are familiar enough, though rarely successful. The dependence of a family on one wage can set limits to, but may also fuel, militancy on wage issues. The legendary militancy of male underground miners would hardly have been possible, in the confrontations of the inter–war years, without the women of the coalfields, almost wholly confined to domestic work for lack of other jobs, organising widespread networks of mutual support between households.

On a larger scale, thinking about the relation with patriarchy may give us some grip on one of the great puzzles about capitalist crisis: why classic economic disasters, the great depressions, have rarely resulted in any major shift towards socialism, while wars repeatedly have. The secret may be that depressions involve massive disruption of capitalist production and working–class organisations (in many areas the unions practically disintegrated in the trough of the 1930s), but not of households, or at least not on the same scale. Indeed a vast amount of energy goes into keeping households going in the worst of circumstances, and the volume of domestic production probably rises in depressions. Modern wars, with conscription, mass killing, strategic bombing and shifts of population, involve widespread disruption of the emotional integration of families as well as the production processes of households. But they involve no corresponding collapse of capitalist production or of class organisation: indeed war booms and accompanying wage gains are familiar. Is anti–capitalist revolution basically a defence of patriarchal households? The mind boggles . . .

The more I think about such episodes, the more difficult it is to keep treating them as crises in capitalism that happen to be affected by its relationship with patriarchy, or vice versa; and the more it seems necessary to think systematically of the two together. I once felt that this might be done by means of a more general theory of social power, from which the structures of class and sex could be deduced as special cases. But as examples of more general theories of power already produced by sociologists such as Blau (1964) and Dahrendorf (1959) show, their tendency is towards an ahistorical abstraction which moves away from practice. And they give no grip on the *interactions* of capitalism and patriarchy that are the focus of the problems raised by socialist feminism. What we need, rather, is an account of a *joint dynamic*; a way of understanding systematically the simultaneous effects of class and gender structuring within the historical process as a whole.

And we need a concept of *joint crisis*. That is, an account of the ways in which the combined structures reach historical limits, changing the possibilities they govern and making their transformation a practical question. This may sound odd; but such a concept can already be found in radical politics. In Marcuse's *Essay on Liberation*, for instance, there is a conception of transition which is simultaneously a breakdown of repressions and a supersession of capitalist production. Much earlier, the dream of 'festival' in Lefebvre's brilliant if erratic *Critique of Everyday Life* was heading in the same direction. More concretely, there is the very existence of political tendencies such as 'socialist feminism' and 'gay marxism'. Unless we see these as accidental conjunctions in the heads of people who happen to be both left and queer, they must presuppose some notion of joint crisis tendencies for their politics to have anything to bite on.

There is a good deal of material for an understanding of this historical dynamic already at hand in the researches of the last fifteen years on women's history, capitalism and the family, and so on. We are by now familiar with some moments of that dialectic. For instance, the interplay of domestic life and economic accumulation in the transition to industrial capitalism, the intricacies of which have begun to be documented, from early industrial England to the contemporary third world, by scholars such as Young (1978). This has sometimes been theorised as if it were simply the impact of a dynamic capitalism on an inert domestic sphere. But we cannot ignore the reciprocal dynamic, shown in the work of McIntosh (1978) and others: the ways family relationships resisted the atomisation of the workforce; the strategic dilemmas created for the state by demands to support the family which conflict with the exigencies of capital accumulation; the struggles to shape the form of the wage as a 'family wage' which provided an important focus for working–class mobilisation.

The conception of a joint dynamic allows a more systematic solution to some of the problems raised in the first section of this paper. The tendency towards functionalism noted there gains much of its strength because it reflects the experience of what, in dynamic terms, would be understood as moments of hegemony—that is, situations where crisis tendencies have been successfully corralled, where the system has been stabilised.

When we look at the intersection of class and sex forces in hegemonic situations, we are very likely to find personal emotions and mass consciousness rooted in a structure of sexual relations that is by no means *optimal* for capitalism. Such a pattern can dampen crisis tendencies in one configuration of class forces, while setting up pressures that are destabilising in another. Again the contrast of depression and war is instructive, and so is their connection. The importance of psychosexual factors in shaping a fascist rather than socialist resolution of economic upheaval in central Europe in the 1920s and 1930s is well recognised. But though this helped save the local ruling classes from the Reds, it also inevitably led, through the black dynamics of the fascist regimes, to further war.

We can also formulate more systematically an alternative to the cross–classification of class and gender categories to which a categorical approach to structures must resort. It is a matter of grasping how, and what, social groupings are actually being produced in a given passage of history. Not all the abstractly possible categories need actually be constructed by practice. As we can speak of processes of 'class formation' in the simpler case, here we have processes of the formation of social groupings by class–cum–patriarchal dynamics, acting through means such as the reconstruction of culture and the hierarchical reorganisation of labour processes. There are now some excellent studies of this, such as Ryan's (1979) account of the formation of middle–class femininity in the mid–nineteenth–century United States, and Gamarnikow's (1978) discussion of nursing in late–nineteenth–century England. In the latter case we see not just a sexual division of labour within a particular class location, but a social struggle which strategically accepted patriarchal domination of the medical industry in order to create a new profession, and thus a new means of class mobility, for women.

How do we understand crisis tendencies in a joint dynamic? It is difficult to formulate the concept of joint crisis without seeming to trespass on the principle of logical autonomy of the two structures, for in this case they do indeed seem to dissolve into each other. On the one hand we find a process of radicalisation spilling untidily from one realm into another. The crisis of the *Ancien Régime* saw Wollstonecraft (1792) and Sade (1791) as well as Paine (1791) and Babeuf (1796); the crisis of the Autocracy in Russia saw Kollontai (1977) and an unprecedented, if fleeting, phase of sexual and cultural liberation. On the other hand we find crisis tendencies in one structure apparently absorbed by the repressive capacities of the other. The student movement of the 1960s (e.g. Reiche 1970) made us familiar with the ways a repressively–organised sexuality can dampen the crisis tendencies of capitalism. The sexual liberation movements now face endless examples of the capitalist absorption of opposition to patriarchy.

To take just one instance, their growth has been closely followed by cooptation of 'liberation' rhetoric by mass marketing and advertising. Cigarette ads in *Ms.* magazine are the classic case. We find more naked commercial exploitation of sensuality, occupying ground won by the radical critique of repression. There is even commercial exploitation of the titillating possibilities of *opposition* to women's liberation, such as the panty–hose ads in the London underground, 'For Girls Who Don't Want to Wear the Trousers'.

At this point we have, perhaps, reached the limit of the usefulness of that way of thinking about historical process which construes class and patriarchy as logically–autonomous–but–interacting structures. In the final analysis, theories of class and patriarchy are both partial ways of grasping the human experience of power, oppression and liberation. It may become necessary to think of the structure of power as a whole, as an overarching structure which can develop crisis tendencies related to its own properties as a whole. Their effects may be focussed in one or other of its parts, without being wholly generated there. The cases of depression and war already suggest one property of the whole, the historically mutable relation between the two major parts, as a determinant of the shape and possible outcome of major crises.

To understand crisis tendencies within such a global structure we need ways of grasping both the ways in which the effects of contradiction may be displaced within it, and the overall constraints on this displacement, that is, the limits set by the structure of the whole to the variation of the parts. Displacement is not a mysterious osmosis between structures. It is a matter of the capacities of those forms of control that are common loci of capitalist and patriarchal relations, being neither alone, but deriving form and efficacy from the state of play between them. The welfare policies of the state, and the cultural content of mass communications, are obviously important examples.

The limit to their capacities, and thus the tendency to generate crisis in the overall structure, in the final analysis has to do with the irreversibility of historical processes. Some cases of this problem have been worked out in the case of class relations. Foster (1974), for instance, speaks of a 'ratchet' effect in working–class consciousness, the English ruling class having been able to buy political stability in the mid–nineteenth century only at the price of an irreversibly increased pressure for shares of the social product. Habermas (1976) speaks of an irreversible expansion of technical knowledge that sets limits to the distortion of culture in the interests of capitalist social control.

We may offer a similar principle for the larger structure. For instance, the accumulation process in industrialisation may create pressures for a reorganisation of the sexual division of labour, biological reproduction and the emotional patterns of domestic life. But once they have occurred, it is not possible to get the old patterns back again—at least not without creating new tensions and problems of control as a result of the resistance of people whose lives are disrupted by the reversal. The resistance to current attempts to drive married women out of the labour market is a significant case in point.

This of course doesn't yet amount to a positive theory of crisis in the overarching structure. But it does suggest we eventually can produce one, since we can state some limits to the indefinite absorption of crisis tendencies. And, most significantly, it allows us to relate the possibility of crisis at the most general level of social structure back to the lives of ordinary people—to the pain and joy, loss and creation, from which at the last all history takes its meaning.

4
How should we theorise patriarchy?

If everything was done in proper logical order, this should have been written before the 'crisis tendencies' paper, perhaps even before the essay on Freud. I had been impatient to get on with it, not bog down in argument about definitions. The difficulty I found in trying to stick together fragments of argument about the dynamics of families, the formation of masculinity, and the politics of change in sexual power structure, showed that the job of conceptual clarification still needed to be done. A paper by Beechey (1979) had admirably shown the confusion of tongues in the literature on patriarchy.

So this essay is intended as an exercise in clarification. It offers a view of the foundations of a theory of patriarchy: its origins, scope, and form, the nature of its categories, the kind of knowledge it embodies and its relationship to history. So as not to disappear in a haze of abstractions, I have tried to work with two illustrative problems in mind: the relationship between patriarchy and capitalist class structure, and the formation and working of hegemonic masculinity. The paper was written in March 1980.

Scope and subject-matter

Though definitions of patriarchy are often quite narrow, the range of issues dealt with in the literature about it is wide. It ranges through the origins of the subordination of women, the cultural practices that sustain it, the sexual division of labour, the formation of character and motive, the politics of sexual object choice, the role of the body in social relations, the strategies of resistance movements, the conditions for an overthrow of male dominance.

I do not think there is any formula that will encapsulate all this, and thus define the scope of a theory of patriarchy. Those speculative abstractions that appear to ('the dialectic of sex', 'relations of reproduction') are more slogans for a particular *way* of theorising the subject than definitions of *what* is being theorised. Not that there is a sharp distinction between the method of a theory and the nature of its object. But I think it is necessary to recognise that the 'theory of patriarchy' is far from being a tightly–knit logical system. It is, rather, a *network* of insights and arguments about relations between various things (e.g. the relevance of the structure of the family to the reproduction of capitalism, of the production of masculinity to the structure of the family). Its scope at any given time is defined by the reach of this network of arguments.

And this corresponds to its history. The contemporary analysis of patriarchy was not established by a great scientific hiccough that revealed a fresh object of knowledge. It grew, rather, out of a complex movement of thought, a struggle to identify patterns and connections, develop ways of seeing them and invent ways of talking about them. I would suggest that its genealogy goes back to the redefinition of a conceptual field that we can see being worked out in Wollstonecraft (1792) and Sade (1791), and that reaches a point of crisis and transition in Mill (1869).

This was the transmutation of an age–old moral argument about the reciprocal rights and duties of men, women, and God. First God was eliminated by enlightenment rationalism, then conventional morality was challenged by revolutionary politics, and then convention was corroded by applying utilitarian criteria which found no grounds at all for 'the subjection of women'. When Mill wrote:

> Under whatever conditions, and within whatever limits, men are admitted to the suffrage, there is not a shadow of justification for not admitting women under the same (1869: 488)

the double negative marked a decisive shift in terms of argument. The presumption was now *for* equality, and patriarchal ideology responded with increasing defensiveness. From this period on in the European intellectual tradition, progressive analysis shifted on to why an unjustified subordination occurred, how it was sustained, and what life would be like without it. Not that moral argument disappeared, or even declined. No–one could mistake the moral passion of Ibsen (1879) or Goldman (1972), or the suffrage movement at large. But it ceased to be the central and defining problem. The growing edge of thought about patriarchy was increasingly in debates about explanation rather than justification.

And in due course, in the liberal and socialist intelligentsia of the early twentieth century, this led to a second transformation of the field. Wollstonecraft, Mill, and early socialist theorists like Owen and Engels, noted how women's (and men's) characters were distorted by oppressive conditions—indeed this is the core of Wollstonecraft's argument. But there was little in their frame of thought that would lead them to question how the categories 'men' and 'women' were in fact *constituted*, how they came to be. Many arguments for political equality suppressed this question by presupposing the sexual distinction and dilating on the virtues women would bring to public life; radicalism on rights often was interwoven with utterly conventional ideas about 'true womanhood' and the proper work of men and women.

These nevertheless came to be challenged, from two main directions. One was developments in science. The work of Darwin found functional explanations for sexual differentiation, but in doing so made them problematic, i.e. requiring explanation. Not long afterwards human sexology changed from the moralising 'sexual psycho-pathology' of Krafft–Ebing (1886) and his ilk, to Ellis' (1897) sympathetic anthropology of sexual variations, and Freud's (1905b) developmental characterology. Freud's arguments especially exploded the notion of fixed characteristics defining the sexes: by showing how their characteristic patterns of attachment and personality structure were constructed in childhood; by the doctrine of bisexuality; and by insisting on the pervasiveness of conflict within the human psyche.

The other source of challenge, which mainly came from feminist socialists, was a rethinking of the sexual division of labour. An increasing recognition of how contingent, how historically specific, was the definition of who does what, and an increasing recognition of the oppressiveness of the division of labour for working–class women, was widespread among socialists in the early 20th century. They came to a head in the debates about the socialisation of child care and housework in the immediate aftermath of the Russian revolution.

Though it took a long while for these developments to come together, they were moving in a common direction. The focus of argument about patriarchy was increasingly the constitution of its categories, the historical process of production of the gender division and of the characteristics of the people caught up in it. These lines of thought eventually meet, and are given their classic synthesis, in de Beauvoir's *Second Sex* (1949). And it was no doubt in response to this changed focus that patriarchal ideologies increasingly took the form of a degenerate Darwinism, insisting on the biological determination of male and female roles, the point of which is to deny that there is any such thing as the social and historical production of gender.

I would suggest that the current literature on patriarchy essentially works within the field I have just described. No comparable re-configuration of the problems has occurred recently. One sign of this is how often theoretical work takes the form of 'rediscoveries'—of Freud, or Ellis, or Kollontai. Nevertheless there have been two important changes.

The first is the extension of the network of arguments to a widening range of topics—for instance, the economics of housework, or the politics of child care. Sometimes, as the second example shows, this is under pressure from developments in patriarchal ideology (in this case Bowlby, 1953, most notably).

The second change is that the argument about the production of sexuality and gender has been connected, in the context of the sexual liberation movements, with the practicalities of structural change. In this setting the theory of patriarchy becomes, centrally, an argument about the conditions for superseding it. Hence the structuring of theoretical debate around strategic ideas: obvious in current debates within the womens' movement, but also implicit in the distance that has opened up between Women's Liberation and Gay Liberation. It is an open question which of the currently contending analyses might lead towards a general reformulation of the field. We can, however, consider them critically in terms of the form in which they cast a theory of patriarchy.

Form

In the 1970s there have been two principal syntheses of the field. To a large extent—though not completely—they correspond to the perspectives of radical feminism and marxist feminism.

In the first, the power of men over women is taken to be an autonomous and fundamental structure of social relations. Autonomous, in the sense that it is not derived from the exigencies of any other structure; fundamental, in the sense that it is (or expresses) an organising principle that governs a large part of social life. (In some analyses, such as Firestone's (1972), it is *the* most basic and important organizing principle of social life; others, such as Delphy (1977), admit other structures of equal importance alongside.) The categories defined by this structure are likewise fundamental and irreducible. It is to stress this point that radical feminists have spoken of women as a class, or have used the term 'sex class'.

The first form of a theory of patriarchy, then, is a synthesis on principles that are capable of yielding, directly, an account of a complete social structure. The classic principle of this kind is the social division of labour; and there are a number of accounts of patriarchy

that use this as their organising principle. Thus Delphy bases an
analysis of the position of women on the way they earn their daily
bread. She sees patriarchy as a structure based on a 'family mode of
production' in which women's labour is appropriated by men,
marriage functioning basically as a labour contract. In a good deal of
feminist anthropology the sexual division of labour has also been
regarded as central, though it has been developed in a somewhat
different way—for instance, in deriving the exclusion of women from
political power from the separation between a sphere of domestic
economy and the main economy.

Alternatively, the sexual division of labour may be treated as
secondary, in effect, a consequence of a power differential whose
roots are in biological differentiation. Mill argued, briskly enough,
that the subjection of women was based on force, began because
women were both weaker than and valuable to men, and was
maintained by a combination of 'bribery and intimidation'. A
synthesis along these lines need not assume that weakness,
vulnerability, childbirth and lactation meant that women have always
been subordinated to men—see Davis' (1971) account of a primordial
matriarchy, for instance. Nor need it assume that some drama in the
mists of prehistory carved a script for the rest of history on tablets of
stone—if (as de Beauvoir especially implies) the biological differences
are such as to produce continuously a particular psychology or power
differential. What it must postulate is the specific character of the
power relations of patriarchy, which mark it off from other structures
of power. It is therefore understandable that such views often go
together with a particular focus on male violence against women as a
crucial political issue in the mobilisation against patriarchy; and with
stress on the creation of autonomous cultural and political resources
by women as a strategy of liberation.

I want to come back to this general formulation of patriarchy later;
here I would like just to signal some difficulties with these particular
bases for a synthesis. Deriving it from a sexual division of labour
means that there is serious difficulty in integrating issues of sexuality
and personal formation—except via some kind of functionalism. On
the other side, deriving social *power* from biological *differentiation*
creates serious difficulties in explaining power relations *within* a given
sex (e.g. the oppression of homosexuals), as well as in accounting for
the history of relations between them.

The second major synthesis of the field proceeds from a very
different starting point. Rather than seeing patriarchy as a *parallel
structure*, equally complete and fully analogous to class structure, it
sees it as the site of *particular kinds of effects* within a social totality,
and not really analogous to class structure at all.

By far the commonest form of this argument in the recent literature, derived from structuralist marxism, sees the family (or sexuality and gender relations at large) as the site of the reproduction of relations of production. These are taken to be the fundamental forms defining the mode of production which characterises a historical epoch or a particular society. But they could not exist without being reproduced, and the performance of this task (dare I say 'function'?) is the principal determinant of the oppression of women.

There are quite a number of analyses based on this line of thought, which became most popular after Mitchell's second book (1975) and Meillassoux (1975) distilled heady brews from anthropology, psychoanalysis and marxism. There is no point here in cataloguing the variations—again, Beechey has done a very useful job—though I do want to note two aspects of the argument which go some way to explaining why a rather curdled piece of structural/functional theory became so popular among socialists. On the one hand 'reproduction' can be seen as the business of bearing children to fit places in production, and servicing the tired worker at the day's end. Reproduction theory thus gave intellectuals a language for some very familiar features of the lives of working–class women, and a way of arguing why they should be feminists.

Alternatively 'reproduction' can be seen as a matter of culture and psychology—shaping people to fit the holes where they are wanted in the system of production, maintaining in good repair the grand social principle of hierarchy and subordination (e.g. Campioni, 1976). And this links to familiar themes in the socialist critique of the distortion of culture to fit the needs of capitalism. When Tolson (1977), for instance, argues a connection between the production of competitive masculinity and the functional requirements of capitalism, the material might be new but the form of argument is very familiar to socialists.

At this point I would like to state, rather baldly, some general objections to this way of theorising patriarchy.

1 It treats patriarchy as a *truncated* structure, either not part of the sphere of production at all, or confined to very limited kinds of production (cf. Rubin, 1975: 167). But we know there is a general patriarchal structuring of production.

2 The exigencies of 'reproduction' are material enough; but they do not at all obviously require sexual hierarchy and oppression. It is in trying to bridge that gap that marxist–feminist reproduction theory ties itself in extraordinary knots, trying to extract explanatory principles from Lacan, Lévi-Strauss, semiotics . . . with, as far as I can see, a complete lack of success.

3 Reproduction theory in general is ahistorical and functionalist; it depends on an indefensible essentialism in class theory; it burkes the key historical question of whether attempts at reproduction will actually succeed.

4 It produces a theory of patriarchy which rests on a *class* periodisation of history (for that is what underlies the concept of 'mode of production'), which forecloses the possibility of research into patriarchy coming up with a new periodisation of the history of production itself.

These objections seem to me to be decisive; and if so, the way of accounting for patriarchy that has been the centrepiece of marxist feminism in recent years must be abandoned. Further, these objections, or something very like them, seem to apply to any attempt to theorise patriarchy that has this kind of logic, that sees patriarchy as the kitchen where particular kinds of effects, required by a social system, are cooked up. So is it back to the parallel–structures model? Yes, if with wary steps. On this question, it seems to me that the radical feminists are the ones who first grasped the right end of the stick. Yet I have already noted difficulties with typical formulations of that position.

These seem to arise basically from an excess of theoretical centralism—from the attempt to organise the whole field around some one master principle. And I think they can be overcome by an approach Mitchell adopts in her first book (1971), and abandons in the second. In *Woman's Estate* she outlines a model of patriarchy where women's situation at any particular time is defined by the intersection and interaction of four different structures (production, reproduction, sexuality, and the socialisation of children), each of which has its own historical trajectory and can move at different paces. Though the term 'structures' is unfortunate—what Mitchell really means here is something like 'practices'—the basic point is extremely important. A theory of patriarchy does not require a 'key', 'core', 'central' relation that organises all the rest. We may regard its unity as a *composed* unity, the (fleeting) product of the history of many processes, which always show some incoherence, some contradictions.

But as critics of the parallel notion of 'relative autonomy' in class theory have asked, what is 'relative' about the autonomy? What entitles us to talk of a unity, a coherence, a system and hence 'patriarchy', at all? I can think of two ways of answering this, though I don't know which (if either) to prefer. One is to do what Rubin does in her superb essay 'The traffic in women': define a zone, a region, a subject–matter for what she calls the 'sex/gender system', and insist that the particular form taken by relations in this zone is highly variable while the definition of the zone itself remains constant. The other (which is rather more consistent with the ideas in the rest of this paper) is to argue that there is indeed a unity, but it is not a logical, definitional one. It is a historically produced unity; and part of the dynamic we are studying is the struggle to *impose* various kinds of order and unity on social relations. Thus, for instance, the father–dominant nuclear family may not actually *be* the pattern of relations that gives rise to all others, but is still the pattern which powerful groups are attempting to enforce, with the result that other relationships get organised by and around the struggle to impose and resist it.

Categories and their production

However this point is resolved, the approach opened up by Mitchell in *Woman's Estate* does seem to commit us to a different view of the social categories in patriarchy from what has been common. The main representatives of both approaches outlined in the last section seem to me to show, to quite a marked degree, traits which in class analysis have been called 'categoricalism' (see chapter 6). They treat a social structure as a set of discrete categories, each with logical 'boundaries', and defining attributes that make each (for the purposes of the analysis) logically homogeneous. Analysis first defines them logically, and then considers the relations they enter into.

There are reasons why the categories in the analysis of patriarchy are still typically couched in a form that has been thoroughly discredited in class analysis. Foremost among them is that the main categories, 'men' and 'women', are not just historical, social categories, but are also biological. However scrupulously we distinguish, like Oakley (1972), between biological sex and social gender—and the distinction *is* necessary, as we know from the experiences of hermaphrodites, transsexuals, and children who are given the 'wrong' label at birth (Stoller, 1968, 1976)—the fact remains that the principal categories are meant to mean both. Like Mahomet's coffin, they hover between the earth of biology and the heaven of history, resident in neither because citizens of both; and the pressure from each realm irons out the wrinkles proper to the other. Thus we get the remarkably simplified set of categories that pass current in theoretical discussions of patriarchy.

I would argue that the categories of patriarchy do not first exist as logical entities, and then enter into particular kinds of relations (such as power relations). Rather, so far as they are social categories, they are produced *as* participants in relations of domination and exclusion, the nature and 'location' of the boundaries between them being defined by social struggle. And they are never logically simple, homogeneous categories.

Much of the literature recognises this point formally, for instance distinguishing the position of working–class women from that of middle–class women; but does not go beyond categoricalism in reckoning with it, merely cross–classifying gender and class categories. (Tolson, 1977, is a particularly clear example in the case of masculinity). Millett (1969) went further, in her definition of patriarchy as a system where male dominates female and older male dominates younger male, thus introducing the notion of a historical relation *within* the gender category. I think we should push this idea further again—much further. As a general rule we should expect to find the categories defined by patricarchy to be a seething mass of internal differentiations, complexities, and contradictions; to have power structures within them as well as between them; and to be redefined not only by struggles between major groupings but by the shifting balance of forces within them.

This must be so, if we see these categories as *really* socially produced, and refuse to fly to one or other of the hundred contending origin–myths to explain them. Analysis of their social production is (and can only be) the history of an ongoing set of practices, in which distinctions are made and sustained, power wielded, people formed. There is no way that these practices can go forward in antiseptic isolation from those that produce the categories of other structures, such as class. On the contrary, we know that they react together in the smallest details of personal life. Real situations and experiences are condensations from these reactions. At the very least, the production of the categories of patriarchy must show turbulence resulting from interaction with other social dynamics.

But more than that: there is conflict, incoherence, contradiction *within* the processes that construct the gender categories themselves. For instance, the creation and imposition of a hegemonic form of masculinity as the social definition of 'man' demands the repression of other psycho–sexual tendencies in hypermasculine men, creates tensions among the large numbers of males who can't quite measure up, and actively oppresses homosexuals and effeminates. None of this is achieved smoothly. The very attempt to transmit hegemonic masculinity within a family dominated by a bull–male father can drive boys into tactics of resistance ranging from becoming a screaming queen to becoming a grass–smoking dropout. Masculinity does not fall from the heavens; it is constructed by masculinising practices, which are liable to provoke resistance, can go wrong, and are always uncertain in their outcome. That, after all, is why so much effort has to be put into them.

Now this is all nicely analogous to Thompson (1968) on class. We see the relations of patriarchy as historical relations, constructed by and in social practices, the categories making themselves as much as they are made ... But there remains a vexatious fact. Those categories, 'men' and 'women', *are* transhistorical in some sense, they *are* simultaneously social and biological. The evidence to which we appeal to prove the social character of gender—such as *berdache* among Amerindians and transsexual careers in western societies—is evidence that entry to the categories is negotiable and not completely settled by anatomy. It is not evidence that the categories himselves are indefinitely malleable. Indeed it can be read as strong evidence of the rigidity of the categories, even in the face of pretty gross violation. For what, say, a male transsexual typically wants, is to *be a woman*, not to redefine or loosen the category of 'men'.

We have, then, to consider the relation of biology to history before we can satisfactorily grasp the nature of the categories in a theory of patriarchy. It is clear, at the least, that they are of a different kind from the categories produced in class dynamics; and that is an important qualification to the position outlined at the end of the previous section.

Historicity

It's not only the categories. Many of the processes at issue also do not seem to be formulable in terms of social practice: menstruation, child bearing, lactation, sexual attachment, arousal, sexual climax, and so forth. It is commonsense that these are non–social, pre–social, or anti–social; and there is plainly something to be said for common sense.

Nevertheless sexual processes do not escape history. We do not have here a haven in a heartless world, any more than in the family. To instance only a few of the ways in which sexuality is social: object–choice, socially patterned to a marked degree, most of all in the definition of who is *not* available as an object; arousal, as we see in the social conventions of seduction; the technique of copulation (Greer, 1971); the period spent with one partner; fantasies during intercourse. Similarly it would not be hard to recite a hundred ways in which body and social process are engaged with each other in the formation of masculinity and femininity while growing up.

Not that this is peculiar to patriarchy. Class processes also involve the body in basic ways. In the most basic issue of all: your chances of surviving birth and associated traumas are distinctly better if you happen to have chosen wealthy parents.

Sartre (1976) offers a general formulation of the relation of the body and social process through labour. In a milieu of scarcity, labour is the form of social practice that determines the shape of history; it also implicates the body in the most direct way. In labour, we use the body as a thing to act on the world of things. This point is important to Sartre, given his attempt to separate levels of social practice so as to rescue the idea of revolutionary transformation from the realm of economic mechanism.

One can see why he does this. Still it seems to me that any doctrine that confines the interaction of the bodily and the social to the lower or more simple or less conscious forms of practice, or which *adds on* the social to the physical (*'Curves Beautified by Berlei'*), is seriously misleading. For two reasons. Complex social constructions, such as hegemonic masculinity, are literally em–bodied in the process of personal formation. And complex and highly conscious social practices, such as liberation struggles, have a bodily dimension. People actually feel different, have a heightened sensibility and greater energy, in the upswing of a major strike or resistance movement. In a revolution the opening of the 'doors of perception' becomes a mass experience.

I would argue, then, that the attempt to fence off biology from history can only succeed by impoverishing history. History implicates the body in all its moments as an active, interactive, participant. It is not just that human biology sets parameters within which history moves (for instance, that we cannot communicate by smell, or that we are capable of reproducing at a certain rate). Indeed biology is a history, of a kind; and if we follow Teilhard de Chardin (1959) or Childe (1954: 7), history is continuous, through qualitative transformations, with organic evolution. This perhaps makes a little less paradoxical the idea of categories which are both biological and social. But there is more to say. The participation of biology and history in these categories is not symmetrical.

Historicity implies a historical process, a social dynamic. Biology enters the constitution of the major categories of patriarchy; but they enter a social dynamic. There is such a thing as a biological dynamic, i.e. organic evolution. But the pace of historical transformations is vastly greater than that, and dominates its effects. Even biological limits, which trigger ecological feedback from population growth and industrialisation, produce essentially social effects (on human beings, that is). Broadly, then, we have a social dynamic which incorporates, uses, and transforms biological differentiation. This will not produce the kind of exponential change and the pattern of transformation

experienced in class relations, because the same biological differentiation is produced afresh in every generation. But by the same
token, the biological 'material' encounters not a constant natural
world, but the new human situations produced from the previous
round of encounters. Thus historical change in patriarchy is not only
possible but inevitable. And there is no reason to doubt that it has an
intelligible dynamic.

But what is it? This I think is one of the most serious gaps in the
current analysis of patriarchy. Some of the things we are presented
with, such as Firestone's 'dialectic of sex', are not dynamics at
all—rather, old–fashioned stand–offs. Others seek the fundamental
dynamic of patriarchy in class relations—a habit not confined to
dogmatists for whom the class struggle is the motor of history, and
also its transmission, gears, steering, and stereo system. Even Reiter
(1977), who most clearly puts the question of the historical dynamic of
patriarchy, periodises it along class lines by identifying as the major
points of transition (a) the creation of state structures, (b) the advent
of industrial capitalism.

This won't do. The transitions in patriarchy of which we have
fullest historical knowledge do not have a relationship to changes in
class structure which would make it sensible to periodise the one by
the other. A theory of patriarchy must gain its historical intelligibility
from nowhere but itself, its own transformations.

This directs us, as a strategic question, to the crisis tendencies within
patriarchy that lead to structural mutation. By 'crisis tendencies' I
mean not just any changes or incoherencies—they can be assumed to
be chronic—but specifically those that implicate the structure–of–
the–whole, the effects of composition already mentioned. For
instance, the shifts in symbols of maleness and collective practices of
teenagers which tied hegemonic masculinity in so closely to the FJ
Holden, mark a significant change, a recomposition, but no crisis
tendency (see Game and Pringle, 1979). But the change in the relation
between hegemonic heterosexuality and marginalised homosexuality
embodied in the emergence of gay liberation undoubtedly was. That
the first impetus of gay liberation has been lost is a useful warning that
'crisis tendencies' are not mechanical trends that work themselves out
inevitably. They are contestable, displaceable, decomposable. The
only assumption that has to be made about them is that they are not
reversible. The structure cannot revert to the *status quo ante*, it has to
deal henceforth with a higher level of tension, incoherence, or trouble
of other kinds.

Can there be a general formulation of the historical dynamic in
patriarchy? Clearly there is a play of power and resistance: not only in
the clash between groups, but also in the process of personal

formation, as this is also the general character of repression. But as the effects of repression remind us, there is also a production going on here—the production of a particular kind of person—and much of that cannot be brought under the rubric of power. The problem is the same as the one about the form of a theory of patriarchy: there is no 'core' that will give a key to the whole process. The dynamic of patriarchy must be understood as a composite dynamic, in which resistance to power, contradictions in the formation of the person, transformations of production, etc., interact. On the structure of that dynamic no-one, as far as I am aware, has yet done any work.

This leads me, finally, to a problem about liberation. If Sartre is right that the intelligibility of a historical process resides in its dialectical character, in the connection of analysis with the project of transcendence; and if a significant part of the dynamic of patriarchy concerns the formation of persons; then what is the meaning of 'transcendence' here—what is the sense of 'liberation'?

Marcuse's (1972a) stress on the revolutionary character of Freud's notion of polymorphous perversity (a concept of liberation perversely projected backwards into unformed children) is heady stuff; but doesn't it mean the transcendence of form towards formlessness? And we know that sexual delight depends not on formless release but on an erotic dialectic of constraint and freedom. I am not sure that I want to give up my neuroses; or that I would be a better, or freer, person, without my armoury of compulsions, fears, fetishes, fixations, prohibitions and enthusiasms. I might not even be a person at all. On the other hand I know that some of this acts as a habitus, to use Bourdieu's term, generating oppressive, or potentially oppressive, practices. And I know that freedom is a social fact, or it is nothing.

Somehow the concept of liberation must be embodied in practices that work *through* the structures of the person, towards the abolition of relations of oppression and exploitation *between* people. And that is where socialist feminism, and feminist-influenced socialism, have to work. They got carried off by the structuralist bus ten years ago. It's time they got moving again.

5
Class, gender, and Sartre's theory of practice

While on study leave in 1979 I finished wading through the *Critique of Dialectical Reason*. It seemed to me to offer some real help in getting beyond structuralism—not surprising, on reflection, since much of Althusser and some of Lévi–Strauss was based on a rejection of Sartre. At all events, here was an important resource which had been practically neglected in the theoretical debates of the Anglo–Saxon world in the 1970s. It seemed worth recovering and attempting to refine the useful parts. 'How should we theorise patriarchy?' made a small start with the knotty problem of the relation of biology to history, and this essay develops that theme as well as others. It was written in August 1980 as a paper for the Sociological Association conference in Hobart, and considerably revised after a very useful discussion there.

In the last decade, as the impact of the women's movement on western socialism has deepened, there has been a good deal of argument about the connection between class and gender relations. Among the attempts to grasp the issue has been an extended debate about the economic significance of housework, somewhat ponderously known as the 'domestic labour' debate (see Molyneux, 1979, for a summary of the literature). Among other attempts have been Delphy's materialist feminism (1977), arguing the independence of patriarchy from class relations but modelling a theory of the former on marxist accounts of the latter; and Mitchell's attempt (1975) to synthesise the two using psychoanalysis and ideology–theory as solvents. There have also been accounts of 'capitalist patriarchy' as a specific kind of social order (Eisenstein, 1979), and attempts to develop a general theory of social reproduction in which everything should fall into place (Centre for Contemporary Cultural Studies, 1978). Hartmann (1979) has an excellent statement of the general intellectual problem.

To say that this literature is abstruse would be a serious understatement: some of it is amazingly esoteric and obscure. Yet it matters; there is a lot at stake. Feminist theory has mounted a fundamental challenge to the way socialists set about analysing society, just as feminist politics challenges the way socialists have traditionally organised themselves and thought about strategy (see particularly Rowbotham et al., 1979). Getting the class/patriarchy problem right is not just a matter of squaring off some timbers in a back room of the socialist theoretical edifice. It bears on immediate and difficult questions of political practice, from how far Labor should support separatist womens' refuges to whether women should campaign for separate representation in socialist party structures. And through them it bears on strategic questions that will decide whether socialist and feminist movements are aligned or opposed in the politics of the 1980s, and ultimately whether socialism itself can be regenerated.

In most of these writings the assumption has been that there are two structures, two sets of relations—capitalism and patriarchy, relations of production and relations of reproduction, class and gender—which are somehow articulated. In short, that there is some kind of hinge between two systems, which occupy conceptually different spaces, but which turn upon each other. Commonly the one structure gets analysed in terms of the way it functions in reproducing the other. Thus a kind of systems theory is smuggled into the argument about patriarchy, slotting in with the implicit functionalism that is common in socialist–feminist discussions of class (see Kuhn and Wolpe, 1978 for a marked example). To get beyond this way of thinking is obviously important. But it is also difficult; we have to go back some steps from positions apparently established. The problem of the articulation of structures, I would suggest, is stuck at functionalism unless we re-think the 'structures' themselves in terms of the practices that compose them. And for that, we need an adequate conception of practice.

A related problem arises within the theory of class. Some approaches conceive of classes as, basically, groups of people (defined according to taste). Others conceive of classes as, basically, positions in a structure of relations (e.g. relations of production). And both of these ideas seem to be necessary. The former is wanted for understanding what a class actually does, i.e. for any theorising of collective action. The latter is wanted for any understanding of what happens to a class, and hence the reasons for its collective action and the limits to what it can do. Yet it has proved extraordinarily difficult to reconcile these conceptions theoretically, or even to use them together. Treatments of class constantly fall towards structural determinism on the one hand, empiricism and voluntarism on the other. (Chapter 1 of Connell and Irving, 1980, develops this argument.)

A partial reconciliation can be found in the work of Thompson, Gutman and other practitioners of 'the new labour history', i.e. the history of the working class. Class, argues Thompson, is 'something which in fact happens ... in human relationships' (1968: 9); it is above all a process of constitution. Class is, in this approach, the way one gets from structure to group, from common fate to collective action. Here again we can see a move towards a conception of practice in order to resolve dilemmas about structure. But it remains unsystematic. For instance, Thompson's brilliant insights into the process of class mobilisation give us very little grip on the problem of class de-mobilisation—i.e. the decline of cultural distinctiveness and politicisation that is so central a feature of class dynamics in the last generation. Here too, it would seem, we need a rather more systematic and sophisticated theory of practice.

The basic idea of this essay is that in wrestling with these problems and others like them, there is a great deal to be learned from the later writings of Sartre, particularly the *Critique of Dialectical Reason*. Much of Sartre's philosophical writing is turgid and dull in the extreme; and I'm afraid some of what follows will be too. But many of his ideas are very powerful. And every so often, even in his most technical prose, a shaft of pure sunlight breaks through the cloud. I hope I can convey a bit of that, too.

It is, on the face of it, curious that the most sophisticated of all modern theories of practice has had so little impact on Anglo–Saxon social science. It's not just in the literature just sketched that Sartre's work is pretty comprehensively ignored, but also in debates about the state, the labour process, psychoanalysis, mass communication, and the dynamics of revolution, on all of which he has penetrating things to say. This is all the more striking in that at the time he wrote the *Critique* he was certainly the most influential intellectual figure in Europe. His journal *Les Temps Modernes* was the most important forum for the attempt to thrash out a sophisticated radical interpretation of the contemporary world (it was, soon after, where Debray's theory of Latin–American revolution was first published); and his earlier work was enjoying something of a vogue in English. Nor is it principally a matter of the inaccessibility of the work. The full text of *Being and Nothingness* has been available in English since the mid–1950s, and *Search for a Method*, an extended essay closely related to the *Critique*, since 1963. Though the *Critique* in full was only translated in 1976, a good condensation of it by Laing (in Laing and Cooper, 1964) has been available since 1964.

If Sartre's work hasn't been used, then, it must be partly because people didn't want to use it. One reason is the anti–communism of the Anglo–Saxon intelligentsia in the wake of McCarthyism and the post–war boom. Given that the *Critique* is an attempt to find an epistemological basis for marxism, and Sartre's postwar politics centred on his fluctuating relationship with the French Communist Party, it was more convenient to ignore it than explore it. Beyond that, a couple of widely–held misunderstandings may have contributed to the silence.

One is the image of Sartre–as–existentialist, the metaphysician of *angst*, wandering around with hand to brow agonising over the loneliness of consciousness in the world. Ironically, some of the few Anglo–Saxon social scientists to have paid serious attention to Sartre have reinforced this image. The so–called phenomenological school of sociology, stressing the subjective construction of social meanings, have sometimes made Sartre an honorary founding father of their enterprise. Even Laing (1960, 1967) and Cooper (1968, 1971), despite their knowledge of the later work, drew their main inspiration from the exposition of existential psychoanalysis in *Being and Nothingness*. The notion of Sartre as a theorist of subjectivity remains in much more recent left–wing critiques, such as Aronson (1978).

This image does Sartre a serious disservice—even for his earlier writings. They certainly don't treat consciousness as separate from social relations. For example, in the terrifying study of schizophrenia in his short story 'The Room' (1939), Sartre dwells on the formal relationships and conventional interactions, the socially–determined incomprehensions, that surround the mad man. And the story enters his delusions, not through an account of his subjectivity, but through the practices by which his wife participates in his world. In *Being and Nothingness* (1943) one finds, repeatedly, ontological questions being worked out through analyses of social situations: such as the famous sketch of the café waiter in the discussion of 'bad faith'. In *Nausea* (1938), the novel that established Sartre's literary reputation, the same thing occurs repeatedly: as in the long, funny and savage set–piece about the provincial bourgeois promenading on the main street of Bouville. Before Sartre's 'discovery' of class struggle, then, his writings showed a strong concern with social practice. Even, one might say, with a specific kind of class practice, as his target repeatedly was the process of objectification in the convention–ridden interactions of the bourgeoisie.

He did make a conscious turn towards class politics after World War II, starting on the track that led towards the *Critique*. Yet a related misconception has been spread among those who might have been expected to take a close interest in the later writings, i.e. English–speaking marxists. To Althusser (whose *Reading Capital* is in part a reply to Sartre's *Critique*), Sartre was one of the main villains in the idealist and humanist perversion of proper, scientific marxism. With the extraordinary vogue of Althusserian ideas among the English, Australian, and to a lesser extent North American radical intelligentsia, this characterisation seems to have been accepted on trust. Sartre–the–Hegelian was created as a companion dolly to Sartre–the–existentialist, and pins stuck in both.

I don't want to enter the fratricidal debate about what is and is not rigorous materialism, though I do have an opinion on how many angels can dance on the point of a pin. The point is simply that this opinion has led people very much concerned with class to ignore an extraordinarily rich discussion of the character and constitution of classes, the nature of labour, the problems of class membership and collective practice. We can't afford to ignore it any longer.

I should make clear that what follows is not an attempt to expound Sartre. He was not exactly backward in expounding himself (the *Critique* runs to 750–odd pages; *The Family Idiot*, which followed it, is three volumes; and there is a huge mass of other writing). There are now also some useful English–language summaries, such as Poster (1979) and Desan (1974). Rather, what follows is an attempt to *use* Sartre, to tease out the leads which his arguments give for the analysis of several intractable problems in social theory. Let us start with the nature of class.

The constitution of a class

In a long section towards the end of the *Critique*, Sartre offers an account of the working class 'as institution, fused group, and series'. These are technical terms developed earlier for a more general purpose. Sartre's basic purpose in this book, as indeed in his massive study of Flaubert, *The Family Idiot*, was epistemological. In the one case he wished to show the intelligibility, through dialectics, of the entire social world; in the other the complete intelligibility of an individual life. I have some doubts about the epistemological answers arrived at, but this isn't the moment to tackle them. What this paper is concerned with is the machinery he sets up to get them. For he has to develop a substantive theory of practice in order to demonstrate the intelligibility of all its forms.

Sartre draws fundamental distinctions between three levels or structures of practice: individual practice, the collective but passive activity he calls the 'practico–inert', and the developed phenomena of groups. The *Critique* expounds them in that order. Sartre is careful to say that that implies neither a historical sequence nor methodological individualism—it is simply an order of understanding. Individual practice comes first because it is most directly and uncontroversially comprehensible by dialectical methods.

Things become more interesting when Sartre moves on to the 'practico-inert', those aspects of social reality which are the consequences of human action, but which oppose, or set limits to, the pure freedom of individual action. This is the world of alienation; but Sartre has in mind a larger realm than is usually included in modern discussions of 'alienation'. He includes, for instance, the state of technology, human–made, which defines a particular labour process and hence what it is to be a worker at a particular time and place. Thus he suggests the nineteenth–century 'universal machine' (a machine which can be turned to many purposes, like the lathe) is 'a passive structure of the proletariat', requiring a certain kind of organisation among workers, the subordination of larger numbers of unskilled to an elite of skilled workers.

Human practice produces a world of passive being, formidable in its inertia, which in turn produces a definite kind of social grouping, which Sartre calls a 'series'. A series exists when people are defined as being severally in one and the same situation, by an object or a logic outside them. Examples: a queue; the audience for a radio broadcast; all those laid off when General Motors closed down its car–assembly plant at Pagewood in Sydney. The unity–in–dispersion thus imposed on them, Sartre calls 'seriality'; and he suggests that this is the basic character of 'class being'. At this level class is passivity, or—since everything in the social world is human activity and its products—'passive activity', activity which receives the imprint of an alien logic and carries it out. As, in different ways, both workers and managers submit to the logic of capital accumulation in the firm; though that logic cannot exist except through their work.

For Sartre, seriality does not occur by itself in pure form; it is simply one structure of the social. Out of it arise various forms of what we might call positive social structuring, groups and institutions.

Not, be it noted, through new features being added to a simpler form—as in the tired old formula of the class-in–itself being transmuted into the class–for–itself by adding the wonder ingredient, class consciousness. There is nothing simple about the matters Sartre deals with under the rubric of the practico–inert. In no sense do his distinctions concern different orders of complexity. The shift to the level of the group involves not an addition to, but a *negation of*, aspects of seriality.

In describing, for instance, the 'fused groups' that engage in social struggle at crisis points such as the storming of the Bastille, Sartre vividly describes the overcoming of the otherness, the dispersal, characteristic of the series, by the course of events that prompts the revolutionary mass to act as one. Similarly, further negations are involved in moving beyond the fused group. The revolutionary mass, for instance, finds in the moment of its victory the threat of its own dissolution. Its transience must be overcome by new forms of unity: and here Sartre introduces the phenomena we are accustomed to think of as the subject-matter of sociology—solidarity, leadership, institutions, bureaucratisation—along with some that aren't so commonplace—terror, sovereignty, militancy. The problem of intelligibility now concerns the relationship between the constituent practices of the members and the constituted practice of the collectivity. Sartre gives the example of a football team, where the free creative practice of each member must interlock with those of all the others before it has any meaning at all. The line of argument expounds the more and more complex series of negations and mediations that are required to understand large-scale social structures in terms of practice, winding up with the state and colonialism.

The is a very quick sketch of a very complex argument; but it is, perhaps, enough to give a grip on Sartre's argument about the nature of a class. The key methodological point is that

> the complex forms assumed—by what are conventionally called *social realities*, need not be confined to any one specific level of intelligibility. (1976: 678-9)

The working class, in the phrase already quoted, is institution, fused group, *and* series. And something more:

> The working class is neither pure combativity, nor pure passive dispersal nor a pure institutionalised apparatus. It is a complex, moving relation between different practical forms. (1976: 690)

At one level, then, class can be understood in the way stratificationism and categorical marxism conceive of it ('pure passive dispersal'). At another level, in the way Thompson and some kinds of radicalism do ('pure combativity'); and at another, in terms of unions, companies, parties and governments. But each of these is inadequate, and simply adding them together is also inadequate. Class, fully understood, has to be understood as the developing *relation* among all these forms of practice, the way they give rise to each other, oppose each other, and collapse into each other, in the movement we call history.

And this 'moving relation' is not an abstraction: it is itself practical, a new type of practice, composed by the others. Class is to be understood through the concept of a multi-dimensional *class practice*. This deserves a new section.

Class practice

This 'new type of *praxis*' is so complex, so intricately mediated, that it cannot immediately be grasped as practice in the sense we understand individual practices or even group practices. It appears to us, rather, as if it were a process in nature, something external to us. Recognising this, Sartre sometimes refers to this multi-dimensional development as 'praxis-process', and sometimes suggests that it is genuinely less intelligible than individual practice. That, however, is a matter of the limits to our comprehension. History never really turns into a natural process (as mechanistic marxism and theories of social evolution or sociobiology would make it).

In this account of the internal complexity of class practice Sartre has, I think, given us a way through some of the antinomies produced by simpler and more abstract conceptions of class. In the process of class formation, we don't have a mobilisation superimposed on a category, with its unity defined in advance by the production relations. We have, rather, a mobilisation addressed to the *disunity* created by the practical reality of a system of production, an open-ended process whose eventual form is settled by social struggle. Thompson's example of the Luddite machine-breakers is very much to the point here (and relevant to current struggles around word-processors), mobilising on the basis of existing social networks to confront and contain the disruption caused by the exploitative use of new technology.

Nor is class formation finally achieved at any given point. Sartre stresses the ways each kind of group and organisation can relapse into seriality; for instance, falling apart by internal conflict, or handling the problems of disunity in a movement by setting up a bureaucratic apparatus. Political parties can represent a return to seriality as well as a more complex form of class mobilisation. Indeed Sartre creates a strong impression that there is always a tendency to relapse into seriality, and that the continued existence of other structures of practice is always something of an achievement. One way or the other, his account gives us some useful tools for understanding the process of *de*-mobilisation—and it's hardly possible to over-estimate the importance for socialists today of getting some kind of theoretical grip on that.

Sartre's own uses of the concept of class practice normally refer to a class as a whole, or some sub–group that is taken to stand for it. The concept is, nevertheless, useful in getting a grip on class phenomena in much smaller groups that in no sense represent classes, for instance families.

In analysing social process we must often go back to the individual life and its immediate environment of other people, as Sartre argued in *Search for a Method* and did in *The Family Idiot*. We then often talk of the 'class position' or 'location' which a person or family occupies. Yet spatial metaphors are no more than metaphors, often misleading, and constantly slip towards stratificationism (see Chapter 6). Strictly, we should still speak of practices which are organised in a class way; which are constrained by, and oriented to, the larger class process (or praxis–process). We need, in short, to speak of the class practices of units which are not classes, such as individuals and families.

Yet it often seems unreasonable to do so, because the activities we wish to relate to class structure are often incoherent, or involve practices not consciously directed to class questions. An example may help clarify this. The Walkers, a ruling–class family I interviewed a few years ago in a wealthy suburb, send their son, Ian, to a well–known elite private school. There the boy is being carefully trained in mathematics and science, and equally carefully as a footballer. His mother gave up her job on marriage, and spends most of her time keeping an elegant house and providing social and emotional support for her husband's career as a top executive in a high–technology industry. Both the relation between Mrs Walker and her husband, and the specific content of Ian's schooling, are highly relevant to their class situation. The patriarchal household is characteristic for senior executives, and important in getting them to the top—Mr Walker couldn't function as a boss in the way he does if it wasn't for Mrs Walker's conventional femininity and domestic subordination. Ian's training in mathematics is plainly related to his task of getting to university for an engineering degree so he can repeat his father's career. So, less obviously, is the football, as that is one of his school's chief techniques for producing the competitive, macho personality structure required for corporate executives. At times, however, the different bits come into conflict. Mrs Walker hates the violence and stress of the football, as many women do. Ian has to rupture his original attachment to his mother in order to fit into the masculine world of competitive striving—and that has produced some psychic stress, which seems to be undercutting his school achievement.

A more detailed account of this research is available in Connell et al. (1982) and Kessler et al. (1982), but this fragment is enough to illustrate the problem. Sartre's stress on the multi–dimensional, multi–layered character of class practice is very useful in understanding what is happening in cases like this. It helps us formulate the coherence of the apparently incoherent. It clarifies the way deliberately class–organised practices (such as the Walkers' sending Ian to a private school) arise out of a field of inertia (such as the fact of living in a ruling–class suburb). It helps us see, indeed, the different levels of mobilisation through which even so small a group as a family may pass, fleetingly, in its constant grappling with the problems endlessly posed it by its class situation.

Some problems

Why does Sartre, in contrast to other theorists of practice such as Bourdieu (1977) or Giddens (1979), lay so much stress on the different levels or structures of practice? There are, I think, two main reasons.

One is that Sartre, writing at a time when official marxism was dominated by a dead economism, wanted to sustain for the world of social relations the thesis of human freedom and creativity that was always basic in his thought, and that gave his politics their anarchist flavour. The terrible constraints of history have to be recognised, indeed stressed—to the extent that Sartre sees terror as necessary in transcending them. But freedom can arise beyond them: not in the distant future as communist eschatology has it, but here and now. Somewhat as, in *Being and Nothingness*, human freedom arises as negation from the ground of the in–itself, so here the collective projects of the social struggle for liberty arise as negation and transcendence from the ground of the practico–inert. For the group,

> freedom is not the free activity of an autonomous organism but, *from its origins*, a conquest of alienation. (1976: 558)

To sustain the thesis of radical creativity, while recognising the weight of inertia in history, pushes Sartre towards the stratification of practice.

The second is Sartre's sense of the truncated intelligibility of history. He assumes the translucency, the immediate intelligibility, of individual practice. Of course he is aware this is an abstraction, but it still sets up a standard of intelligibility which history fails. History is comprehensible only via second–order constructions—the 'constituted dialectic' in Sartre's terms—and we have already seen, in the notion of praxis–process, an acknowledgement of the partial incomprehensibility of what is constituted. Given his model of knowledge, Sartre is pushed towards a stratification of practice in order to account for the opacity of social processes.

One can see the point of a conception of levels in practice. But Sartre's version still seems to leave severe problems; and the epistemological priority of the 'constituent dialectic' is one of them. What appears translucent to Sartre's X-ray eyes is full of shadows to others. If one takes seriously the psychoanalytic idea of the unconscious (which Sartre rejects), there is an epistemological layering within individual consciousness. And if one accepts any part of the range of arguments that the unconscious is partly a social structure—from the early Reich, through Marcuse's arguments on surplus–repression, to Mitchell's argument that the unconscious is where patriarchy and class relations intersect—that layering also is social. Social forces thus must enter as a constituent at the point where Sartre's analysis of practice departs. Some, at least, of the clarity of his distinctions disappears.

Another problem has to do with the classic problem of sociology, how to account for the coherence of a social order. Attempts to build an analysis of social process by moving from individual to collective always run into this problem, and this is where functionalism often enters, and with it a systematic exaggeration of the unity of the whole. Sartre genuinely escapes functionalism, but partly at the cost of incoherence (the second volume of the *Critique*, which was to supply coherence through a positive study of history, was abandoned—I suspect because it was impossible to write), and partly through a purely formal solution derived from the notion of scarcity as the general condition of human society.

This part of Sartre's argument has been extensively, and I think justifiably, criticised. The concept does a lot of work for him. It is scarcity, necessary rivalry for resources, that makes matter an external mediation between human beings, worked matter the medium of a fundamental opposition between them. This is the basis of much that Sartre has to say about seriality. It is the postulate of scarcity that makes classes the fundamental structures of social life, that gives unity to classes, and that gives history its unity as the intelligibility of a struggle. So it affects his account of group practices too.

But scarcity is not the general condition of human life that Sartre makes out. Scarcity can only be defined as inadequacy of means in relation to definite purposes; and as anthropological discussions of 'primitive affluence' indicate (e.g. Sahlins, 1972), we can all too easily fall into ethnocentric views of both what human purposes are, and what are adequate material means. Further, scarcity is not only a natural distribution of resources, it is also socially produced. Indeed Sartre is well aware of this, and spends some time analysing the case of agricultural development in China where the uncontrolled extension of peasant agriculture produced deforestation and hence devastating floods. This requires us to think of scarcity as a condition produced *in* history rather than a condition *of* history; and if so, we cannot regard class or a class relation constructed around scarcity as a *necessary* structure.

A second difficulty is that setting up the argument around the theme of scarcity leads to a curiously impoverished view of the way the body is implicated in social process. In *Being and Nothingness* there was an extended analysis of the body, in relation to consciousness and the relation between consciousnesses. In the *Critique* the body has shrunk to the status of a tool, and a locus of vulnerability.

For an attempt to give a general materialist account of practice and its intelligibility, this quite strikingly ignores the way the body is implicated in social practice through the construction of gender. Even more striking, since precisely that had been spelt out in considerable detail by de Beauvoir in *The Second Sex*, and by Sartre himself in the analysis of character and sexuality in *Saint Genet*.

I presume the reason is something like this. Sartre works from a basic assumption of free action that must lead to total incoherence in the picture of history unless it is reined in by some general restriction. He is also, as a marxist, stuck with a model of class as *the* basic structure of social relations, and the relation between classes as the key to the unity of history. He has to work out this problem in a way that won't produce complications and incoherencies along another dimension—for if that happens, his project of demonstrating the intelligibility of history will collapse. The theme of scarcity gives him this solution, or appears to: materiality can be handled mainly through the analysis of need and work. Hence the marginalisation of the body, except as tool and as bearer of need; and hence the systematic ignoring of problems of sexuality.

But these problems won't go away, just because they are read out of the world of the *Critique*. If the last ten years have shown anything in theoretical sociology, it is that class cannot be understood except in connection with gender. Nor need Sartre have taken the path he did, as if his approach to practice were incompatible with an analysis of patriarchy. I would suggest, on the contrary, it has much to offer; in particular, because it grapples with the general problem of how to understand social categories that are both passively suffered and actively constructed.

Practice and patriarchy

Like theories of class, theories of patriarchy suffer from a deep-seated antinomy. On the one hand are various kinds of biological determinism, which derive the social relationship of power between men and women from ancient differences of physical strength or differences of function in reproduction. On the other hand is the stress on the social construction of gender—massively reinforced by comparative anthropology—which argues that categories are elaborated from bodily distinctions by a social logic not a biological determinism. The second line is the only one that can seriously be sustained. But a position of total social determination is untenable, for the same bodily distinctions have remained an axis of social differentiation throughout history. Can this be recognised without falling back into biological determinism?

Sartre's theory of practice suggests the way this kind of problem can be handled. The gender category is, like the class category, a construction of more than one type of practice. (Usage here follows the convention that 'gender' refers to the social category, 'sex' the biological.) The biological differentiation is a passively–suffered condition. Men cannot bear children, infants require suckling, etc. To these conditions correspond a limited range of practices, and their consequences, that have some of the characteristics Sartre assigns to the practico–inert. At this level, 'women' and 'men' are social categories with some of the characteristics of seriality, an array of parallel situations in which action is defined by an external (in this case biological) logic.

But these aren't the gender categories as we encounter them in social practice—far from it. Indeed the biological *differentiae* of fertility are often quite remote aspects of the social encounters in which gender is constructed and sustained. (This is obvious in the case of the imposition of gender on children.) There are other levels of practice involved.

Sartre's analysis of the relation between levels of practice points us here to a crucial feature that has not often been recognised in discussions of gender. The developed gender system is not a matter of the social being *added to* the biological, or group practice added to the practico–inert. What we see, again, is *negation*. The social gender category involves a negation and overcoming of the serial dispersion of the bodily category, in practices that create the solidarity of a gender or sub-gender. There is a continuing effort to sustain the social definition of gender, which is necessary precisely because the biological logic, and the inert practice that responds to it, *cannot sustain the gender categories.*

Thus we must have masculinising practices throughout the rearing of boys—such as Ian Walker's induction into football—and feminising practices for girls. And they demand forms of repression that often must run *counter to* the biological statute. Girls in early adolescence, though usually bigger and stronger than the boys in their school classes, must be made passive and fearful in relation to males.

To sustain masculinity and male power on the largest scale requires an arbitrary differentiation among men, that constructs some of them as hyper–masculine and others as effeminate; thus part of the dominant group is selected for oppression as queers, poofters and ponces. (Useful analyses of these processes are to be found in Weeks (1977) and Plummer (1981).) Sustaining the myth of sacred motherhood for women in Western Christianity has required institutionalised virginity for some, notably in convents.

More examples could be given, but the point is perhaps made. The gender categories, far from being externally given under a biological statute, are constantly under construction, and internally contradictory; indeed, a 'moving relation' between various sorts of practice.

Yet none of that would make much sense without something that operates at the level of the whole—the power relation between members of the major categories, the overall subordination of women by men. Much of the argument about the concept of patriarchy turns on how to explain that general fact. Possibly this has been a red herring. I'm not sure that we either can, or need to, give an abstract general reason for sexual exploitation, any more than we can for class exploitation. Sartre's effort with 'scarcity' is about as sophisticated an attempt at the latter as anyone has yet come up with, and the result is hardly encouraging. What matters about oppression is not an ultimate 'why', but the fact that it exists; that it has a history; that it is possible to explore its dynamic; and that it is possible to fight it. We can see the power relation of gender, as I suggest we should see the power relation of class, as a historically composed structure whose (always partial) unity is imposed by nothing except its own logic of development.

One thing is crucial in this: the continuation of a structure of oppression is not a fact of nature, it is a practical achievement. As Sartre argues of class,

> exploitation ... could not be maintained, and the process of capital could not develop, if they were not sustained by *the project of exploitation*. (1976: 734)

So also with patriarchy. It could not be maintained except by the project of oppression, sustained collectively among men. Whatever the complicity of women (and, in the case of the survival of capitalism, the complicity of the working class), there should be no doubt where the main responsibility lies—among those with power.

The 'articulation' of structures

We can now come back to the problem raised at the start, of how to understand the relation between gender and class. Sartre's own treatment of 'structure' isn't particularly helpful, as it focusses on the minor issue of the ways the practices of sub-groups or group members are directed to an organisation as a whole, and I suspect it is circular anyway. But the general notion of structures as consisting in multi-levelled practices that are constantly forming and re-forming ('totalising', in Sartre's jargon) seems to me an important tool for grasping the problem of 'articulation' as something more than the exteriorities of a sort of systems theory.

It often seems to be assumed that terms like 'class' and 'patriarchy' refer to different types of practice or at least different spheres in the practical world. Patriarchy, for instance, is referred to the home, class to the workplace; or patriarchy to sexual and ideological activities, class to production and the state. This surely is wrong. There is a patriarchal structuring of production, as is obvious from a glance at any study of sexual divisions in the paid workforce (e.g. Game and Pringle, 1983), even before we consider the division between paid and unpaid work and the sexual division of labour as a whole (see Barrett, 1980: 152-86). And there is a class structuring of sexuality, if anything like Marcuse's or Reich's arguments are correct, and a class differentiation in sexuality, as has been known since the first Kinsey studies. Plainly, we can't think of class and patriarchy as occupying separate spheres of practice.

Rather, we have to think of class and patriarchy as forms of structuring that can be discovered in the same kinds of practice. They are concepts that refer not to peculiar species of practices but to particular patterns of relationship among practices, which create characteristic situations with characteristic constraints. More: as the example of the Walkers indicates, class and patriarchy are forms of structuring that can be discovered in the same practices at the same time. Mrs Walker's relation to Mr Walker is both patriarchal subordination of the most direct kind, *and* the way Mrs Walker participates in the class practice of the family as a whole.

When we speak of the 'articulation' of structures, then, we are speaking of the simultaneous presence of two patterns of determination within one set of practices, on the assumption that each conditions the history of the other through the practices to which they jointly give rise. (In a different context, this is similar to the notion of over-determination adapted from Freud by Althusser (1969: 87–128). That conception however lacks a developed account of practice.)

The simultaneous presence of two patterns of determination within one set of practices is not an exceptional situation. In fact it is difficult to think of any system of practices in our society that is *not* conditioned both by class and patriarchy. Joint determination, and reciprocal influence, is the normal situation. This is clear in practices of childrearing. In the research already alluded to, it has struck us that there is no such thing as *the* situation of working–class or ruling–class *adolescents* in the school or in the family. The situation of working–class *boys* is systematically different from that of working–class *girls*; and for both, their class fate is worked out in and through their gender; and vice versa.

At a higher political temperature, it is notable how class combativity among men is associated with hyper-masculinity, both in macho militancy on the Left (see Burgmann, 1980, on union militancy), and tough management styles in business; while hyper-femininity among women seems to go with passivity in class politics. Here we have a more complex case, where divergent group practice in relation to one structure conditions on the one hand group practice, on the other inert dispersion, in relation to the other structure. It is clear that investigation of the relation between structures cannot stop with demonstrations of functional interconnections at only one level of practice.

This leaves open the question whether, in a particular situation, one pattern of relations may be dominant—a question that cannot be settled *a priori*, for all its importance. It also leaves open a question that has repeatedly been raised when I have talked about the articulation of structures, which is, why stop at two? Why not throw in race, age, or any other structure of difference among people? And, if it comes to that, why start with class and patriarchy? What tells us that they are the most important, or most general, or most necessary?

The general answer is that there is no *a priori* reason to stop at two, or start with these. Sartre's attempt to derive class as a necessary structure of history from general considerations about the context of human life doesn't work, and I doubt that any other attempt at such a demonstration would. The judgment is a practical, not a logical one. These structures are as a matter of fact the most general and powerful, and understanding them gives us the deepest insight into the way the world works and the best chance of changing it. A practical judgment can still be compelling, while blood is being spilt.

Coda

I don't think Sartre's theory of practice, as it stands, provides an adequate basis for a theory of class or patriarchy. The derivation of the necessity of class seems to be wrong, the approach doesn't lead to an adequate treatment of the unity of a system of relations, and the distinction between levels of practice can't be completely sustained. Sartre repeatedly postulates what needs to be demonstrated, and then excuses himself on the grounds of the necessary circularity of dialectical investigation.

But his work does supply at least a starting–point and a direction for an enormously important component of an adequate social theory, which escapes many of the dilemmas of structuralism, and allows us a much more sophisticated understanding of the nature of class and patriarchy and their interconnection in the movement of history. Social science, if it is worth having at all, is about the conditions of human liberation. Sartre's work, for all its flaws, is the most sustained attempt we have to illuminate what now seems to be a growing darkness.

PART TWO

6
Logic and politics in theories of class

While working with Terry Irving on *Class Structure in Australian History*, I had been taking for granted the superiority, indeed the necessity, of a historical approach to class. The common currency of academic sociology, and hence of discourse in the semi-professions that drew on it (welfare, teaching, and the like), was an ahistorical stratificationism. Apart from the brilliant but brief introduction to the second edition of Thompson's *Making of the English Working Class*, there was nothing much to which one could point that would explain what the difference between historical and ahistorical class analysis actually was.

I had long felt that the difference was not mainly in subject–matter, was not even a question of duration at all (for you can get cross–sectional stratificationist studies that talk about time via repeated cross-sections, as in 'panel' surveys like Lazarsfeld, Berelson and Gaudet's *The People's Choice*). It was a matter of the inner logic of conceptions of class, which determined whether or not they could grasp class *dynamics*. And thus it was the logic of class analyses that ultimately decided their political meaning. But how to explain the different logics? Some years earlier I had begun to read Chomsky's linguistics, and it seemed that the distinctions he made in *Syntactic Structures* between different kinds of grammars had some bearing on the problem I was facing. An adaptation (rather than an application) of his models helped to formulate the distinction between dimensional and generative theories that is the basis of this paper. A short first version was written in April 1976, a much expanded one for the Sydney Class Analysis conference in

August that year, and another revision was tried on my
long–suffering students in a course on Class Analysis in early
1977.

The distinction between the concepts of 'class' and 'stratification',
and the theories rallied in disorderly ranks around them, is one of the
more tangled issues in theoretical sociology. There is, as usual, gross
confusion of terms—'class' is often defined in a way that makes it
equivalent to 'stratum'—but there are also more substantial disputes.
We learn from one school that 'stratification' is the more general
concept, and 'class' a special case that arises in particular
circumstances (circumstances which, in some versions of the
argument, have now passed into history, making the continued use of
class concepts a mere ideological anachronism). We learn from
another school that 'class' is the basic social category arising from the
scientific analysis of a mode of production (at least the capitalist one),
while stratification theory is an ideological misrepresentation of class
effects. We learn from some more hopeful souls that the two
approaches can be married, for instance by introducing notions of
elites into discussions of class, or concepts of class consciousness into
accounts of strata. Any of these arguments can of course be made true
by judicious definition.

I will avoid arguing about definitions, because I think there is
something more fundamental here than definitional arguments about
the matter seem usually to have reached. Class analysis and
stratification theory, broadly speaking, represent different types of
theory with different internal structures and different capabilities. In
this paper I hope to clarify some of these differences by examining the
characteristic logical operations that are embedded in their theoretical
arguments.

This is, perhaps, an unusually abstract way of approaching the
question. But it is an approach that has large implications: for the
formal structure of a social theory is intimately connected with the
way it arose, the kind of knowledge it can embody, and the
consequences to which it leads. The capabilities and limitations of
theories are set by their internal logic, and in these capabilities and
limitations much of their political meaning is to be found.

The literature is vast, and life is short. I will develop the argument
around two relatively clear–cut examples, a group of dimensional
stratification theorists on the one side, and marxist class analysts on
the other. I think the argument can be readily extended to 'relational'
stratification theory and at least some post–marxist class analysis, but
will not attempt to show that in any detail here.

The dimensional logic of pure
stratification theory

Stratification theory starts with the discovery that there are differences between people in their command of the benefits their societies offer, 'social goods' as Krauss (1967) called them in an attempt to be absolutely general, and works outward from that. Runciman (1974), in a sophisticated restatement of the approach that I will take as a principal text, defines stratification in this light as 'any and all institutionalised differences of privilege among the adult members of society'.

This is, I think, pretty much the understanding of stratification, or at least of what stratification theory is about, that is basic to the literature. It persists through various controversies about why institutionalised differences of privilege occur and persist, what types of differences there are, and so forth. There has been, for instance, considerable argument over the claim, advanced by Runciman among others, that stratification 'consists in a ranking in three dimensions—the economic, the social (in the sense of social prestige), and the political'. The controversy is about whether three is the right number, it being assumed that stratification means a ranking in *some* number of dimensions. It is important to realise how widespread this view is, even among theorists such as Parkin who talk most of the time about 'class'. Parkin's (1972: 18–19) concept of the class structure and its 'backbone'—'a hierarchy of broad occupational categories'—is strictly within the boundaries of Runciman's definition.

This definition, though simple, establishes a framework within which quite complicated analyses can be conducted. Consider, for instance, Runciman's argument for going beyond statics to dynamics:

> But in general the adequate description, let alone the explanation, of any system of stratification requires not simply a specification of the relative position of all persons within it at some one given moment but also an account of the mechanisms which determine their positions over the course of their lives, whether through individual mobility within the system as it now is or from changes in the degree of privilege attaching to the positions available to be occupied. Formally, therefore, each member of the system should be assigned a place in 'stratification space', whether three-dimensional ... or more complex ..., and his/her movement along the several axes plotted over adult life from an initial position of parental or quasiparental origin. (1974: 58)

Weber, as the quasiparent of stratification theory, might not have approved entirely; but this rigorously follows out the implications of the definition. Dynamics can be analysed in this framework as the movement of people, or positions, or collectivities, along the dimensions of difference, a formulation that incorporates and broadens the usual concept of social mobility.

The definition is elaborated into a theoretical model in the following way. Stratification is conceived of as a system of (institutionalised) differences between people. These differences are inequalities, and can formally be represented by the inequality relation (<) of mathematical logic. A crucial assumption about such a relation is that it is transitive. (Everyone will remember transitivity from the IQ tests they did when being stratified in school: if John is taller than Bill, and Bill is taller than Fred, then John is ... than Fred.) The transitivity axiom is absolutely basic to stratification theory. It allows a set of people to be sorted into an ordered array,

$$A < B < C \ldots < N,$$

which allows the definition of a scale (by specifying units of wealth, prestige, etc.). And this scale is taken to measure or represent an underlying 'dimension'. The same set of people can be mapped simultaneously onto more than one scale and thus arrayed in more than one dimension.

If the inequalities are given an arithmetic interpretation (by introducing a postulate of equal intervals and giving the scale a metric), then the dimension can be taken as strictly analogous to a line in Euclidean geometry. And if several such dimensions are used simultaneously, they become the axes of a Cartesian space, within which every person can be identified by a particular set of coordinates. Boudon's procedure illustrates this particularly clearly:

> 1. We assume that stratification generates and actually describes a number of differences between people. The lower the social status, the poorer the cultural background—hence the lower the school achievement, and so on. These are what we have called the primary effects of stratification.
> 2. The primary effects of stratification may be represented in a Cartesian space. Indeed, let us assume that one of the dimensions of this space is achievement at the elementary school level and that a second is age upon reaching high school. The list could be continued ... Lower class children tend to be located in one 'corner' of the Cartesian space (low school achievement, older age at the end of elementary school, etc.). Conversely, upper–class children are more likely to be located at the opposite 'corner' (high achievement, etc.). (1974: 29)

Boudon here is dealing with a particular sub–set of stratification variables, of course, but he has brought out the general logic of the approach. It does not matter whether the axes are imputed to the social structure by the theorist, or are supposed to be in the heads of the people themselves, as in Goldthorpe and Hope's procedure for modelling judgments of occupational prestige as 'a distribution of points in a Euclidean space of minimal dimensionality two' (1974:

146). Such a dimensional space is a postulate of a great deal of the analysis of multidimensional stratification studies which uses parametric statistics. It is, however, not necessary to make this strong arithmetic interpretation. Runciman's development of the theory is for the most part compatible with a non-metric ordering, and there are mathematical techniques which can handle this in several dimensions at once. What *is* essential is that there is a transitive inequality relation, without which the central idea of a dimension of differences breaks down. A set of such relations defines a homogeneous space within which people can be located; the Cartesian space of these examples is merely a special case.

All of this applies regardless of what the units arranged are— whether people, families, roles, positions, occupational groups—and also regardless of what the relation between them is, provided only that it meets the criterion of transitivity. Thus the view sometimes expressed by marxist critics, that stratification theory deals with distribution and consumption but not with production, is not strictly correct. Parsons (1954) for instance is able to incorporate relations of production into a strictly stratificationist theory.

What we have, to this point, are dimensions of difference. The idea of 'stratification' is plainly more than this; and Runciman's definition is incomplete, because it does not particularise *strata*. However the meaning of 'strata' is now easy to define. Strata are sets of people (roles, families, etc.) who are located at a particular point, or within a particular range, of one of the dimensions. Thus Lenski, who defines a stratum (he calls it a 'class') as

> an aggregation of persons in a society who stand in a similar position with respect to some form of power, privilege, or prestige. (1966: 74-5)

The image of a society as a series of layers like the strata of a geological succession is thus given a precise meaning.

Two characteristic problems arise from the fact that strata are so defined within the homogeneous space of dimensional analysis. The first is the difficulty of settling how many strata (or 'classes') should be distinguished. Lenski, for one, is very open about this:

> The critical reader will ask how much similarity is required and will find, unhappily, that there is no definite answer ... In most cases human populations simply are not stratified into a limited number of clearly differentiated, highly discrete categories. Rather, they tend to be strung–out along continua which lack breaks that can be utilised as class boundaries. ... In general, students of stratification have found it more advantageous to employ a smaller number of larger and more inclusive classes. (1966: 76)

Lenski tries to make a virtue of it, but the problem arises from the basic model. On a homogeneous dimension, the specification of boundaries must *in principle* be arbitrary; and what appears 'advantageous' to 'students of stratification' is no *theoretical* specification at all. Statisticians have devised ingenious clustering techniques to make empirical judgments based on where, on the various scales, most people happen to fall (for a recent example see Broom and Jones, 1976: 106 ff.); but in no sense is this a result yielded by the theoretical stratification model. More often, and quite reasonably, the cut–off points are defined by *fiat* and have no significance in the analysis. In fact, we have reached here one of the limits of pure stratificationism. The issue can only be handled theoretically by stepping outside that logical framework, and a number of theorists have done so precisely at this point.

The second problem is really a special case of the first: how does one deal with elites? Stratification theorists often wish to speak of elites (one reason why will appear below); but they have no way of incorporating them into the basic model except by defining an elite as the set of people occupying the top range of some dimension. For example:

> the highest ranking segment of any given social unit, whether a class or total society, ranked by whatever criterion one chooses. (Lenski, 1966: 78–9)

Lenski acknowledges that the boundaries of elites 'are usually imprecise'. One could better say, in stratification theory, they are always arbitrary; and one finds a characteristic imprecision even among the most careful theorists when they reach this point. It is even difficult to pin down the proper number of elites, for an indefinitely large number can be defined for any social order according to the number of criteria which, in Lenski's phrase, one 'chooses' to study. Thus the plurality of elites in attempts to apply stratification theory, such as Keller (1963) or Encel (1970).

To speak of an elite *being* something is quite possible in this framework, but to speak of an elite *doing* something is to step outside it. Yet this is what Runciman is obliged to do when he confronts the question of how a particular dimensional system gets to be there in the first place. This problem was handled by functionalist theorists by a kind of hidden–hand argument, the hand being variously attached to the arm of system survival, system integration, or technological evolution. All, be it noted, locate the constraint outside the stratification system itself. Runciman, no functionalist, attempts to tie the explanation back to his strata, but winds up in a kind of bootstraps argument. It is open to industrialising elites, apparently, to decide what kind of stratification system they—or more exactly their non–elites—are going to have (1974: 94). But how those elites arise, and come to be in a position to make such decisions, is left without explanation in the theory.

There is in fact good reason why this problem should be difficult for stratification theory, and why it is usually solved by appeal to some extrinsic cause. To give an *internal* account of the generation of a stratification system requires some notion of dialectics, which must break the bounds of dimensional logic. At the least, it requires a claim for the special significance of some link in the chain of inequalities, which violates the general transitivity axiom on which the very concept of a dimension is built. Dahrendorf seems to have understood this. Wishing to build a dialectic into his reformulation of class theory on the basis of the Weberian concept of authority—a relation that normally fits the stratification model—he was obliged to attribute a (quite arbitrary) special significance to one link in the chain, specifically the relation between those with no authority and those with any (Dahrendorf, 1959: 238, 265). This does not, I think, yield a satisfactory account of change in a class structure, but at least it escapes the impasse to which pure stratificationism leads.

A strict dimensional theory without a dialectic can still handle history, though in a very specific way. Let us return to the passage about dynamics in Runciman quoted above. He notes that there can be change by the movement of individuals or positions within a stratification space. The theory accordingly does not fix any necessary distribution within this space. It follows that a particular society can be characterised by the distribution (at a point of time, or a range of distributions within a range of time) of persons (or positions, etc.) within the space. We may then, moving to a meta–level, define a system of *differences between distributions* which represent differences between societies. (For the purposes of this exercise, the dimensions themselves must be assumed to be standard.) Runciman does just this, classifying societies on such variables as the degree of concentration of power, and the rate of elite turnover.

These meta–level differences can themselves be ordered, and the ordering yields a new system of scales—just as the differences between people were treated, except that the units now being classified are whole societies. This provides the basis for a typology of societies. Runciman works out such a typology for a range of industrial societies, but the logic can of course be extended beyond this. There is a close parallel here with the procedures of French structuralism. If, instead of treating these meta–level differences as forming scales, we treat them as categorical variables, the model produced is exactly equivalent to the 'combinatory' that is the basis of Lévi-Straussian theory, and which appears also in the treatment of the elements of a mode of production in some recent marxist writing (e.g. Balibar, 1970; Terray, 1972).

Stratification theory can thus be developed to incorporate the past as well as the present, for such a typology can be made sufficiently general to extend to all known societies and all periods. But it does so, as critics of structuralist theory have often pointed out, at the cost of suppressing historical process. The criticism has been levelled at structuralist combinatories, rather than meta–level dimensional structures, though as the former are merely special cases of the latter the argument is not hard to develop. What it means in the present case is that the theory does not of itself yield an account of the actual historical transformation of any one type into any other. They merely coexist in the combinatory. The *logical* transformations necessary to produce one from the other can readily be specified (as far as I can see they will take the form of the permutation group as discussed by Piaget, 1971b). But these transformations have no *historical* content, no necessary ordering or irreversibility.

Intransitivity and the market

When Weber remarked that class situation is 'ultimately "market situation"' (1958: 182), he was summarising a decisively different approach. The idea of class as a position in a market—a shared position, of course—is capable of yielding an account of the hierarchies of which stratification theory speaks, but it is not based on the same logic. This concept of class is based on transactions between people which do not and cannot obey the postulates of the stratification model.

Let us consider the particular kind of market which is central to both Marx's and Weber's account of class structure in capitalism, the labour market. When, as Marx puts it in *Capital* (I, 6), 'the owner of the means of production and subsistence meets in the market with the free labourer selling his labour-power', and establishes the relationship in which capitalist production will be carried on and surplus–value produced, it is clear that they are not establishing a link in a stratificationist array. The relation is not transitive. The person who is capitalist to someone else as wage–labourer, is not in principle wage–labourer to some higher order capitalist, which would be necessary to yield an ordered array. A small capitalist may certainly be driven out of business by a bigger one and thus become a wage–labourer, as Marx anticipated would happen to most—but only by virtue of ceasing to be a capitalist of any size. This would merely change the numbers of people in the positions or 'places' (to wax Althusserian) of capital and labour, it would not create intermediate strata. The labour market may be *segmented* (as in American theories of the 'dual labour market'), but it is not logically *ordered*, in the manner of stratification theory, by its fundamental relation.

A theory of class based on market exchanges, then, must obey a different logic from one based on comparisons or hierarchical relations. A first approximation to it is that the relationships involved can be conceived of as *oppositions* between the people or groups involved (e.g. Poulantzas, 1973: 86). This immediately suggests a dichotomous class structure, and dichotomy is indeed central to Marx's analysis of the capitalist mode of production, the dichotomy of the owner of means of production and the worker bare of all but labour–power. The same logic is strongly suggested by Weber's (1958) observation that '"Property" and "lack of property" are, therefore, the basic categories of all class situations', regardless of the type of market in which these two categories are found. Giddens is correct that Weber's view leads to a pluralistic conception of classes (1973: 42), provided that one observes the plurality is in large part a plurality of markets, within each of which a dichotomous property relation can be found. (To the extent that the different forms of property become transferable, the markets merge: which is of course the burden of Marx's argument about the long–term tendency of capitalism to transform all other forms of production into its own.)

It would, however, be a mistake to take dichotomy as *defining* class analysis. Ossowski's tendency (1963) to sort class theories according to the numbers of classes recognised does not get to the bottom of the matter. Numbers of strata are arbitrary in stratification theory, and it is quite possible to have a stratification model with only two: elite/mass theories are familiar examples. It is also possible to produce a market analysis in which more than two fundamental places are recognised, as for instance by Giddens:

> There are three sorts of market capacity which can be said to be normally of importance in this respect: ownership of property in the means of production; possession of educational or technical qualifications; and possession of manual labour-power. In so far as it is the case that these tend to be tied to closed patterns of inter- and intragenerational mobility, this yields the foundation of *a basic three–class system* in capitalist society: an 'upper', 'middle', and 'lower' or 'working' class. (1973: 107)

One should not be misled by stratificationist terms such as 'upper', 'middle', and 'lower', which have more to do with the *consequences* of transactions in a market (such as money income). These can be mapped on a dimension; the basic relations themselves cannot.

The intransitivity of fundamental relations is what allows class theory to overcome one of the characteristic problems of stratification theory, the indeterminacy of the number of classes and their boundaries. This is not to say that it is always *easy* to specify classes and determine their boundaries in a given historical situation. In historical class analysis such problems regularly arise in giving an account of class formation, where boundaries are naturally uncertain because they are in process of being constructed. In the highly formal version of class theory due to Althusser and Poulantzas, classes are clearly defined in the abstract analysis of a pure mode of production, but problems of enumeration and demarcation arise wherever this is to be tied down to a concrete social formation (see Poulantzas, 1975). Other cases could be given. The point is not that the job is easy; simply that the specification of classes is not arbitrary in the logic of the basic theory.

A more positive way of putting this would be to say that it is the category of *class structure*, rather than the category of class, that is fundamental to class analysis. Classes arise within a social order which has given birth to certain kinds of oppositions, and develop as a structuring of that social order by processes of mobilisation around specific oppositions. Class formation in the sense of Thompson's *Making of the English Working Class* involves the bringing–to–consciousness of the basic oppositions and their consequences, and is itself a crucial step in the development of a full–blown class society.

Generative logic:
the example of marxist theory

A concept of class based on position in a market is not in itself a decisive advance over stratification theory; this too can remain a static and ahistorical concept. If class is, as Thompson argues, an event, 'something which in fact *happens* ... in human relationships' (1968: 9; my emphasis), class theory must be something more. It must be able to deal with historical process, and do so through its central concepts. In this section I will outline some features of Marx's approach which give it this capacity, and which must in some form or other be shared by any historical theory of class.

> It follows from Marx's ontology that research has to be directed to discovering the transformation rules whereby society is constantly being restructured, rather than to finding 'causes', in the isolated sense that follows from a presupposition of atomistic association, or to identifying 'stages' or 'descriptive laws' governing the evolution of totalities independent of their parts [as in evolutionary stratification theory — RWC]. Marx thus directs our attention to the processes of inner transformation in society. (Harvey 1973: 289-90)

Or, as other commentators have observed in language closer to his own, Marx approaches the analysis of society from the point of view of its reproduction. In one of its aspects *Capital* is an attempt to detail the transformational rules according to which capitalist social relations are reproduced and, in their reproduction, changed.

The concept of transformations (in reality) or transformational rules (in a theory) is a very general one, though its recent popularity has come from a specific usage. In his account of the grammar of natural languages, Chomsky (1957, 1965) shows how the structure of sentences can be analysed in terms of a set of transformational rules. These specify steps by which one can get from a relatively simple starting point (a 'kernel' sentence in the earlier version of the theory, an abstract 'base phrase–marker' in the later) to the complex structure of actual utterances. In Chomsky's usage the transformations are purely logical devices meant to simplify the grammar, and are not taken necessarily to represent real–world processes; in this they differ from some psychological usages and certainly any historical usage. The model is useful, however, in characterising the logic of any theory that speaks of the production of a structure out of another structure; and this plainly is what class theory does. We may identify a general type of theory which incorporates rules that specify possible transforms of a given structure and rule out others, which thus 'generates' the possible transforms by specified operations. Marx's theory is a generative theory in this formal sense.

We see this in the well–known chapter of *Capital* on 'simple reproduction', where Marx concludes:

> Capitalist production, therefore, under its aspect of a continuous connected process, of a process of reproduction, produces not only commodities, not only surplus–value, but it also produces and reproduces the capitalist relation; on the one side the capitalist, on the other the wage–labourer. (Vol. I, Chapter 23)

Marx offers the concept of a cycle of activity, starting with the meeting of capitalist and worker in the labour market, proceeding via the labour process and the payment of wages, the extraction of surplus value and the marketing of the product, the entire circulation of capital—the cycle getting more and more complicated in successive volumes—always returning to a new meeting in the market and the reproduction of class relations.

Of course this is only the beginning. In itself it is only an identity transformation and would merely model the persistence of class relations through time. (Though even that is an improvement on the 'institutionalisation of differences' in stratification theory.) The same concepts also yield an account of 'reproduction on an extended scale', the *accumulation* as well as the maintenance of capital, and a host of consequences thereof.

Two are particularly important. The first is the series of changes linked with the growing productivity of the capitalist system, its destructive competition with older production systems, and the creation of unemployment, by which more and more of the population are swept up into capitalist class relations. Marx does not develop this side of the theory formally, but we have here in principle a set of transformations specifying what might be called the lateral extension of class relations. The second, which is worked out in more detail in *Capital*, deduces changes within the system: the rising organic composition of capital, the tendency of the rate of profit to fall, which in turn 'breeds over–production, speculation, crises, and surplus–capital alongside surplus–population' (III, 15). A definite historical trajectory, and not just an open–ended process, is thus deduced from the transformations specified in the analysis of extended reproduction.

A great deal of marxist writing has been devoted to working out the later stages of this trajectory in terms of Marx's generative logic. Theories of finance capital and imperialism were produced in Lenin's era; then theories of fascism and the state; and most recently, theories of urban structure and changes in the labour process. It may be illustrated by a case as far removed as possible from the technology of Marx's day, Greenbaum's (1976) study of the computer industry. Computers were introduced in American business in the 1950s, and the work force was originally undifferentiated. Machine languages were typical, and they required skilled workers, often drawn from research backgrounds, who formed a freewheeling group that mixed programming and operation and commanded very high rates of pay.

A marked change set in in the 1960s, particularly associated with the IBM360 series of computers which had much wider commercial applications, and the development of specialised programming languages such as COBOL. Greenbaum argues that this resulted in a *downgrading* of average skills (in contrast to what is usually thought about cybernation) and a marked differentiation between types of jobs, producing a hierarchy of systems analyst, programmer, computer operator and keypunch operator. This was not inherent in the technology, but was inherent in the capitalist context in which the technology developed. It was a consequence of management's drive to lower labour costs and achieve labour stability, and centralise key information in the hands of a small professionalised group of workers who could be linked tightly to the interests of capital. In the 1970s, with a period of labour oversupply, wage rates were checked and much computer work was converted into routine semi–skilled operations.

This is, I think, a particularly interesting case, not just because it deals with the technology that a good many thinkers—on the left as well as the right—believe is breaking down class patterns; but also because it shows very clearly the way a job hierarchy of the kind spoken about in stratification theory is actually produced. The categories of class theory here specify the constraints (profitability, leading to a drive to lower average wages; control, leading to a drive to centralise information) under which a labour process is developed and a new set of production relations created. Greenbaum's study is by no means isolated: a similar story, set further back in history, is told by Stone (1974) about the origins of the modern job structure in the American steel industry—here the breaking down of earlier production relations by capital required bloodshed—and Braverman (1974) offers a general argument covering 'white-collar' office work and 'service' work as well as industrial labour.

This analysis, however, has a fundamental problem. How do such generative processes get started? As Marx also observed,

> The class relation between capitalist and wage–labourer therefore exists, is presupposed from the moment that the two face each other in [the labour market exchange]. It is a purchase and sale, a money–relation, but a purchase and sale in which the buyer is assumed to be a capitalist and the seller a wage–labourer. (*Capital,* Vol. II, Chapter 1.)

Wealth, to Marx, is not capital until it is used precisely in this exchange and in the production process structured by it.

In what sense do we have a generative theory of class, when the principal groupings whose formation is to be explained are presupposed in the basic relation of the theory? Marx goes into this *empirically* in considerable detail, tracing through European history the ways in which the immediate producer was separated from the means of production and the characteristic production relation of capitalism was itself created. To represent this *in theory* it is necessary to move to another logical level, where the unit of analysis is no longer the commodity but the mode of production as a whole. The generative theory of capitalism then rests on a second–order theory, in which we find formulations of the transition between modes of production.

This has a formal similarity to the meta–level dimensional theories of comparative stratification theory. To the extent that they differ—and some marxist theoreticians come very close to the other school at this point—it is along the lines stated by Habermas:

> Historical materialism now proceeds from the assumption that the productive forces and relations of production do not vary independently of each other but, rather, form structures which, firstly, correspond with each other; secondly, which produce a finite number of developmental stages which are homologous in their structures so that, thirdly, the succession of the modes of production reveal some kind of developmental logic. (1979: 139)

In short, a generative theory of modes of production is required. The 'kind of developmental logic' is crucial, for a notion of simple technological succession here would produce a theory not very different from Lenski's evolutionary stratification theory.

Marx's formula of a contradiction between the forces of production and the relations of production provided a starting-point. He worried at the issue, especially in the later sections of *Capital* where he attempted to produce a theory of crisis that was consistent both with the internal 'laws' of capitalist development (the lower–level transformational rules in the theory) and with his general formula. The issue has recently come back into focus in Marxist theory (see e.g. Hindess and Hirst, 1975). Marx's aspiration was to produce a unified analysis that operated at both levels, which would indeed be a mighty feat of theory construction. But there is no need to suppose that the logic of the one will closely resemble the logic of the other.

Historicity and politics

In his remarkable study *Class Struggle and the Industrial Revolution*, Foster (1974: 3) speaks of the necessary 'incompleteness' involved in the study of a social system seen at a particular moment in time. It is well illustrated by Foster's own theory of false consciousness, a consciousness based on particular historically developed levels of consumption, which contains destabilising possibilities for the future, and (in specifiable ways) constitutes a block to any ruling–class attempt to revert to previous conditions.

It is the incorporation of this incompleteness in the basic structure of theory, I would suggest, that constitutes the historicity of class analysis, and can be represented (in terms of the formal properties of theory) by the concept of a sequence of transformations. It is not there by chance. Socialist class analysis developed a generative logic, not because Marx was a half–baked Hegelian drunk on the dialectic, but because socialist thinking embodied a specific social experience in which real transformations were focussed. It arose from the experience of workers at the heart of the process of capitalist industrialisation, and crystallised the politics of resistance and revolt to which that experience gave rise.

Stratification theory, as I have argued, is capable of historical application, but its treatment of history is almost exactly the reverse. Time flows *through* the categories of an analysis such as Boudon's, it is not inherent in them. Time is actively suppressed by the comparative stratification theory that produces a permuted typology of societies. And if introduced by specifying a sequence of types (as in Lenski's 'evolutionary' theory), time is necessarily external to the categories applied in the analysis of any type in the sequence, so long as the stratificationist approach holds true.

The ideological significance of stratification theory has a great deal to do with this suppression of historical process. One is not surprised to find, at the end of Runciman's long paper, a nod towards the politics and ethics of the matter in which he says that the stratification theorist cannot say which type of society is best:

> All he can say is that whether for better or worse institutionalised competition for privilege will be universal among post-industrial as among industrial societies; or as Michels concluded in a more limited context, the 'cruel game' is likely to continue without end. (1974: 95)

A nice peroration, and this is indeed the nub. Suppressing history, stratification theory lacks the specific incompleteness of historical theory, and with it the concept of a *future* produced by that incompleteness. History has come to an end, or perhaps was never there, and what we know now we will always have, though perhaps in different combinations and permutations.

The connection between the theory and the politics is in fact the reverse of what Runciman suggests. It is not the conclusion of his theory that he has stated here, but one of its postulates. He wrote at the start of the same paper, in a passage which he had presumably forgotten when writing its conclusion, 'Stratification, like kinship, is a cultural universal ...' (1974: 56). One begins to see the political significance of the marked voluntarism noted earlier. Runciman is saying, in effect, that everyone has to have stratification, but industrialising elites can choose which sauce they will have it with; he offers a vision of class relations from the point of view of the exploiters.

Class relations will continue to mean exploitation, violence and probably war as long as class societies persist. Of course, historical class theory no more guarantees that class society will end than ahistorical stratification theory guarantees it will continue. What it does—and this is still a vital function for socialism—is to provide a way of thinking the possibility of an end. Not an end to history, as ruling–class ideology always tries to persuade us. Perhaps, as Marx suggested, an end to the pre–history of human society.

7
Complexities of fury leave...
A critique of the Althusserian
approach to class

> At midnight on the Emperor's pavement flit
> Flames that no faggot feeds, nor steel has lit,
> Nor storm disturbs, flames begotten of flame,
> Where blood-begotten spirits come
> And all complexities of fury leave,
> Dying into a dance,
> An agony of trance,
> An agony of flame that cannot singe a sleeve.
>
> Yeats, 'Byzantium'

'Logic and politics' tackled the relationship between stratificationism and historical class analysis. But for a good many people that issue was already passé. In the early 1970s a remarkable number of English–speaking socialist intellectuals began to abandon ship for another life–raft, structuralism. More and more students who were concerned with class analysis were now taking it to mean exegesis of Althusser, Poulantzas, and their followers.

The reasons for this shift are complex. Some people who had been radicalised in the student movement and the campaign against the Vietnam war were dissatisfied with a vague radicalism and were in search of a more rigorous analysis of capitalism. Some were no doubt attracted by the splendid air of confidence with which age–old problems were solved. And structuralism was in the air—Lévi–Strauss in anthropology, Chomsky in linguistics, Piaget in psychology, and structuralist literary critics, were all reaching the peak of their influence in the Anglo–Saxon world about this time.

I was, frankly, exasperated by the fashion for structuralist marxism. For a few, who could clamber through the maze and come out the other end with some useful experiences and still able to think for themselves, it was exhilarating. For most, it was a retreat into dogmatism, a refusal of both experience and history, and very often a refusal of real politics. But I didn't have much success in conveying these reactions. In April 1978 the students in our Class Analysis course asked me to explain them in detail, and the result was the first version of this essay. It was shorter, and much more irritable, than the version presented here. Discussion showed that many points needed to be worked out in detail, given the complexity of the texts. And some of the exasperation was worked out in the process of writing the critique. I still think the structuralist episode of the 1970s was a disaster for radical intellectuals, and that many intelligent and active people are still trapped in its by–ways and aftermath.

Since what follows is a close argument about a set of texts, questions of sequence are sometimes important. It should be borne in mind that the dates in the citations are those of the English translations, not the French originals which are sometimes referred to in the text. I should also note, since what follows is very negative, that there *are* some insightful and useful passages in Poulantzas' work, especially in his last two books when he was moving rapidly away from the theoretical framework discussed here. It is a pity the earlier texts are still the ones by which he is mainly known.

One of the most remarkable things about the revival of socialist theory in the last decade has been the influence of the French school of marxism which formed in the early 1960s around Louis Althusser. Serious criticism of their ideas has mostly come from within marxism, and has naturally focussed on what appeared to be novel within that intellectual framework—their epistemological doctrine, their account of 'the break' in the history of Marx's thought, their theory of ideology and the state. Criticism (at least in English) has mostly overlooked their position on an issue that many socialists would regard as rather more fundamental—the theory of class.

Partly this omission has to do with the history of the school itself: its positions were first worked out as philosophical doctrines. As Althusser retrospectively remarked (1976: 146), 'the class struggle does not figure *in its own right* in *For Marx* and *Reading Capital*', and

the same is true of *Lenin and Philosophy*. Books within the
Althusserian framework explicitly devoted to the theory of class did
not appear until 1974 (Poulantzas' *Classes in Contemporary
Capitalism*) and 1977 (Carchedi's *On the Economic Identification of
Social Classes*). Yet there is a definite approach to class to be found
even in the philosophical texts, which after all use the term, if they
don't examine it, on every second page. It was crystallised in 1968 in a
highly influential forty pages of Poulantzas' *Political Power and
Social Classes*; and can be followed in a more explicit and elaborated
(and in some respects modified) form, into the texts of the 1970s.

The other reason why the Althusserian approach to class has not
figured prominently in critiques is that many of the critics share it—or
at least, hold assumptions about how to think about class that are
strikingly similar. Criticism is very definitely a process with a subject.
The following discussion is conducted from a position at a fair
distance from the Althusserian; further, for instance, than that of
marxists like Wright (1976), Hunt (1977) and Clarke (1977) who have
addressed Poulantzas' views on class; in short from a non-marxist,
though explicitly socialist, position. I wish to evaluate the
Althusserians, not as candidates for the apostolic succession to Marx,
but as voices in an enormously more important debate among
socialists about the nature of capitalist society and the future strategy
of the labour movement. That, I take it, is what the theory of class is
really about. The focus of the discussion, then, will be how an account
of the class structure of capitalist society is constructed in the
Althusserians' writings, and what the politics of that account might
be.

Their approach cannot be extracted from one or two quotations.
The sociological views expounded by Poulantzas and Carchedi rest on
canons of method developed in the earlier philosophical writings. But
these writings themselves rest on assumptions about class, more
exactly on positions taken within the theory of class and political
organisation. There is, then, a rather complex network of arguments.
I will certainly not attempt to expound it *in toto*; but I hope at least to
have teased out from the philosophical writings the main themes
which were to govern the development of a theory of class, and
conversely from the sociological writings the main positions in which
the methodological arguments issued. At all times the networkish
character of the arguments should be borne in mind.

A word, before launching out, on the sense in which one can talk of
an 'Althusserian school'. It is notable that almost every member
of it, including Althusser, has at some point or other announced a
departure from the original positions. There are divergencies between
the texts, some of which will be explored later. Yet I think it would be

widely agreed that these are differences in the working–out of a common approach, rather than fundamentally distinct positions; and it is the common ground that is the subject of this essay. Though the point of the argument is political, it is not meant in any sense as a commentary on the political vicissitudes of Althusser, Poulantzas, and the others in their personal situations. It is strictly an attempt to evaluate the significance of that part of their work that has gained international circulation, and that has had a considerable impact on the modern theory of class. In what follows, 'Althusserian' can be read as meaning simply what is common to the texts under discussion. I would also like to acknowledge here a general debt to the ideas of Callinicos, whose *Althusser's Marxism* is the best analysis of the Althusserian system I have seen.

Althusser's project

As he has explained carefully and often, Althusser began to formulate his distinctive views in response to a definite situation, that of intellectuals close to the French Communist Party at the end of the 1950s. It was a moment when that party was groping for a strategy, in the fug of de–Stalinisation in the world communist movement, and vast uncertainty in the left at large after the postwar restabilisation of capitalism. The context encouraged a basic reconsideration of socialist ideas: either in the form of attempts to reconstruct them (this was the time and place that produced Sartre's *Critique of Dialectical Reason*, Mallet's marxist syndicalism in *The New Working Class*, and Cardan's 'The meaning of socialism', as well as the rhetoric of 'humanism' in official communist circles); or in the form of a strenuous reaffirmation of orthodoxy.

Althusser's choice was for orthodoxy, but not a simple one. His response took the form of a search for the class line in theory, a new way of demarcating what was authentically marxist and proletarian from what was not. What was not, included marxist humanism. To Althusser, this represented contamination by bourgeois ideology, which had now succeeded in penetrating the communist movement in a big way. The theoretician's task was, as he put it in *Reading Capital*:

> to repel the humanist and historicist assault which, in some circles, has threatened Marxism continuously for the past forty years. (119)

His project was, in short, to purify marxism: to free Marx's science from its crust of distortions; to reject 'false solutions' to political and economic problems; and thereby to vindicate the proper principles of

proletarian politics. These he summarised in another context some
years later, in talking of parties

> which apply a mass 'line' of struggle for the seizure of State Power, a 'line'
> based on 'the concrete analysis of the concrete situation' (Lenin) in which
> they have to fight (this 'analysis' being achieved by a correct application of
> Marx's scientific concepts to the 'concrete situation'). (1971: 72)

If the detection of Marx's 'scientific concepts' can be taken as the
main theme of his philosophy, their 'correct application' is
undoubtedly the master theme of the sociology that followed.

Beginnings are not everything, but they are important; and two
related aspects of this one are striking. The first is the intellectual
frame of reference established by a communist theoretician setting
about the business of purifying marxism. Though Althusser draws
from some unexpected sources, including Freud, it is notable that the
socialist thinkers he draws on are, almost exclusively, men canonised
by the communist movement: mainly Marx and Lenin, secondly
Engels, Gramsci and Mao. Many of the most important socialist
thinkers of the century are either never mentioned, or treated briefly
and with scorn. To anyone except those committed to a strict
communist loyalty in politics, this must appear an approach that is
radically impoverished from the start. Its effects can readily be traced
in the starkness of the later Althusserian account of class.

The second point is that the project in its philosophical beginning is
already governed by an implicit, and highly political, conception of
class. Althusser constantly wished to draw class lines in the realm of
theory—for instance in his early distinction of ideology (governed by
class interests) from science (which is not), and in his later definition
of philosophy as the class struggle in theory. To give him his due,
Althusser explicitly rejects in principle the crude 'proletarian science
vs bourgeois science' schema held by Stalinists in the 1940s. But in
practice it does not seem very different, when we look at what
Althusser designates as scientific and what ideological. Marxism is
assumed to be scientific, other political and sociological positions to
be ideological. Indeed all positions within marxism that are opposed
to the mainstream marxist–leninist position Althusser holds, are taken
to be the effects of bourgeois ideology. In short, a class line is used to
reject opposing positions, but the class line itself, what is bourgeois
and what is proletarian, is defined politically. Thus we get an
unblushing identification of scientific truth and approved communist
leadership, of which perhaps the ripest example is Althusser's claim
that *The Development of Capitalism in Russia*, an admirable if rather
obscure work of Lenin's youth, is 'the only work of scientific
sociology in the world' (1971: 100). (The 'Rudiments of a critical

bibliography', in which this splendid remark occurs, illustrates Althusser's tendency to refuse discussion of a question on which he actually adopts a rigid and restrictive position. The recommended reading on *Capital* consists exclusively of texts by Marx, Engels and Lenin, and ends, without explanation, at 1917. The explanation is all too obvious.)

The project of purification was directed, in the early 1960s, against the two trends that Althusser saw as the chief dangers in marxism: the old enemy, economism, and the new one, humanism. The argument against humanism (in which most of his characteristic positions were developed) required a heavy stress on Marx as scientist.

> In conformity with the tradition constantly reiterated by the classics of Marxism, we may claim that Marx established a new *science*: the science of the history of 'social formations'. To be more precise, I should say that Marx 'opened up' for scientific knowledge a new 'continent', that of *history*—just as Thales opened up the 'continent' of mathematics for scientific knowledge, and Galileo opened up the 'continent' of physical nature for scientific knowledge. (1969: 13–14)

In *For Marx* the history of Marx's thought was reinterpreted to show where his new science broke from his previous moral philosophy; and in *Reading Capital, Capital* was re-read to read out the ideological hangovers (i.e. all those bits which would support a humanist interpretation), and read in the missing bits required by the new scientific framework.

In Althusser's view each science has its own particular object of knowledge; and his view of what the object of Marx's science actually was, is most important. It did not include the purposes, wants, needs, reactions, ideas or consciousness of people as people, or indeed as collectivities, i.e. much of the content of what we would ordinarily think of as 'history'. Any argument which used such categories was, to Althusser, governed by the 'problematic of the subject' and not properly part of Marx's science of history. People *as subjects* did not figure in that science, because its true 'object' was the system of objective *relations* which govern the lives of individual people. These relations are defined in the analysis of a 'mode of production' which is an abstractly–defined structure of relations among elements (such as the direct producer, and the material means of production) which themselves have no existence (for marxist science at least) outside the structure. Real people appear not as the *elements* of these structures, but as their 'bearers' or 'supports'. Althusser goes so far as to characterise Marxism as a form of 'theoretical anti–humanism'.

This was not originally a sociological doctrine, i.e. one that made people out to be *in fact* the puppets of social forces—like those doctrines hammered in Wrong's famous essay 'The over–socialised conception of man in modern sociology'. It was originally an epistemological doctrine, simply part of the effort to specify what Marx's science was about and what it was not. But it rapidly slid into being a sociological doctrine, indeed at times quite a stringent sociological determinism. The slide was no doubt aided by the Althusserians' scientific conviction of the truth of marxism, and their political acceptance of the marxist–leninist rejection of spontaneity and grass–roots initiative. The *sociological* doctrine is not argued for; one is simply left with the impression that the epistemological argument validates it.

The search for a class line in theory, the emphasis on marxist orthodoxy, the stress on science, the dispute with humanism, come tightly together here in a node which is the heart of Althusserian theory and the origin of its way of doing class analysis. Its effect is to claim that mainstream marxism in politics has strict scientific warrant; and the urgency of defending it is obvious if

> the greatest event in the history of the class struggle—i.e. practically in human history—is the union of Marxist theory and the Workers' Movement. (1971: 41)

There are well-known dangers for orthodoxy in too heavy a stress on science. Sciences periodically revolutionise themselves, promote scepticism towards received truths, are intellectually untidy and anarchic, and encourage people to go looking for fractious and unruly facts. The reconciliation of faith and reason is an ancient problem; and Althusser responded to it with an almost equally ancient solution—redefining reason. In what I am still inclined to think his most ingenious intellectual move, Althusser redefined the concept of science. He vigorously rejected 'empiricism', any idea that facts exist in the world ready to be stumbled over by the questing scientist, or that science proceeds by a series of confrontations of tentative scientific ideas with the brute facts of reality. Rather, he suggested, the development of science is a process that occurs entirely within thought; and what distinguishes a science from other bodies of thought is the nature of its 'problematic'—i.e. the system of concepts and questions that underlies it. In a science the problematic allows an open–ended development of questions and answers; an ideological problematic by contrast is closed, its answers pre–determined by the social interests that govern it.

The scientificity of marxism then consists, not in any form of correspondence with contemporary facts (the fallacy of empiricism), but in its being based on a scientific problematic. The construction of this new problematic—the development of concepts such as mode of production, productive forces, surplus–value, etc., and the questions through which they are linked—was 'Marx's immense theoretical revolution', which began in 1845. For modern marxists scientificity is guaranteed, if they keep within the problematic, and repel all boarders. If they are running into theoretical problems, it is either because they have allowed some contamination from ideology and are therefore suffering from 'deviations', or because they have not yet developed the necessary concepts within the problematic.

This doctrine of science has a number of interesting consequences for the theory of class. Most immediately it dissolves the problem of the *correctness* of marxism as a source of concepts and laws for class analysis. Althusser denounces the problem of the 'guarantees' of scientific knowledge as part of the problematic of empiricism; but he replaces it with little more than metaphors about thought appropriating the real. In effect, he gets his guarantees with his party card. In one of the very few places where he even recognises that there may be a question about whether marxism is right, he suggests that we *recognise* marxism as a science 'because it provides *objective knowledge*', producing 'results which can be proven by scientific and political practice' (1976: 110). What scientific practice can verify the theoretical results without some confrontation with the world of facts is left mysterious. But Althusser at least specifies that the political verification refers to the 'fusion' of the Labour Movement with Marxist theory, as expounded by Lenin, Gramsci and Mao. It appears, then, that somehow or other the history of the communist movement provides the verification of marxism. To other socialists it might appear that the history of the communist movement is, on the contrary, extraordinarily embarrassing for marxism. But that is all the argument we get. Althusser leaves us with 'an unimpeachable and undeniable *scientific* core in Marxism' (1976: 117), which practically speaking provides its own warrant, while exercising police powers over all other concepts within its domain.

The second consequence of this doctrine of science is a heavy stress on the primacy of theory, and indeed the most abstract levels of theory. There is a grain of good sense here—it is now a commonplace of the sociology of knowledge that facts in science are partly constituted by the process of investigation itself. But Althusser's position offers little resistance to the tendency to regard facts as *entirely* constituted that way, to take the world as having the shape that theory says it ought to have. The effect has been, quite strongly, to discourage original investigative research by those influenced by his thought. The rejection of empiricism, and the necessity of 'producing' concepts by refining the ore–body of the marxist classics, has meant that Althusserian class analysis has developed as an elaboration of abstract conceptual argument on a truly awe–inspiring scale, hardly to be matched in the social sciences since the palmy days of Talcott Parsons. But, like Parsonianism and for much the same reasons, it has added very little in the way of new discoveries. Most of the practical themes of the Althusserian literature on class—the relative autonomy of the state, cultural control of the working class, the importance of the new middle strata, etc.—have been common themes of socialist debate (and for that matter academic sociology) for a good long time.

Thirdly, this doctrine of science places extraordinary importance on the theoretical starting–point, as proper scientific conclusions can only be arrived at by argument within the problematic. In our case this starting–point is, by and large, *Capital*—at least, those things which are 'settled' in Marx's analysis of production in that book. Althusser himself displays a fascinating ambivalence towards Marx. On the one hand he praises him to the skies, using language about him (and Lenin) that is quite embarrassing in its fulsomeness. And there are many places in Althusser's writings, and also in Poulantzas and Carchedi, where a quote from one or other of the great men is taken as quite sufficient to settle a disputed question. (I do not want to burden the text with examples of such points; yet, lest the remark be thought unfair, see the following examples in Carchedi, 1977: 13,34,35,48,75,140.) Yet Althusser rejects much in Marx as ideological, and devised the procedure of 'symptomatic reading' to justify dropping much from the famous texts, and supplying other things that they did not say. The net effect is to select out as a starting–point that part of Marx that corresponds to Althusserian notions of marxist science—but to give the full force of divine revelation to that part.

The problematic thus retroactively constructed by Althusser, Balibar and the others, centres on the concept of a 'mode of production', and this is the base on which the Althusserian theory of class, methodologically speaking, rests. It is a concept constructed at a very high level of abstraction indeed, at a good distance from historical detail. One might therefore be tempted to think of concepts like the 'capitalist mode of production' or 'feudal mode of production' as ideal–type concepts *à la* Weber. But certainly Althusser did not think of them that way. He thought that in analysing the mode of production, Marx had penetrated to 'a deeper, more concrete reality' (1969: 110). The concept of the mode of production in this view is not a hypothetical construct, easily to be changed as the course of argument demands; it is a great scientific 'discovery'—as Althusser explicitly calls it.

The first step in building a systematic theory of class on this base is provided by the Althusserian analysis of what a mode of production is. And here the polemic against the second deviation in marxism, economism, becomes important. From the time of his 1962 essay 'Contradiction and Overdetermination', Althusser was clearly aligned against any notion of simple economic determinism, or the inevitable unfolding of stages in history. In that essay he argued forcefully that the revolutionary situation in Russia in 1917 was not a matter of the economic system brewing up a social crisis; it was a coming–together in one time and place, a 'conjuncture', of a whole series of contradictions of different kinds. This theme was spelt out more formally in his conception of a mode of production and a social formation as systems composed of several different 'levels' or 'instances'—economic, political and ideological, in the usual formulations—each of which had a 'relative autonomy' from the others, and each of which shaped the others. (For this network of reciprocal influences he borrowed Freud's term 'overdetermination'.) Each of these instances was seen as having its own history, and its own pace of development, though never existing outside the context of the others. A toe–hold in marxist tradition was kept by insisting that the economic was determinant 'in the last instance', which meant that it was supposed to be what settled the relationships of dominance among the instances, without necessarily being the dominant one itself. Though there is relative autonomy between the instances, there is also 'structural causality', i.e. the effects of the way the social whole is organised—which stated the general constraints on which marxist analysis rests.

The scheme of the three 'instances' was introduced somewhat tentatively—Althusser later referred to it as a 'metaphor' (1976: 129), and there is some oscillation in his own writings about how many are needed. But it rapidly became canonical, in fact the most distinctive formula of Althusserian social analysis. Poulantzas, to take only one case among many, couches his general definition of class in terms of the three instances (1975: 14–15). Its point is to give, at least in principle, great importance to ideological and political considerations in understanding classes, which had commonly been understood in marxist literature as fundamentally economic categories. It decisively rejects the rather simple–minded notion of historical progression implied in the traditional formula of the change from 'class–in–itself' to 'class–for–itself'. Classes in the Althusserian model are not first economic, and then political and ideological entities. They are always all three.

This is good sense, and agrees with a great deal of recent theoretical analysis and empirical research (such as Thompson's) on the importance of culture and political organisation in the formation of classes. But like many of the Althusserian ideas, a good (if common) insight soon becomes a conceptual straightjacket. From the sound argument that classes are simultaneously economic, political and ideological the analysis proceeds as if they are *only* economic, political and ideological. Other dimensions of social reality and experience are dropped from the picture. Once again, these exclusions are not argued for; they are simply a tacit consequence of the science being defined by its problematic, and the problematic being defined by the 'marxist classics'. The scope of Althusserian class analysis is limited to questions that can be handled within the conceptual language of Marx and Lenin. Thus Poulantzas' (1974) long treatise on fascism systematically ignores the psychological dimension of the class politics that produced it, though this is widely recognised to be of great importance and has been the subject of a good deal of research. More importantly, the sphere of sexual social relations is practically excluded from the world which this theorising describes; and it also seems to have been purged of housework, child–rearing, and all like matters. Only an Althusserian could publish, in 1977, a book *On the Economic Identification of Social Classes* which entirely ignored ten years' debate on the place of women in class structures, and the economic role of domestic labour.

This may give the impression of an extremely rigid theoretical postion, which in some respects it is; yet there are other features of the Althusserian model that give it immense flexibility. The top–down method of argument, which has already been stressed, requires movement through a number of levels of abstraction (different formulations specify four, three, or two, but the point remains the same), at each of which new qualifications and complications can be introduced. When we get down to the most concrete level, where elements of different modes of production are intermingled and a unique history has to be taken into account, no automatic conclusion can be read off from the theory of the abstract structures. There is always the possibility of the kind of 'conjuncture' which Althusser recognised in the case of 1917; and if that was an exceptional situation, he asks, 'are we not always in exceptional situations?' (1969: 104)

Well, yes, we are. With three relatively autonomous instances, each with its own history rolling along in a state of 'dislocation' from the others; with three or four logical levels of analysis applicable to any mode of production, none of which can be understood by pure deduction from the level above; and with actual social formations made up of a mixture of several modes of production; with all this, the Althusserian formalisation of marxist theory begins to admit a truly formidable number of possible situations and schemes of analysis, which makes it possible to treat every situation as the exception it is.

Conversely, the analysis of any actual one requires a mighty effort of cross–classification to place it correctly in its unique niche in the Althusserian system. It is no wonder that Laclau (1975: 102) was impressed by the 'taxonomic fury' with which Poulantzas reacts to the complexities of social structure. That reaction is quite strictly entailed by the way the Althusserian model of things works.

Let me push this argument one step further, before leaving Althusser's generalities for the specifics of class. Though his stated intention was primarily to defend marxist orthodoxy, it is plain enough that he was unhappy with its current state and wished also to extend and modernise it, to make it able to speak about the manifold of unpredicted situations that had arisen in the course of the twentieth century. The main apparatus he provides for social analysis—the top-down order of analysis, the distinction of structure from conjuncture, the notions of relative autonomy and dislocation between instances, and the concepts of 'structural causality' and overdetermination—are precisely concepts that allow these two aims, the one explicit and the other tacit, to be met simultaneously. While not 'structuralist' in the precise sense of Lévi–Strauss and Piaget (1971b) (on this point I think Althusser is right and a number of his critics wrong), these ideas do function in a reasonably similar way as a set of *translation devices*, which allow one to talk about any actual situation in the language of traditional marxism without threat to its basic doctrine. The received truths of marxism are mostly relegated to the realm of the structures, where they have little more than a rhetorical relation to real situations. In effect, orthodox marxist are allowed to believe much what other people believe about events in the world, without needing to alter their rhetoric or their conviction of the scientific truth of Marx's general model.

The importance of this will become evident when we examine the historicity of the treatment of class. But before doing that, it is necessary to examine the class concepts that are employed. At this point the focus of the argument must shift from Althusser to Poulantzas and Carchedi. It is not a complete break, because (as I have suggested) the philosophical doctrines are active in the sociology, and there is at least a rough sociology of class already active in Althusser's philosophy. Althusser also, on occasion, offers a view directly on the sociological issues. In his 'Reply to John Lewis', for instance, he argues that classes exist only in the class struggle, adding (falsely) that this is a view that distinguishes revolutionaries from reformists. But for the most part we must turn to the younger authors for a systematic theory of class. While pointing out some differences between their positions, or the themes they develop, I will focus for the most part on points that are common within the whole approach.

The class concepts

The first thing they all agree on is, of course, the importance of the concept of class as the basic constituent of a rigorous social theory. As Poulantzas explains,

> Marxism indeed admits the existence of fractions, strata and even social categories ('state bureaucracy', 'intellectuals'). But this in no way involves groupings alongside, marginal to or above classes, in other words external to them. Fractions are class fractions; the industrial bourgeoisie, for example, is a fraction of the bourgeoisie. Strata are class strata; the labour aristocracy is a stratum of the working class. Even the social categories, as we have seen above in relation to the state bureaucracy, have their class membership.
> ...The division of society into classes precisely means, both from the theoretical and methodological point of view and from that of social reality, that the concept of social class is pertinent to all levels of analysis: the division into class forms the frame of reference for every social stratification. (1975: 198–9)

In the light of the discussion so far, it will surprise no–one to learn that the classes initially recognised in Althusserian discussions are those that populated the world of Marx; basically, those that emerged as major categories in Marx's schematic model of capitalist production. A representative list is given *en passant* in an early essay by Althusser on the theme of the accumulation of contradictions:

> How else could the class–divided popular masses (proletarians, peasants, petty bourgeois) throw themselves *together*, consciously or unconsciously, into a general assault on the existing regime? And how else could the ruling classes (aristocrats, big bourgeois, industrial bourgeois, finance bourgeois, etc.) who have learnt by long experience and sure instinct to seal between themselves, despite their class differences, a holy alliance against the exploited, find themselves reduced to impotence...? (1969: 99–100)

These categories are, so to speak, the small change freely used in an informal way in Althusserian discussion, as they are among marxists generally. The formal definitions (to be discussed shortly) qualify the list in some ways, but are mainly intended to provide rigorous logical derivations for these traditional categories. It is, quite rightly, pointed out that the definitions and specifications provided by Marx and Lenin were often informal and incomplete in various ways.

The principal addition to the list is a new class or class fraction to take care of the mass of white–collar wage earners with administrative, clerical, and organisational tasks. This group seems to have been a relatively late discovery; it does not figure, so far as I am aware, in any of Althusser's writings of the 1960s, nor in *Political*

Power and Social Classes, though it makes a fleeting appearance in 1970 in *Fascism and Dictatorship*. When it does arrive, it does so in a big way; much of Poulantzas' and Carchedi's theoretical work in the mid-1970s has been devoted to defining this group and distinguishing it from others. Poulantzas defines a 'new petty bourgeoisie' comprised of non-productive wage-earning or salaried employees, and Carchedi a 'new middle class' which combines the global function of capital with the function of the collective worker. These are not strictly equivalent concepts, though they are plainly meant to refer to much the same people, and to the same familiar historical process by which the evolution of capitalism has produced a mass of clerical and administrative workers.

The first question one must ask about these concepts is where exactly they are located in the analysis proceeding from the concept of the mode of production. Here the suggestions of different writers, who agree on the general logic of the approach, appear to differ. Some, such as Carchedi and Dos Santos (1970), identify 'classes' at all levels of analysis, from the most abstract to the most specific, though making their definition and description more complex as the argument approaches the most specific level. Carchedi suggests, for instance, that at the most abstract level (that of the pure capitalist economic structure) 'classes are definable purely in terms of the economic structure' (1977: 49); the political and ideological are added in at lower levels.

This differs from Poulantzas, to whom classes are at no stage analysable in economic terms alone—a point he argues forcefully and often, and which is certainly more consistent with the general views proposed by Althusser. But the difference is not as great as it seems. When Poulantzas argues (1973: 66) that the 'relations of production ... are not social classes' (i.e. that the categories of capital and wage-labour are not directly class concepts), he is really offering a methodological convention, by which the concept of class is to be confined to another logical field. Carchedi's concept becomes more like this when he moves down one level from the most abstract and introduces ideological and political determinations into his concept of class. The gap is further closed when Carchedi offers to change his class terminology (from 'working class' and 'capitalist class' to 'proletariat' and 'bourgeoisie') on reaching this level, to signify the new bits in the picture (1977: 82). In stressing the point, however, Poulantzas formulates a new concept, that of the distinction between the structures on the one hand, and the 'field of social relations' (in which classes are constituted) on the other, which will be important later on in following his approach to history.

These different formulations converge on one idea, which is central to the claims made by Althusserian class analysis: that of the structural determination of class. The essential idea was stated by Balibar in *Reading Capital*:

> The definition of the capitalist class or of the proletarian class therefore does not precede that of the social relations of production, but *vice versa*, the definition of the social relations of production implies a 'support' function defined as a class.
>
> ...Classes are not the subjects of this mechanism [of distribution] but its supports, and the concrete characteristics of these classes (their types of revenue, their internal stratification, their relation to the different levels of the social structure) are the *effects* of this mechanism. (1970: 233)

Poulantzas puts the same point as a general formula in his own terminology:

> *More exactly, social class is a concept which shows the effects of the ensemble of structures, of the matrix of a mode of production or of a social formation on the agents which constitute its supports: this concept reveals the effects of the global structure in the field of social relations.* (1973: 67-8, italics in original)

Or more baldly, in a later book:

> Social class . . . is a concept which denotes the effects of the structure within the social division of labour. (1975: 14)

It is not always completely clear what these pronouncements mean. In particular they could be interpreted as definitional statements following from Althusserian epistemology (as suggested, for instance, by Balibar's phrase about the 'definition' of class); or as substantive claims about causal priority in reality (as suggested by the term 'effects', and as implied more clearly in arguments such as Carchedi's about the structural determination of the income of the new middle class, which is supposed to vary according to the balance between the functions of capital and labour performed). If they are causal claims they are never substantiated by evidence or argument. Nevertheless it is plain that *some* kind of priority is being attributed to the categories that arise in the abstract analysis of the mode of production over the categories yielded by the concrete complexities of history; and that the latter are *in some way* determined or governed by the former, that they must be understood as 'effects'. This is the basis of the Althusserians' claim to be able to say anything significant about history. We shall be concerned with a number of the implications, variations and transmutations of the idea of structural determination from now on.

What *are* the classes so listed and so determined? The literal sense of a number of the remarks already quoted (such as Poulantzas on fractions, strata, and categories) would be that classes are groups of people who can be identified by certain criteria and sub–divided by other criteria. Much the same is, literally, implied by the definition of class by Lenin which Carchedi takes as his starting–point: 'large groups of people' differing from each other by their place in production, relation to the means of production, role in the social organisation of labour, and share in social wealth.

Yet this conception would violate the deepest taboos against empiricism and the problematic of the subject; and every Althusserian explicitly rejects it. Carchedi (1977: 107) goes so far as to correct Lenin: 'Actually, instead of "groups of people" it would be more correct to speak of "production agents" '. Balibar is even more explicit:

> But these classes are obviously not sums of individuals, which would not change anything: it is impossible to make a class by adding individuals together on whatever scale. Classes are *functions of the process of production as a whole.* (Althusser and Balibar 1970: 267, original italics)

Poulantzas, in *Classes in Contemporary Capitalism*, spells it out a little more by suggesting that a class is defined by its 'place' in the social division of labour as a whole, and that this corresponds to the structural determination just discussed. The concept is applied, for instance, in giving a brisk solution to the grand old problem of whether propertyless managers are part of the ruling class under capitalism:

> It is the place of capital, defined as the articulation of relationships that bear certain powers, that determines the class membership of the agents who fulfil these 'functions' . . . The directing agents who directly exercise these powers and who fulfil the 'functions of capital' occupy the place of capital, and thus belong to the bourgeois class even if they do not hold formal legal ownership. In all cases, therefore, the managers are an integral section of the bourgeois class. (1975: 180)

People, in other words, form classes only insofar—exactly insofar—as they are the 'agents' of the system, the bearers of a structure which defines class places for them and distributes them among these places.

This seems clear enough. It is an Althusserian version of the general socialist claim about the objective reality, the intractability, of class and class structure. It avoids 'classes' defining themselves by the bootstraps, i.e. by their own images of class–ness, and thus dissolving into subjectivity as they do in much of the modern survey research on class (e.g. Davies, 1967). And it avoids 'classes' which are shapeless sets of people who merely share a common characteristic, and thus have no necessary connection with an account of social structure, as in much of the 'social stratification' literature in academic sociology (see Chapter 6).

But in escaping these familiar traps, has the argument arrived at a stable and defensible solution to the thorny problem of defining classes? It seems to me it has not. The admirable concept of structural determination dissolves in practice into one of two positions, either functionalist or categorical, or some amalgam of the two in which the latter finally dominates (as in Carchedi). They are equally ahistorical; and I will suggest that the Althusserian approach to history is the basic reason why their class theory falls into this dilemma.

The element of functionalism in Althusserian argument has often been noticed, and I don't want to labour the point here. I merely want to call attention to its definitional importance in a number of cases where a class is construed, essentially, as the personification of a function-that-has-to-be-performed-for-the-system. Balibar's definition of classes as functions of the process of production as a whole has just been quoted. If it be objected that that is merely a phrase referring to the structural determination of class, it is worth recalling Poulantzas' definition of a class by its class place which is equivalent to its structural determination. (So there can be no doubt about the matter, Carchedi explains for us what dialectical determination is; and his first point is that 'the determinant instance . . . determines the determined instance . . . in the sense that the former calls into existence the latter as a condition of its own existence', a definition Carchedi thinks important enough to repeat with emphasis (1977: 47–8, 143). Parsons himself could hardly have given a clearer account of a functional imperative.) To move beyond definitions, we repeatedly find in practical analyses that the places which define classes are themselves defined by a function performed in the system and its reproduction. Poulantzas' solution to the problem of the managers, quoted above, is a crystalline example of this. Carchedi's solution to the problem of the new middle classes involves a much more elaborate functionalist argument, which develops the idea of the 'global function of capital' and the 'function of the collective worker', and defines this class as those whose jobs involve performing *both* functions (albeit at different times). It would not be hard to give a couple of dozen further examples, but they would lead us away from the concept of class.

To be fair, both Poulantzas and Carchedi are aware that there is something wrong with functionalism (Carchedi's very inadequate attempt to deal with the problem will be discussed later), and they claim not to be functionalists. Certainly the picture of society that they draw is poles apart from that drawn by Parsonian sociology. Like all socialists, they describe classes as fundamentally antagonistic, class society as based on exploitation, class politics as the child of conflict. Poulantzas, having located classes in the field of social relations in the passage quoted above, went on to explain that

Social relations consist of class practices, in which social classes are placed in *oppositions*: social classes can be conceived only as class practices, these practices existing in oppositions *which, in their unity, constitute the field of the class struggle.* (1973: 86)

A functionalist definition does not require consensus. In this case, rather, it is implicit in the way these platitudes about conflict are understood and developed in actual analyses. Indeed it is implicit in the circularity of Poulantzas' definition of classes in terms of a field of social relations, and definition of social relations in terms of class practices; what gets this circle moving is the hidden presence ('in their effects') of the functional categories from the field of the structures.

The conception of a 'class practice' could lead in a very different direction if one took the trouble to make a close, historically concrete, study (as Mallet, Gorz, Braverman, Beynon, Sennett and others have) of what various groups of workers actually *do* in their daily lives. But none of our theorists has done this. Their fear of 'empiricism', and the priority they accord to the most abstract level of analysis, insistently pull them back towards a functionalist understanding of class practices and hence of the class categories. In effect, it is the function to be performed that decides *which* of the many actual practices of a given group is taken into account in analysing its class determination.

The functional and the categorical tendencies are not strictly separate—in Carchedi, for instance, the functional analysis is the means by which the main categories are defined—but the latter is the more striking, if only because it was so explicitly rejected from the formal definitions of class at the start. Again, in practice, the concept slides. This tendency can best be seen by considering what are the characteristic problems and debates that arise in the Althusserian literature on class. Two of the most important, indeed perhaps the two most contested, are the question of class alliances and the question of class boundaries. Poulantzas, for instance, has been deeply concerned with the former in all his books. (His development of the concept of the 'power bloc' in *Political Power and Social Classes*—an alliance of classes and class fractions in relation to the state—is an early and important example.) His critics have dwelt on the latter. The two are essentially linked. As Poulantzas sensibly observed in a conference discussion on the matter, where you put the class boundaries decides whether you need a class alliance or not (1977: 114–116). This is no trivial matter, either of practice or theory. The issue is, in fact, how you basically define a class *for* practice, as Hunt realises:

Any fundamental criteria of class determination must meet one essential test. Does it [*sic*] succeed in revealing the most fundamental and pervasive boundaries within the social structure? (1977: 92)

Now, twist and turn it how you will, I do not see how you can construe a debate over the theoretical definition of class boundaries as anything other than a discussion about the defining criteria for *sets of people*. It is, to use an Althusserian phrase, a question that reveals a categorical problematic within the theory of class. And you cannot have alliances between 'functions' or 'places', only between groups of people. Normally, indeed, between groups that have reached a reasonable level of organisation and class consciousness, though the process of mobilisation is hardly ever discussed in the Althusserian theoretical literature, which usually treats the matter in the abstract form of an alliance between categories.

The categorical tendency in all this becomes clearest in the work of Carchedi. An almost chemically pure example of categorical reasoning is provided in his discussion of how to go about 'placing the doctor or the nurse, working in a state hospital, in the class structure'. There follows a complicated list of criteria for the classification of such people, and then not only the workers but also the organisations they work in. More generally, Carchedi elaborates a system for classifying people which becomes increasingly elaborate as we move down the levels of analysis, producing many blinding sociological insights, like:

> In terms of the first element [of the definition] it is no longer just the producer who is exploited but we include also the non–producer as oppressed. This is the agent who, even though taking part in the labour process as a whole, does not produce surplus value; this agent should not be confused with the non–producer who does *not* take part in the labour process, who thus performs the (global) function of capital and thus who cannot be oppressed. (1977: 83)

The system also becomes more elaborate as we move forward through the stages Carchedi arbitrarily identifies in the evolution of capitalism.

This passage was not chosen particularly for satirical purposes. The bulk of Carchedi's theoretical effort, and a good deal of Poulantzas', is directed towards elaborating and refining distinctions which are essentially criteria for the theoretical classification of people— refinements, in short, of a solidly categorical conception of class. I have quoted Laclau's remark about Poulantzas' 'taxonomic fury' in respect of political theory. This is, if anything, too mild for the theory of class. We are confronted here with a kind of categorical frenzy, an elaboration of criteria so abstract and intricate that one cannot even seriously argue with their later stages. One can only gape in wonder. Look at Carchedi's 66–category table (1977: 86) for economic identification, and reflect that this is only for two classes and only on the basis of production relations. If we add in just one more class, and multiply by three to allow for political and ideological criteria in comparable numbers, we get something like 297 criteria for the identification of classes under capitalism . . .

Once again, it must be recognised that this is not strictly the same as the categoricalism of, say, stratification theory. The categories are built on a conception of necessary antagonisms inherent in the structure of capitalist production relations. Yet even the class struggle, so far as the theoretical work goes, seems to be occur by definition

> social classes coincide with class practices, i.e. the class struggle, and are only defined in their mutual opposition (Poulantzas, 1975: 14)

rather than by the exertions of real antagonists. Real antagonists, after all, sometimes get tired, or lose, and stop struggling; without thereby ceasing to be members of classes.

For a body of marxist writing, the theoretical work of Althusser, Poulantzas and Carchedi oddly lacks the dimension of political economy, the historical analysis of the actual course of capital accumulation, the transformations of the labour process and the distribution of the social product, and of course an analysis of mobilisation. When the question of relationships between classes has been addressed systematically it has mostly been through abstract models of the ways class domination may be mediated (Althusser on ideological state apparatuses, Poulantzas on the capitalist state) or through a classification of forms of production relations (Carchedi), all governed by a definitional postulate of class oppositions.

The themes of this discussion of class concepts can brought together in a simple example. In the *Communist Manifesto* there is a well-known passage where Marx sets out an account of the experience of the European working class in the process we might now describe as class formation and political mobilisation. The proletariat, he says, goes through various stages of development, where the struggles of individual labourers with their exploiters are gradually generalised to the factory, to the trade, to the locality, to increasingly wider spheres, and in so doing, increasingly take on the form of collisions between two classes. This is quoted at the beginning of Poulantzas' initial discussion of class theory (1973: 58–60, 75), where he notes its importance (along with other texts) in suggesting (by a 'literal and direct reading of Marx's texts') a historical approach to class, an analysis of the genesis of social classes and class structure. The point is Poulantzas' response to this line of thought. It is utterly, vehemently, and repeatedly rejected.

Making it work:
historicity and the field distinction

With a literal understanding of it strictly ruled out, how does one apply Marx's Science of History? The aim of the enterprise is, after all, to yield an analysis of actual historical situations and ways of transforming them. There is an answer to this in the Althusserian framework, which is in fact the basic reason for the tendencies in the concept of class just described. Let us go back a step or two.

Marxism in the late nineteenth and early twentieth century had a profound intellectual impact by asserting the importance of economic processes in the pattern of historical change. In the course of polemic and political conflict, this theme hardened into the 'economism' which Lenin and others rejected, and which Althusser wished to oppose in theory. In order to do so, and to produce credible accounts of the flux of history and the complexity of conjunctures, while holding to the orthodox marxist doctrine of determination–by–the–economic, Althusser produced the various translation devices I have already outlined: the distinction between instances, the idea of their relative autonomy, overdetermination, and determination in the last instance by the economic; and the distinction between logical levels of analysis, between the level of the structures and the level of their effects, between the abstract analysis of the mode of production and the concrete analysis of conjunctures in history.

It is the last of these that is crucial in the application of the theory of class. To follow the way it works, and the way it solves the dilemma of historicity, it is necessary to go into a bit of detail. I will concentrate mainly on one crucial example, the treatment of the problem by Poulantzas in *Political Power and Social Classes*. Analogous distinctions are made by other authors, and in other of Poulantzas' writings; but it is worked out in greater detail and explicitness here than anywhere else.

Poulantzas accepts the general Althusserian distinction between three instances (or levels) within a mode of production or social formation; and he accepts the general distinction between an abstract level (the mode of production) and a more concrete level (social formation) in which several modes of production may be combined. In constructing the concept of class, as we have already seen, he introduces a third conceptual distinction, which, so to speak, operates at right angles to the others: the distinction between the field of the structures and the field of social relations.

This distinction is in fact built into his definition of class in the passage already quoted (page 112 above), which continues:

> In this sense, if class is indeed a concept, it does not designate a reality which can be placed in the structures; it designates the effect of an ensemble of given structures, an ensemble which determines social relations as class relations. (1973: 67–8)

(To translate roughly: there is a field of social relations, which gets organised along class lines by the combined influence of all the structures.) The field of social relations is 'circumscribed by the limits set by structures'—i.e. structural determination operates on classes—and being so determined, it also has its three instances. Yet it is distinct, with its own characteristics and dynamics, and is capable of becoming 'dislocated' from the structures. For this is the field in which the class struggle occurs. This struggle in fact *is* the opposition between the practices of the different classes, which come to a head in class politics ('political class struggle'), the 'nodal point' of the process of transformation of the whole system. The analysis of this field of conflicting class practices requires new concepts (e.g. 'interests' and 'power') which do not appear in the analysis of the structures. This field is the site of the 'conjuncture', the current situation in which classes and other groupings appear in the guise of 'social forces', and which is the object of political practice—notably, attempts to revolutionise the lot. (This exposition is a summary of points from Poulantzas, 1973: 68–98, where the quoted phrases will be found.)

As noted earlier, the field distinction at first led Poulantzas to deny that the concept of 'class' was strictly applicable within the field of the structures. In *Classes in Contemporary Capitalism* he retreated from this austerity. But he retained the field distinction, in slightly altered terminology, as the distinction between the class 'place' in the field of structural determination and the class 'position' in the conjuncture, adding a little diagram to make it all clear (1975: 15):

Practices/Class struggle		
Structural determination/ Class places		Conjuncture/ Class positions
Social division of labour Social classes, fractions, strata, categories	*Ideology* relations of ideological domination/subordination ideological struggle *Politics* relations of political domination/subordination political struggle *Economics* relations of production/ relations of exploitation economic struggle	Concepts of strategy: social forces, power bloc, "people"

Poulantzas is very clear that place and position need not coincide; in

fact a great deal of his analysis, in both books, turns on the idea that
they don't.

It is worth reflecting on what this theoretical evolution has given us.
Starting from the general analysis of the mode of production, we have
(within the field of the structures) the more concrete level of the social
formation, which need not correspond with all its constituent modes
of production in the classes it gives rise to. Within social formations
(and within the field of social relations), we have three distinct and
relatively autonomous instances which may be, in fact normally are,
dislocated from each other, and on each of which a class may or may
not have a distinct existence. We have, beside the field of the
structures, the field of social relations; the two may be, in fact
normally are, dislocated from each other. Poulantzas rather breath-
lessly suggests that in a particular case we have 'a set of relations of
dislocation between two systems of relations of dislocation' (1973:
91).

To put it in another light, we have here a truly formidable engine
for generating variations on the original marxist themes, while still
preserving the *language* of marxist analysis and the *form* of ultimate
determination by the economic. It is nevertheless a fairly rigorous
development of the concepts of unevenness, condensation, displacement and mutations within the structure introduced in the later
part of Althusser's essay 'On the materialist dialectic', and of his
interesting critique of homogeneous conceptions of historical time in
Reading Capital. Poulantzas indeed applies it directly to the question
of time in denying any necessary sequences in the history of capitalism
and the capitalist state:

> Because of the coexistence in a capitalist formation of several modes of
> production and of several forms of the CMP and because of the complex
> articulation of instances, each with its own time–sequence, the dominance
> in a capitalist formation of one form of the CMP over another is not
> expressed in a simple development. In a social formation we may find a
> stage dominated by monopoly capitalism and the interventionist state
> before a stage dominated by private capitalism and the liberal state...
> (1973: 154)

The distance that has been travelled from the simple evolutionism and
notions of ever–deepening class conflict in vulgar marxism is obvious.

With this historical licence granted them, the classes in the field of
the conjuncture become almost sportive. They form alliances and
break them, follow each other in and out of power, appear and
disappear as social forces. The extent of this flexibility is perhaps best
seen in Poulantzas' account of the 'power bloc', the set of dominant
classes or fractions of classes in its relation to the state. He defines a

'hegemonic' class or fraction, which is the one that dominates the others in the power bloc and holds state power in its unity. But it does not always have to be the same one that holds hegemony in the society at large; nor the one that is actually the ruling class; nor the one that is in charge of the state! All these 'are sometimes identical and sometimes distinct' (1973: 240–50). Poulantzas in fact doubles his flexibility by introducing another, local, field distinction between the field of political practices and the 'political scene'. By this device he is enabled to argue that the hegemonic class may actually be absent from the political scene; and in certain situations the ruling class need not even be part of the power bloc. Politics makes strange bedfellows, and strange absences.

What Poulantzas is trying to do in these arguments is plain enough. He wants to escape simple–minded theories of causality, avoid conspiracy theories of the state, and make his marxism able to deal with the enormous complexities of history. But, we may ask, if the classes in the field of the conjuncture have such flexibility, what connection do they really retain with the firmament of the structures, whence their determination supposedly issues? Hirst, who has raised the question of the 'place' *vs* 'position' distinction in Poulantzas, calls it 'incoherent and unstable' (1977: 133–42). This is a bit strong; the distinction is coherent enough, in its derivation from the general Althusserian position. But it is, I think, fair to call the result unstable. It sometimes stretches the link between structure and event to the verge of incredibility (see the example of the 'ruling class' outside the 'power bloc'). More generally, the argument gives no guide to any systematic pattern in the extent of the 'dislocation'. It suggests, on the contrary, that these are always specific to the conjuncture. Consequently the analyses always appear to be *ad hoc*. On the other hand, the distinction sometimes collapses wearily into an identity, where the class–in–history becomes simply a personification. Odd examples of this can be found scattered widely through Althusser and Poulantzas; a late but fairly extended and important one is the analysis of monopoly and non–monopoly capital in *Classes in Contemporary Capitalism*, where the structural category itself seems to have strategies and desires, form alliances, and experience successes and failures.

Let us consider why this should be so, how this instability in the analysis arises. Obviously it turns on the nature of the relationship between the two fields. This is, specifically, a relationship of determination between the structures and their effects in the field of social practices, where the classes, thus determined, interact. It is worth recalling Althusser on 'structural causality' to get a grip on the relation between the structures and history:

the effects are not outside the structure, are not a pre-existing object, element, or space in which the structure arrives to *imprint its mark*: on the contrary ... the structure is immanent in its effects, a cause immanent in its effects in the Spinozist sense of the term, that *the whole existence of the structure consists of its effects*, in short that the structure, which is merely a specific combination of its peculiar elements, is nothing outside its effects. (1970: 188-9, italics original)

The structures are not entities, things–in–the–world which are separate from other entities called classes or events. Both structure and class are concepts, and the field distinction is merely a distinction in thought, part of the conceptual apparatus that we are offered to help get a grip on all these goings–on.

In one of the few discussions in this literature of the problems of analysing this relationship, Poulantzas observes that classes recognised in the abstract analysis of a mode of production need not be present as an autonomous class in the social formation, or as a social force in the conjuncture (1973: 77-84). A class is distinct there only when its economic existence is reflected in the other instances (of structure or practice) by a specific presence. How do we recognise this presence in the ideological and political instances? By 'pertinent effects'. What are these? The consequences of some 'new element which cannot be inserted in the typical framework which these levels [instances] would present without this element', i.e. which change the pattern of class struggle on these levels. Pertinent effects only appear in specific conjunctures.

There are a number of difficulties in this notably obscure passage, but here I am concerned with only one: its circularity, and the light that throws on the field distinction. The object of the whole analysis is to move from the field of structural determination to the conjuncture in the field of social practices. But the relevance of the structural analysis—structures existing only in their effects—is entirely fixed by the analysis of the conjuncture itself, where 'pertinent effects' are deciphered. One cannot rest the link with the structures on the notion of the 'typical framework' found at various levels. Poulantzas has already explicitly rejected any identification of the structural with the temporally permanent (that suffers from historicism); and anyway, what is 'typical' can only be known through the analysis of other conjunctures, which first have to be deciphered in the same way, whereupon we are trapped in an endless regress. (The first conjuncture, like the last instance, never comes.) On the other hand, one cannot characterise a conjuncture *a priori* in structural terms (even given a complete analysis of the conjunctures immediately before and after the one in question), because that would violate basic doctrines, on time and relative autonomy.

In short, there is no way of establishing coherently the relationship between the fields. The analysis is unstable because it is based on an antinomy embedded in the field distinction itself, an antinomy that *has to be there* because the field distinction, in some form or other, is necessary to make the whole theoretical system work. The dilemma is solved, to the extent that it is, in an essentially *linguistic* way. A tacit convenant is made to speak about social formations and conjunctures in the same language. The link between the two fields is that the first provides the linguistic and logical framework for the definition of the concepts used in the second, and nothing more. 'Structural determination' becomes a logical and rhetorical meta–relation among the concepts of the second field, where all that is actually being said about society is said. The abstract analysis of the first field (based on Marx on the capitalist mode of production) sharply limits the number and names of class concepts that can be deployed in the second field, but puts little other restraint on what can be done with them there.

If this argument is correct, I think it goes a good way towards explaining the peculiar style of Althusserian class analysis, that characteristic combination of a tight–laced conceptual system with a promiscuous application of class categories in practice. And it helps to specify the underlying attitude to history. History becomes a kaleidoscope, whose pieces can be re–arranged by a twirl of the conceptual barrel. Historical events can legitimately be picked up if they are 'relevant illustrations of the subject under investigation', and put down again if they are not, like Poulantzas' facts about fascism (1974: 13). History can be schematised at will, like Carchedi's three stages of capitalism (which never concretely occurred like that). Indeed history becomes to a considerable extent redundant. It is much easier to work out class analysis on the basis of purely imaginary examples, which Carchedi proceeds to do in his central arguments on the definition of the new middle class and its proletarianisation (1977: 90–1, 181–2). We begin to see why the categories of mobilisation and class formation are absent from the theoretical apparatus. They are not needed: the class already exists, ahead of time, as a possibility within the theoretical system; it is simply *recognised* when needed in the analysis of a conjuncture.

Some of the early arguments about conjunctures, such as Althusser's remarks on the condensation of contradictions in a revolutionary situation, suggested that the historicity of class and class relations was to be taken very seriously. But the development of the conceptual apparatus systematically suppressed this. What is actually realised in the theory of class expounded in these texts is a radical ahistoricity. The categorical and functionalist alternatives in the definition of class discussed in the previous section, are simply typical forms of the ahistorical conceptualisation of class, and completely consistent with the working of the theory. They can have no place in socialist theory.

Making it seem to work:
the Althusserian two-step

Because it has no historical method of proof, this literature constantly falls back on sheer postulation. What appear to be important substantive conclusions about the world are often analytic truths, logical deductions from the definitions and postulates. Let us take a simple, though important case: Poulantzas' proposal that 'the bureaucracy has no power of its own', which he argues both in *Political Power and Social Classes* and *Classes in Contemporary Capitalism*. This appears to be an important (and false) claim about the actual state of affairs in capitalist societies. But on close examination it turns out not to be an exposé of hidden impotence beneath the striped trousers, but a purely analytic statement, which follows from his definition of bureaucracy (which he declines to admit as a class or fraction of a class) and his definition of power ('the capacity of a social class to realise its specific objective interests', 1973: 104). So when followers of Poulantzas argue that the state bureaucracy has no power of its own, all they are really saying is that they speak a conceptual language in which, whatever the state bureaucracy does, it will not count as 'power'.

Still on the subject of the state organisations, Carchedi provides another example of the solution of a serious problem by deft postulation. In trying to sort out the class position of state employees he distinguishes capitalist state activities from non-capitalist state activities, and suggests that the former are really no different from privately owned enterprises, and therefore give rise to the same class categories among their employees. This would seem on the face of it to involve some difficulty: surely private companies are owned by capitalists who are trying to extract profits for themselves from the labour of their employees, and this process is the basis of class relations in the firm? And surely such ownership is *not* involved in the case of state enterprises—which is precisely why they can be concentrated in low-profit, infra-structural areas of the economy? But it *is*, in Carchedi's conceptual world:

> While in the individual enterprise the legal ownership belongs to the
> individual capitalist, and in the joint-stock company it belongs to the

stock–holders, in the state-owned enterprise the legal ownership belongs to the whole of the bourgeoisie, rather than to a very limited part of it. This can be seen from the fact that... in the state-owned company the revenue goes to the state, i.e. to the bourgeoisie as a whole ... (1977: 129–30)

The capitalist nature of the state enterprise, and thus the class identification of its employees, is established by postulation, in the form of a tacit definition of the state as the agent of ownership by the-bourgeoisie-as-a-whole.

Similarly Poulantzas' stand in *Political Power and Social Classes* against 'reformist' and 'revisionist' socialism's reliance on the state—a profoundly important and very difficult strategic issue for the labour movement—boils down to the *analytic* link he makes between the state (in its relative autonomy) and the power of the bourgeoisie. *By definition*, the state cannot go beyond the limit set by the interests of the bourgeoisie in the maintenance of its position; though where this limit (the 'line of demarcation') falls may shift from conjuncture to conjuncture. Even if the state is stirring up the masses, encouraging dominated classes to work against dominant one? *By definition*, this is to the advantage of the latter. And even when government and ruling class hate each other? The government still (by definition) functions as the political organiser of the dominant classes. (1973: 191, 272–3, 285) You can't win. In effect, the kinds of strategies now being explored by European socialist and communist parties, the 'revolutionary reforms' proposed by Gorz and Holland, the traditional strategies of the Anglo-Scandinavian labour parties, the strategies of local working–class mobilisations to gain control of the regional state machinery, are all ruled out in advance in this argument—by definition.

It is instructive to watch the definitional two-step by which the key concept for the polemic against reformism, the unity of state power, is presented by Poulantzas:

that particular feature of the capitalist state which makes the institutions of state power ... present a *specific* internal cohesion: this cohesion can be perceived in its effects. (1973: 255)

Following through Poulantzas' argument (282–300), we find that this cohesion is a condition of the relative autonomy of the capitalist state; and relative autonomy is needed for the state to function as a medium of bourgeois class power, which in turn is needed because the bourgeoisie, as we learn from Marx, is incapable of organising itself politically. State power has unity only so far as it is the unity of the dominant classes; the hegemonic class or fraction among them holds power in its unity; which is equivalent to the unity of the power bloc, which depends on the dominance of the hegemonic class or fraction.

But the bourgeoisie can't organise their own dominance (they can't organise their way out of a paper bag, it seems), nor, thus, the unity of the power bloc. Therefore they require the state to be 'the factor of the political unity of the power bloc under the protection of the hegemonic class or fraction'. Finally, 'with regard to the dominant classes and fractions, the capitalist state *presents an intrinsic unity*, combined with its relative autonomy, not because it is the tool of an already politically unified class, but precisely because it is the *unifying factor* of the power bloc'.

After plodding round this little circle for a while, we are not surprised to learn that even when the legislature and the executive reflect different classes, state power is still not divided, whatever common observers might think.

> In this case, in fact, the unity of institutionalised power is maintained by being concentrated around the dominant place where the hegemonic class or fraction is reflected. The other powers function more especially as *resistances* to the dominant power: inserted into the unitary function of the state, they contribute to the organisation of the hegemony of the class or fraction which is reflected as a political force in the dominant power. (1973: 305)

So the 'specific internal cohesion' of the state is still a 'unity' even when there is resistance—or to put it more plainly, class conflict—*within* the state; because *all* state powers are 'inserted' into the 'function' of the state, which is *by postulation* unitary.

Poulantzas' treatment of the relation between the bourgeoisie and the state (the essential logic of which recurs in *Classes in Contemporary Capitalism*) is thus essentially a network of definitional arguments. These elaborate some scathing remarks of Marx on the political incompetence of the mid–Victorian bourgeoisie into a general rule ('everything happens as if the specific co–ordinates of the struggle of the dominant classes contribute to prevent their political organisation'), which defines a function for the capitalist state to perform ('it takes charge, as it were, of the bourgeoisie's political interests and realises the function of political hegemony which the bourgeoisie is unable to achieve'—1973: 284). A system of definitions, translation devices and transformation rules then allows anything and everything to be reinterpreted as being consistent with these postulates.

When I first came across this kind of thing in Althusserian writing, I thought that it was simply a matter of arbitrary arguments being defended from the obvious criticisms by a certain amount of definitional shuffling. I no longer think so. The shuffling is there, but it isn't arbitrary. In writing the text just discussed, for instance,

Poulantzas was not going round that circle for nothing. He wanted people to believe that socialism requires smashing the capitalist state, and a Leninist party to do it, and a dictatorship of the proletariat to follow. And in one way or another he was going to find a way of rejecting any other strategy. If the hegemonic class *always* holds state power in its unity, it is no use doing anything by way of trying to get a little bit of it to use for other purposes—that only helps them organise. The fact that this is a definitional trick rather than a serious argument takes quite a long time to discover, especially as the logic of the whole thing is buried in the appalling jargon in which most of this literature is written. At least Althusser is more transparent:

> Marx thus proves irrefutably that the working class cannot hope to gain from the modern growth of productivity before it has overthrown capitalism and seized state power in a socialist revolution. (1971: 82)

I have never seen a clearer statement of the usefulness of theory for not seeing what is right in front of your nose.

We are now, I think, in a position to understand the much–debated 'functionalism' of the Althusserian school, and the specific form this takes in their arguments about class. To say that their arguments are functionalist does not just mean that they use the term 'function', as when Althusser says that the Ideological State Apparatuses 'function by ideology' and the Repressive ones 'function by violence' (one might as well say 'work by ideology' etc.), or when Carchedi speaks of 'functions' performed in the labour process (one might as well say 'operations' or 'tasks'). As Merton pointed out thirty years ago in a classic essay on functionalism in sociology, the term 'function' is often used for quite different meanings, while the essential idea of functionalism can be conveyed in other words (1957: 20–25).

Though it is not the use of the term that makes them so, both Althusser's and Carchedi's arguments just referred to are parts of functionalist analyses, of ideology and production relations respectively. This follows from the rejection of 'historicism' and the eschewal of historical analysis. To give *force* to the positions taken up by means of definition and postulation, to make it seem to work as an account of the constraints in social structure, and not just as a definitional grid for classifying things, they are repeatedly forced into a functionalist logic. In functionalism, things are analysed in terms of the contribution they make to the wellbeing or continued existence of a larger system of a given kind, and their explanation flows from the idea of their indispensability for that system (or more mildly, their usefulness for it.)

That this kind of argument is common in the works being discussed is hardly open to doubt. It is even embedded in some of the definitions, for instance Poulantzas' view that

> the state has the particular function of constituting the factor of cohesion
> between the levels of a social formation. (1973: 44)

As Laclau has noted, anything that can be analysed as helping to perform the function thus becomes part of the concept of the state. Hence the otherwise extraordinary list of 'Ideological State Apparatuses' offered by Althusser in his essay on that theme, which includes churches, schools, trade unions, mass media, the family, literature, the arts, sports, 'etc.'. To the extent that these materialise ideology and help reproduce, however indirectly, capitalist relations of production, they must be included within a functional definition of the state.

The stress in contemporary marxism on the analysis of the reproduction of capitalism, if it is not resolutely maintained as a historical category, almost inevitably leads to functionalism. This is true, for instance, of the new marxist sociology of the city offered by Castells, Lojkine, and others (see Pickvance, 1976), which is significantly influenced by Althusserian theory. There is quite a strong tendency here to construe the labour force as being called into existence, and maintained, by the functional requirements of capital— by the 'necessity' inherent in the continued existence of the system— which thus provides the explanation of urban forms through the need to provide for the collective consumption needs of the labour force.

A functionalist analysis can also operate at a lower level than that of the whole society—for instance within Carchedi's analysis of production relations. Carchedi's economic definition of his three major classes rests on the function (or in the case of the 'new middle class', the combination of functions) they perform in production. He starts out by defining one function—that of 'the collective worker'— in a non-functionalist way, simply as the increasingly complex set of technical tasks involved in actually producing a commodity, in short, as the organisation of work in a labour process. He then uses the same word, 'function', to refer to the very different business of organising matters so as to extract surplus value from the production of commodities. This is the function of the capitalist, or, as it is subdivided and delegated, the function of the 'global capitalist' (Mr Fat?), or more felicitously, 'the global function of capital'.

> The general, social content of a function under monopoly capitalism is
> determined by either performing the function of the collective worker or the
> global function of capital. (1977: 59)

The features of the second function, e.g. the element of control and surveillance, are deduced from general features of the system, e.g.

'the fact that, under capitalism, the relations of production are antagonistic'. From general features of the system, also, it is deduced that there is a sharp separation between the two functions, such that while performing one you can't perform the other. On this idea rests Carchedi's characterisation of the new middle class and his theories of the determination of its income and the process of its 'proletarianisation'.

Now so far as real history goes, this is plainly wrong. There are many features of capitalist production which show the labour process as inextricably fused with processes of social control: among them, the decomposition of tasks in manufacturing and office work, the centralisation of information and the use of automated production equipment, the production of new technologies and their repressive implementation. There is a socialist theoretical literature on this (*inter alia*, Marcuse (1964) and Habermas (1971) on technology as ideology), a recent body of research (notably from Braverman (1974) and his followers), and forms of struggle in the workplace that address it (such as 'role contestation' in the movement for workers' control). But all this *cannot* register in Carchedi's analysis, because his model of the production process requires two distinct functions to be performed, in order that there should be both material commodities and surplus–value. The labour process must therefore be such that the functions can be exclusive.

Here the element of argument by postulation is hard to distinguish from the element of functionalism. They merge together in the context of a highly abstract model of capitalism which is simply assumed to represent the reality of the world. The general point in which all this issues, can be put this way: the economically–defined classes in Carchedi, the state in Poulantzas, the ideological apparatuses in Althusser, are all theorised in terms of the function they perform in a social order *whose class nature is known a priori*, as it is specified in the analysis of 'the structures' at the most abstract level. The constraint in the Althusserian theory of society is the necessity to have those functions performed which will preserve or reproduce that known structure.

Since a pattern of causation usually cannot be demonstrated (in the absence of a historical method), the analysis constantly falls back on 'as if' arguments. Thus Althusser, in his first essay on the subject, explaining the functional necessity of ideology:

> It is as if human societies could not survive without these *specific formations*, these systems of representations (at various levels), their ideologies. (1969: 232)

Or Poulantzas, on a theme already discussed:

Everything happens precisely as if the state permanently played the role of political organiser of the power bloc. (1973: 299)

Or on the theme of education in mass schools:

Everything takes place as if, even when the petty–bourgeois agents [i.e. children] are educated in apparatuses [i.e. schools] that appear from formal considerations as overwhelmingly designed for the working class, their forms of education are still radically distinct from the forms of the latter. (1975: 260–1)

In this last case, the 'as if' argument allows Poulantzas to evade the facts to the extent of interpreting a statistical tendency in intra-school streaming as a class boundary, and to ignore the specific integrative politics of common schooling. (The latter is a curious omission, for him.)

The converse of this line of thought is the 'only–an–effect' argument. The centralisation of decision–making in companies seems to be an important change in power structure, perhaps linked with computers, which might seem to need some reconsideration of orthodox marxist views (as observed above); but don't worry, Poulantzas explains, it is only–an–effect of changes in the relations of production. Classes themselves, in economic life, seem to take the form of gradations of income, not fundamental cleavages; but don't worry, the hierarchy of levels of income is only–an–effect of the relations of production (1975: 18, 20, 130, 182). In the 'as if' argument, the missing but required facts are conjured up in mid-air; in the 'only–an–effect' argument, the present but unpleasant facts are conjured away. How these 'effects' are produced is never explained. Here the systematic ambiguity of the relationship between fields, discussed in the last section, is decidedly convenient.

I have given only a few examples of these arguments, though literally scores could be produced. The question of forms of argument is far from being a verbal quibble, for it is in such dress that the Althusserian approach, normally developed at an extremely abstract level, touches ground; and here its fundamental character can be deciphered. To me, the most telling moment of all comes when Carchedi is expounding his theoretical framework, and explains that determined instances over-determine the determinant instance, but the determinant sets the limits to its own overdetermination... we have heard this before. But then comes the illustration:

For example, the non–capitalist sector must always be subordinated to the capitalist one, or the capitalist system will cease to be such. (1977: 48)

Or the capitalist system will cease to be such! There it is, in a nutshell: the point that links functionalism, definitional argument, ahistoricity, top-down abstractions, and marxist orthodoxy all together. We know the system is capitalist; we have a model of it which, because it comes from Marx, must be right; therefore those things which the model tells us about must be there in reality, or the capitalist system will cease to be such. The non–capitalist sector must be subordinated to the capitalist, the labour process must be subordinated to the surplus–value producing process, the state must present an intrinsic unity, reformist parties must contribute to the organisation of bourgeois hegemony, the ideological apparatuses must function to insert workers in their class places, and so on and so forth, or the capitalist system will cease to be such. It is, indeed, unarguable—given the definitions, and a completely closed conceptual system.

At a couple of points in his book Carchedi addresses the question of functionalism. At one, having specified that the capitalist is in fact involved in doing some of the world's work, he says that nevertheless the fundamental role (in the package defining the capitalist) reverts to the element of ownership, and that it was necessary to stress this 'in order not to be accused of functionalism'. A little further on he suggests that in studying the income of the new middle class, we should avoid 'a functionalist explanation' of the type that says that the more important functions get the higher incomes, à la Davis and Moore's (1945) theory of stratification. (Carchedi promptly suggests two functionalist explanations of his own, however, on the next page—1977: 88, 95–6). It would seem that Carchedi's notion of 'functionalism' equates it with consensus theory, and that he thinks if you stress issues of ownership and exploitation, you are adequately protected from functionalist ideology. Plainly, that is an adequate protection from the specific version of functionalism that we find in Parsons or Davis and Moore. But as Merton pointed out in the essay already mentioned, functionalism as such does not depend on postulates of social consensus, and is not necessarily aligned with political conservatism. There can be a marxist functionalism. Where it differs from Parsonian functionalism is in its a priori assumption of class society, and in its analysis of everything in terms of functional relations to the reproduction of the postulated class structure and implicit relationships to the Revolution.

To coin a term, this is a bipolar functionalism. By this I don't mean anything to do with Carchedi's two 'functions' in the production process, which is indeed a simpler conception and quite compatible with orthodox functionalism. It is rather the position implicit in his remark that:

> In the case of the labour aristocracies, it is the economic which assigns the dominant role to the ideological because the capitalist economic structure, in order to reproduce itself, needs to introduce within the working class several types of bourgeois ideologies (e.g. reformism). (1977: 145–6)

What is implicit here, shadowing the successful performing of this function, is a kind of anti–function whose functionaries are the bearers of the revolutionary line. Indeed this was mentioned only a moment before, where Carchedi suggested that a complete definition of the proletariat must involve the ideological and political as well as the economic, and therefore would include only that part of the working class which had developed a proletarian class consciousness, and also had joined 'the worker's party' and joined in proletarian political practice. (Incidentally, if Carchedi means by 'the worker's party' what marxists usually do, then in a country like Australia his definition of the proletariat would embrace one–fortieth of one per cent of the economically active population, approximately. On the loosest definition possible, it embraces a little over one per cent.) A more elaborate example is given when Poulantzas, running down his version of Althusser's list of ideological state apparatuses, comes to 'the political parties, the unions', and adds, in parentheses,

> (with the exception, of course, of the *revolutionary* party or trade union organisations). (1969: 77)

The naivety of this, in a world where 57 different sects each proclaim themselves *the* revolutionary party, is charming; but the implications are not. The effect of Althusserian bipolar functionalism is to claim that every practice outside that of the revolutionary party *actually* subserves the reproduction of the capitalist system. I am not making a merely logical point here, but a very practical one, because this theoretical position comes through again and again in the statements that Althusserians, or other marxists influenced by Althusserian notions, make about all kinds of practical issues. Examples that come immediately to mind are urban politics where, as Pickvance (1976: 204) notes, this approach refuses ever to see 'the authorities' as a source of change or concession until they are forced, and hence systematically devalues any strategy of working–class mobilisation to capture local state power; and welfare, where the effect is to make any achievable welfare measures appear only to stabilise and help reproduce capitalism (Trainor, 1977). The obverse of this is to claim scientific justification for one line and one line only; in short, to imply that anyone interested in any moderate reform, let alone socialism, must join 'the' revolutionary party. The specific form of Althusserian functionalism, then, has a definite political point. It is closely connected with a conventional, October–in–Petrograd, big–bang theory of the transition to socialism.

The politics of theorising

If class analysis is, as I suggested at the start, fundamentally the social theory produced by and for socialist politics, the ultimate significance of a line of class theory is political. This view would undoubtedly be accepted by Althusser, Poulantzas and Carchedi; so let us consider the political tendency of their theorising about class. Althusser of course began with a political act in the realm of theory, the campaign to defend marxism against humanism. It was in the course of this that he developed his critique of the 'problematic of the subject', and his melancholy doctrine that the socialist theory of class society cannot be about people and their action on history, but that

the structure of the relations of production determines the *places* and the *functions* occupied and adopted by the agents of production, who are never anything more than the occupants of these places, insofar as they are the 'supports' (Träger) of these functions. (1970: 180)

What is the political significance of this apparently abstruse epistemological doctrine? It begins to be spelt out especially in Althusser's and Poulantzas' work on ideology. What ideology is about is 'inserting' people into a place already defined for them by the structures, a class place. Classes can *not* be understood properly as created by the process of mobilisation, in which, for example, working people struggle to take control of their own destiny. We have already noted Poulantzas' rejection of Marx's view on this: construing classes in terms of a process of class formation is historicist, empiricist, subjectivist, ultimately idealist, and not quite *comme il faut*. Being thus inserted, the working class cannot formulate correct theory on its own, because it is (by definition) permanently dominated by bourgeois and petty–bourgeois ideology. Marxist science must be imported from outside to criticise what the working class itself thinks, set it straight, and rescue it from the 'deformations' to which it is naturally heir. Guess who will do this? Why, folks, our old friend the revolutionary party, which will eventually lead us forward to 'the socialist democracy of the dictatorship of the proletariat'. (Poulantzas, 1973: 183–4, 204–6, 356)

The methodological position from which class theory is constructed thus leads, indirectly but inevitably, to an account of the working class that justifies the vanguard–party theory of socialist organisation, and systematically discredits any strategy based on spontaneity, self–management, and popular mobilisation. This trend of logic is strongly supported by an atmospheric effect in Althusserian writing which is quite important, though I have mostly ignored it in order to concentrate on explicit ideas about class. I refer to its convoluted methods of argument and its abominable literary style. It may be that the French texts suffer somewhat from bad translation into English, though I am informed that they are not regarded as examples of classically limpid French prose either. But no-one can say it is an effect of translation (or writing in a foreign language) when Carchedi takes forty mortal pages of definitional waffle to introduce the banal observation that in advanced capitalism some people do the work, other people organise them in order to extract a profit, and other people do a bit of both. (No satire intended—this is, literally, the guts of his theory of the economic identification of classes.) The whole literature has almost totally corrupted the language of a good many English–speaking followers of the Althusserian school.

The political point of this is that there is no way that people who write class analysis like this can be intending to address the working class, or even the socialist movement at large. People who do wish to serve the mass movement, and be corrected by it, must constantly struggle to clarify, to speak in the plainest possible language. If someone doesn't, then there must be a different audience and role intended. Occasionally one finds a defence of all this obscurity:

> It is not surprising that the resurgence of a strengthened Marxist theory should sometimes be difficult or even inaccessible; this is a small price to pay for the existence of a viable and healthy discussion that is now taking place *within* Marxism. (Hunt, 1977: 8)

It is not surprising that this arrogant and complacent statement comes from the report of a conference of the 'Sociology Group' of the Communist Party of Great Britain at which all speakers were academics. But the point is not that this stuff is mainly written by academics. The point is that reading it must intimidate workers, if they can be bothered with it at all. With the supposed theory of the workers' movement written in a way that is utterly 'inaccessible' to the rank and file, the political consequence can only be a reinforcement of the cultural dominance within the movement of an elite of intellectuals—the 'real initiates' mentioned in a little–quoted discussion of this point by Althusser (1969: 24)—who take upon themselves the task of formulating strategy. The hegemony of the educated within workers' parties is of course a problem in other contexts than European marxism. Hindess, for instance, before being converted to Althusserianism, made an excellent empirical study of this process in the British Labour Party (1971). But it seems most likely to become entrenched where the creation myth of the movement centres around intellectuals. (No joke, incidentally: see Althusser's offhand statement that 'Marx founded' the First International (1971: 95). All those French and English workers apparently were just standing round the walls.)

The cultural character of the putative vanguard is sufficiently indicated by the Althusserian attitude towards other intellectuals. I have already mentioned the re-reading of Marx to purge him of anything smacking of passion and humanity; the purification of marxism which purified it of most of Gramsci, Lukacs, Korsch, Sartre, Reich, the Frankfurt school, Trotsky, in short most of what was interesting and innovative in marxism in the last sixty years. The attitude to Trotsky is particularly instructive. To Althusser he is practically an un-person, not mentioned at all in *For Marx* or *Lenin and Philosophy*, and only once in his contribution to *Reading Capital*, in passing in a list of marxist political leaders. In *Political Power and Social Classes* Poulantzas adopted the same attitude. Trotsky is mentioned only once in its text; and it is worth quoting the passage in its entirety:

> Moreover, theoretical research [on the state apparatus] has been widely distorted because of the errors of Trotsky's analyses and in particular because of the ideological rubbish churned out by his successors. I shall therefore try to avoid the ideological terrain of this discussion by staying close to the scientific analyses provided by Marx, Engels, Gramsci and Lenin on this subject. (1973: 351)

Keep close to mother! By 1970, when he wrote *Fascism and Dictatorship*, Poulantzas was adopting a much kindlier attitude to Trotsky. Partly he had to take him seriously because there is simply no way you can miss Trotsky in discussing communist views of fascism in the 1920s; but also, in the meantime, Poulantzas had moved politically towards a position in which criticism of the Soviet Union was more respectable.

In making these attitudes credible, some importance must be assigned to the ahistorical functionalist theory of class and the state. Having such a theory allows one to go back through the history of socialism with a kind of timeless mark-sheet, handing out awards for strategy and tactics: this person is right here, that one is wrong there, someone else is inevitably wrong. The reason for being wrong politically always has to do with having 'deviated' in theory, failed to appreciate the relative autonomy of the state, built too much on the spontaneity of the workers. Fighting over lost battles this way is a great pastime among marxist theorists, which has the useful effect of bolstering the importance of theory in the present. Above all it confirms the impression of there being one and only one line which will bring about the overthrow of capitalism, which is awfully difficult to discover and hold to even within the revolutionary vanguard.

The political effect of the bipolar functionalism discussed in the last section is, as I suggested there, to reinforce a particular view of the transition to socialism, a big-bang theory of revolution. In Carchedi's words,

The characteristic element of the transition from capitalism to socialism is that the socialist production relations can be established only through a revolution which gives first of all the political and ideological power to the proletariat. (1977: 148)

Remembering that Carchedi's 'proletariat' is a tiny politically-organised minority, this easily fits with an elitist view of how the revolutionary rupture is to be encouraged:

... it is impossible for the working class to achieve a developed class consciousness without an organisation which wages an economic, political, and ideological fight against the class enemy under the leadership of a vanguard. (1977: 41)

All of this is good grey marxist–leninist orthodoxy, and was there long before Althusser and his school. Their originality was not in producing any new political strategies (as they have produced few new ideas of any kind), but in building a massive theoretical system which made *this* strategy appear not the dubious choice it actually is, but a logical necessity stemming from the innermost nature of capitalism.

To be generous, the functionalist tendency at least encourages a kind of militancy, a focus on changing the whole class system rather than getting bogged down in the bits. The effect of the categorical tendency in the conception of class is to render this an abstract militancy. To the extent that classes are understood essentially as sets of people (or even 'production agents') who meet a particular criterion (as in the whole debate over class boundaries), they are not seen as groups that in any sense constitute themselves by their actions and hence by a transforming practice. The necessity of militancy, in other words, is not generated from the lived experience of the class. (The categorical logic of theory here corresponds to the traditional bolshevik disdain for the limitations of the spontaneous consciousness of the working class.) Rather it hangs in the air, as a kind of categorical imperative deduced from the structures.

When we now take into account the distinction in the theory of class between the field of the structures (whence this militancy about social transformation arises) and the field of practice and conjunctures, a further political conclusion emerges: it is that *no* political conclusion can be deduced from the structural analysis, except the demand for militancy itself. The conjuncture is, as Althusser and Poulantzas make very clear, the site and object of political practice; and, as they also make clear, the characteristics of a conjuncture can never be deduced from an analysis of the structural determinations of the classes in it. In short, we have a militancy without substance, in the sense that it cannot ever, of itself, propose what is to be done. At least in the present. The game Poulantzas plays, of going back and correcting theoretically the strategy and tactics of the socialists who actually had to improvise a response to fascism in the heat of a complicated, violent and unexpected struggle, can only be done retrospectively. And we cannot draw from it rules for the future. As Althusser said—and it is one of his most profound insights—'are we not always in exceptional situations?'

Let me draw these points together. The implicit politics of Althusserian class theory as theoretical practice is an abstract militancy, without a political 'line' of its own, providing a general justification for a revolutionary vanguard party led by an educated but fairly intolerant elite who are the bearers of marxist science; and a general devaluation of strategies connected with spontaneity, mobilisation from below, incremental change, or use of the existing state.

That sounds, on the whole, pretty familiar. It sounds not very different from what Althusser came out of, i.e. European stalinism. The ear-marks of stalinism are visible enough: the justification for a revolutionary elite within the labour movement; the denunciation of most of the creative (and therefore heterodox) work in twentieth-century marxism; the bland assumption that there is one proper revolutionary party, and so on. At a deeper level, the theory works in the same direction; the priority of the structures, the bipolar functionalism, the abstract militancy that they produce; in the Althusserian world, the revolution itself—a transformation of the structures, scientifically speaking—seems to occur behind the backs of the workers. That terrible intervention of living, sweating, bleeding human beings in their own history that is the basis of all radicalism, is methodologically ruled out of 'marxist science' by Althusserian marxism. Here, I think, is its fundamental affinity with stalinist politics, which is precisely characterised by the combination of a notional militancy with a practical suppression of grass-roots socialism.

I stress 'fundamental affinity' rather than making a direct equation, for two reasons. First, it is plain enough that Althusser and the others do not mean deliberately to defend stalinism. Althusser personally has had a complicated and ambiguous debate with the ghost of Stalin, in the course of which he has attempted to identify stalinism as a deviation (basically an economist one) within authentic marxism. Opinions may reasonably differ about this exercise; basically I am inclined to agree with Callinicos (1976: 89ff) that the distancing hasn't gone very far, that the fundamental affinity is still there. The second reason is more general. The political meaning of an intellectual position cannot be read off directly from its content. To do that would be to adopt an ahistorical method, exactly the kind of essentialism into which the Althusserians fall in denouncing humanism, historicism, and the rest. Rather, its political significance must be judged also in terms of its context, the situation in which it is active, and the possibilities and intractabilities of that situation.

Generalising very rashly, I would like to suggest that there is at least one important difference between situations in which Althusserian theory has recently been active, which gives the system significantly different meanings. In contexts where there is a mass communist party, Althusserian theory provides an abstract justification for a mainstream stalinist leadership; to the extent that its theoretical militancy inflames young intellectuals, it will tend to urge them into political activity in such a party or on its fringes, trying to change its direction if it appears to be lacking a little in orthodoxy or militancy. But in contexts where there is no such party, where all the mass labour organisations plainly fall under the ban of 'reformism', the result is likely to be very different. Here the theory is most likely to lead to sectarianism or political alienation.

As this is the situation in those English–speaking countries where Althusserian theory has had a significant impact (i.e. England and Australia), this is the effect that must concern us here. I have mentioned some of the forms already. The impact of the Althusserian theory of class, the state and ideology on discussions of the education and social welfare systems in which a majority of our radical intellectuals actually earn their daily bread, is systematically to undercut any hope of achieving social change through them. The impact of the Althusserian theory of class and political organisation is to undercut any motive for participating in the available mass organisations, *and* any hope that the working class will generate its own socialist consciousness and thus transform the organisations. The impact of Althusserian epistemology is to discourage intellectuals from doing research that might actually be useful to unions and parties; and the impact of Althusserian language is certainly to discourage the workers from talking to *them*. What it does positively encourage them to do is sit around and theorise, militantly.

The reception of Althusserian theory was undoubtedly a response to a need felt by many intellectuals, in the context of the backwash from the radical mobilisation of the late 1960s, for a systematic, solid, incorruptible theory of the social world and the need for revolution. I have no doubt that it did some good by way of encouraging people to read Marx and Lenin carefully; and of course there are things in Althusser worth reading anyway, such as his discussions of historical time and the working of ideology. There were some things to be gained. But in supplying them, the system led its readers nowhere politically, and never will. As a general theory of society, it is incapable of development except by ever more intricate exegesis of ever more abstruse concepts. For the sake of the working class, who do actually need (and often want) a decent contribution to socialism from the intellectuals, it should be ditched, as soon and as thoroughly as possible.

Afterword

This discussion has been almost exclusively critical, which is in itself unfortunate; the main point is to do better. Of course the criticism is implicitly based on a view of how to do that, though in a paper of this (already overblown) size I can do no more than gesture towards it by way of slogans. It would imply a concrete rather than an abstract militancy, that is, commitments rooted in a knowledge of the actual situations that make up this violent and exploitative society; a thoroughly historical understanding of class, whose core is the relation between collective experience and the structure of situations; and an approach to socialist strategy in advanced capitalism that is based on the remobilisation of the working class and the generalisation of local struggles for workers' power and sexual equality, and which, among other things, has some respect for the workers' own views in the matter and for the organisations they have built. Of course this is no private position of mine. It corresponds to the practices of a large part of the socialist movement, though it has not been very articulate in theory. It includes, I might say finally, the political practices of some socialists who have formerly been adherents of Althusserian positions in theory, and this tendency is important. The more people who move in this direction from the positions criticised in this paper, the stronger the socialist movement will be.

8

The black box of habit on the wings of history: critical reflections on the theory of social reproduction, with suggestions on how to do it better

Poore cousened cousenor, *that* she, and *that* thou,
Which did begin to love, are neither now;
You are both fluid, chang'd since yesterday;
Next day repaires, (but ill) last dayes decay,
Nor are, (although the river keepe the name)
Yesterdayes waters, and to daies the same.

Donne, 'The second Anniversarie'

With structuralism came reproduction theory. A whole series of questions—the nature of ideology, the sociology of education, the relationship between capitalism and patriarchy—had by the mid 1970s been re-worked as problems of social reproduction, the reproduction of the relations of production, even 'relations of reproduction'. Bourdieu's work became as influential in discussions of schooling as Althusser's in discussions of ideology. The 'new left', counter-cultural movements, progressive education and welfare activism were all heavily criticized as contributing to the reproduction of capitalism. A deep pessimism began to settle on the theoretical left. It was as if *not* accepting reproduction theory was a sign of hopeless naivety.

Like many other people, I found some of these arguments convincing—at first. But as it went on, I came more and more to feel that it was not only politically immobilising, but also bad theory. This became clear in a specific case as we worked on our interview material in the School, Home and Work project, and found it very much at odds with the arguments of Bourdieu and

the structuralists. It seemed to me, more generally, that along
with some of the innocence of the 1960s, some important
insights and practical lessons about the nature of liberation were
also being lost. And it was time to try to bring them back into
the theoretical picture. The essay was written in England in
August 1979.

Where the issue comes from

The concept of 'social reproduction', or the 'reproduction of the
relations of production', has become very influential in socialist
theory in the last fifteen years. It has been the central idea in analyses
of the education system and its exasperating link with social class. It
has been a key idea in a number of socialist attempts to understand the
subjection of women, and the way the family is linked to capitalism. It
has become unexpectedly prominent in discussions of the structure of
cities, the concept of ideology, the nature of the capitalist state. It has
even been proposed by a leading French marxist as the basis for an
entire re–thinking of socialist strategy.

A concept that has acquired such a workload is bound to show some
signs of strain; and in this case I think they are more than passing
twinges. The basic problem with which analyses of social reproduction
are trying to grapple is immensely important—how an oppressive and
exploitative social system is stabilised; what holds it together, in the
face of the resistance it produces, and its own irrationality and
incoherence. But a given way of setting the problem up may create
more difficulties than it solves. We have to be alert not only to the
topic, but also to the way the arguments are put together, the
understanding of capitalism they rest on, and their implications for
practice.

There is nothing new about the issues. That the capitalist system of
economic exploitation was supported by, and depended on, forces
outside 'the economy' itself, has been familiar to socialists from the
jump. The early socialist movement was born in a milieu where
military force was widely used to keep the workers in their place, and
where official culture was stacked against them. Early nineteenth–
century unionists and radicals were commonly rationalist and atheist,
not just because they had read Tom Paine and the *philosophes*, but
also because they recognized the church as a moral police and buttress
of the system of property. (This role of religion—and formal
education was at this time mainly an adjunct of religion—was equally
well recognized by the ruling class of the day; it is thrown into sharpest

relief in those parts of the imperial system where the problems of social control were concentrated, like the convict colonies in Australia. See Connell and Irving, 1980.) It is striking that when the great anarchist Bakunin wrote his Revolutionary Catechism in 1866 he put the abolition of state religions *before* the abolition of class among the conditions for freedom (Dolgoff, 1971: 77–8). A biting criticism of bourgeois culture was one of the great themes of anarchist and anarcho–syndicalist movements in the next two generations—most familiar to English speakers in the songs and satire of the I.W.W. (1955). Some of the most creative socialists of the late 19th and early 20th century, such as Morris and Carpenter in England, set themselves not just to oppose capital but to work out alternative forms of daily work and domestic life (Rowbotham and Weekes, 1977). A theorist such as Sorel could win international fame with an argument about the new 'myths' that the labour movement had to create, and the ethics of a worker-controlled society, in the course of which he explored the role of art as a model of liberated production (see 'The ethics of the producers' in *Reflections on Violence*).

As this temper was mostly lost by the socialist movement for fifty years after World War I, it is worth recalling this pre-history. Lefebvre (1976) is wrong to suggest that the underlying problem has only recently been clearly recognised, or that it first took shape in the work of Reich. Even among psychoanalysts, that is to ignore Adler, a socialist who posed the question of the link between social hierarchy and the dynamics of personality considerably earlier; and managed to be the first heretic booted out of Freud's circle.

But it would be fair to say that it has only comparatively recently come into focus in marxist socialism, and that it is this tradition that has given it the form of a theory of social reproduction. The general historical conditions for this were, as Lefebvre makes clear, the failure of the Leninist strategy of world revolution after the Russian one, and the successive reconstructions of capitalism through the twentieth century. And it seems as if the particular conditions were another dose of the same, if there is any significance in the fact that the three most influential theoretical statements (by Althusser, Bourdieu and Lefebvre) were all produced in the years immediately following the French crisis of 1968—that melodramatic moment when an advanced capitalist system did indeed seem on the point of revolution from within, but triumphantly survived.

The theory of reproduction, then, did not arise as an abstract necessity of social theory, a pure emanation of science. It is an intellectual response, shaped by a particular sociological and political tradition, to a definite problem. Before exploring this further, it may be useful to have a potted version of the main lines of argument.

Reproduction theorists:
Althusser, Lefebvre, Bourdieu

Every society—Althusser (1971) argues in his celebrated essay on ideology—based on a given mode of production, must reproduce both its own productive forces and the existing relations of production. The former means not only reproducing material goods like tools and machines, but also labour–power, The production of the right kinds of that, is increasingly a matter of formal schooling. The school not only teaches basic skills, but also the rules of behaviour and attitudes appropriate for the positions in production the children are destined for, as workers or as agents of capital.

To account for the reproduction of the *relations* of production, Althusser sets about reformulating the marxist theory of the state and ideology. Reproduction of class relations is the business of the state, acting through two kinds of mutually-supporting institutions: the 'repressive state apparatuses' and the 'ideological state apparatuses'. (Meaning, roughly, force and fraud.) The educational apparatus has become the dominant ideological apparatus in mature capitalism, and is now the key means by which capitalist relations of production are reproduced. Within it occur the practices and rituals which allocate a person to a class fate, and obscure from her the truth of the relations she is entering. In Althusser's poetic phrase, ideology 'calls to' the person; and the person living in ideology mis–recognises her real conditions of existence, being provided with an imaginary version of them. In the school, technical knowledge is learned wrapped up in the ruling ideology; more exactly, a different version of it provided for the different categories of people sorted out by school selection. Thus the school prepares, for their various functions, the mass of manual workers, who leave first; next technicians and white–collar workers, who get a bit more training; and finally the higher intellectuals, ideologists, managers and capitalists, who reach the summit of the education system. The fact that it does this is, however, systematically obscured by the school's own official ideology of neutrality and impartiality—which the great majority of teachers accept.

Given that they are sharply opposed on a whole range of political and philosophical issues, it is striking how much of Althusser's analysis is shared by Lefebvre. They start from the same premise— that a theory of production, on which socialist theory has been centred for a century, is partial and hence misleading; that reproduction is the larger, more comprehensive process. They make the same distinction between reproduction of means and reproduction of relations, both focussing on the latter. And they see this as being mainly accomplished in a realm of everyday life that has in the past seemed marginal to class analysis—for Althusser, education; for Lefebvre, urban space. (Not that Lefebvre contests the argument about schooling—he offers a short discussion of it that agrees in all essentials with Althusser's—merely thinking it less central.) Both of them, finally, see the state as the co-ordinator and organiser of the process.

Lefebvre departs from Althusser, however, on a critical point of method. He refuses to take the 'capitalist mode of production' as an already-constructed, logically coherent system whose reproduction can be explored theoretically. Rather, he sees capitalism as an incoherent, fragmentary, vastly uneven trend in the history of the world, whose coherence is a goal of strategy of the ruling classes (acting through the state), rather than something that can be taken for granted in a theoretical analysis. There is, he argues, no 'logic of reproduction'. It is not an automatic process; it is something achieved in the course of a social struggle whose outcome is by no means pre-determined. Hence the theory of reproduction is historically specific. Only at a certain point in history, after the level of economic development and class tension reached about the end of the nineteenth century, was the reproduction of the means of production displaced by the reproduction of class relations as the key problem facing the ruling classes—and the proper focus of socialist theory and strategy.

How has the ruling class won, to date? In *The Survival of Capitalism* Lefebvre runs through a spectrum of proposals about how social domination is achieved in everyday life. The radical critique of education and mass media; Foucault's and others' arguments about the controlling power of language, of 'discourse'; the radical-feminist argument about the centrality of patriarchal relations; Reich on the same theme; and others. All attempts to find a 'generative nucleus', an institution or process in which the business of social reproduction is concentrated, Lefebvre finds radically incomplete. They still presuppose the power structure as a whole. Further, the process of social reproduction is not concentrated, but extended—both in the sense that it is now a matter of struggles that are world-wide, truly global in scale; and in the sense that reproduction is located in the organisation of space itself. Capitalism has invaded, fragmented, and re-organised both countryside and city; and the business of living in this differentiated space reproduces the class relations that give rise to (and constantly transform) it. Power relations are implicit in the production of space, as they are in the production of the person growing up in a patriarchal family.

These are simply leading points in a sprawling, and not always completely consistent, argument (a complaint that would probably not disturb Lefebvre). Bourdieu, by contrast, is so rigorously formulated as to be, at first reading, almost incomprehensible. In the first half of *Reproduction* he and Passeron offer a portfolio of propositions about 'symbolic violence' couched in a language of truly remarkable obscurity and abstractness, intended to provide a framework that could apply to any society whatever. It is, nevertheless, mainly based on a decade's research on education in capitalist France (plus Bourdieu's ethnographic studies in Algeria); and is best read backwards to see what the authors are getting at. (This approach can be justified by Bourdieu and Passeron's own statement of the provisional character of their theoretical system, and the way it was produced—see 1977: ix–x.)

At the core is the fact that so impressed Althusser, class inequalities in educational outcomes; and the belief, also shared with him, that these are central to the stabilisation of the class structure at large. The second half of *Reproduction* is a discussion of French education called 'Keeping Order'. By that the authors mean the business of assigning people to their class locations, and persuading everybody that those are their right places. The general theory of reproduction is built up by deducing the conditions required for this to be successfully done—or, if you like, what presuppositions have to be made in order to explain it.

At the most concrete level, this requires an education system able to do the job; and here Bourdieu's line of thought begins to diverge from Althusser's and Lefebvre's, both in his treatment of education, and in his attempt to analyse what 'the job' actually is. For the reproduction of a structure of social relations is above all a matter of perpetuation of social practices, and practices are not churned out of a machine like sausages. They are what people do in improvising the course of their daily life. In his *Outline of a Theory of Practice*, published shortly after *Reproduction* and an essential part of the argument, Bourdieu spells out what is required to explain the reproduction of a structure without falling into the traps of structural determinism or voluntarism:— a way of accounting for 'invention within limits'. He formulates this in the concept of 'habitus', the system of dispositions, inculcated in the growing person, to generate the appropriate kinds of actions in later life. This is the means by which a family can hand on its 'symbolic capital' to the younger generation; and this is the business also of pedagogy in schools.

In their treatment of class effects in schooling Bourdieu and Passeron are I think unique in their simultaneous grasp of two principles: this is indeed oppression, 'symbolic violence' in their own terms; and it is not only not planned by the educators, but is largely produced by the action of the dominated classes themselves, or more

precisely by their interaction with a conservative educational
environment. Neither the mass education system nor the people
entering it are homogeneous. The children each have a habitus already
shaped by primary pedagogic action within the family, arising from
the conditions of their various class milieux, and expressing the
tendencies within them—such as the greater stress on symbolic
mastery in families whose upper–class economic position frees them
from practical need. Such a habitus becomes symbolic capital if it
meets a market–place in which that kind of mastery is valued—which
the education system is. Not that the education system is homogeneous,
far from it. But within its rivalrous parts and clashing principles, a
dominant position is held by those sections that most closely reflect the
culture of the class that holds power in the society at large. (In France,
the *grandes écoles*; in Anglo–American systems, no doubt, the elite
universities.) From there, the principles of teaching and examining
that govern the selection of people for elite education (and the future
rôle of educators) filter down; and these principles correspondingly
devalue other kinds of education and the people who get them.

Class inequalities, then, are not imposed on the masses by the
education system—that might indeed provoke a revolution, given the
value workers place on education!—but are achieved by *what is tacitly
presupposed by the teaching*. Specifically, the higher you go in the
system, the more strongly does it presuppose the kind of habitus
(tastes, skills, and so forth) liable to be produced in an upper–class
milieu. For this to work, it is of course necessary that that kind of
pedagogy be accepted by all concerned as legitimate; and a good part
of the theoretical apparatus erected by Bourdieu and Passeron is
devoted to this point. The education system, they suggest, succeeds in
concealing its own objective character as the broker of power relations
between classes. It is a feature of pedagogic authority in general that
teaching legitimates itself and thus legitimates the dominant culture on
which it is based. The arbitrary character of its content is concealed,
made to look 'natural'. And indirectly, the whole social order is
legitimated at the same time and through the same means that its
power relations are reinforced and inequality perpetrated.

Assumptions about class:
the problem with history

The first question that can be asked of a theory of reproduction is,
what exactly is being reproduced? In Lefebvre and Althusser, it is the
means and relations of production. These are not always easy to

distinguish—in Althusser's account of the reproduction of means he talks about the production of a hierarchically differentiated labour force, and children learning the rules of good behaviour, which sound uncommonly like questions of social relations to me. Anyway, the main stress in both theorists is on relations of production, which in the marxist tradition means class relations, and on the fitting of people to them. Bourdieu and Passeron, pedantic about so many points, are curiously inexplicit about the meaning of their own title; but it would be hard to deny that the main burden of their discussion is the reproduction of the power relation between classes, and of the 'cultural arbitrary' characteristic of each. In short, what these theories are about is (a) the characteristics of classes, (b) the pattern of relations between them; principally the latter.

Theories of reproduction, while analysing reproduction, have taken the nature and pattern of these relations for granted. This assumption is almost absolute in Althusser and Bourdieu. The former takes for granted the definition of a structure of class places within a mode of production when analysing the means by which people are inserted into them. Bourdieu and Passeron, however subtle they are about the way schools work, blandly presuppose a set of classes and a distribution of power between them, at every level in their analysis of the educational system, its sources of legitimation, its own power structure, its recruitment patterns, its effects. In the *Outline of a Theory of Practice*, where Bourdieu develops an account of reproduction in the context of Kabyle ethnography, the equivalent assumption is made by adopting the convention of the 'ethnographic present', i.e. talking as if traditional forms were being exactly preserved (surely an astonishing convention to adopt for Algeria in the 1950s!).

Lefebvre's position here is rather more complex. He is much more conscious of class dynamics, poses the question of the identity of a structure through time, and stresses that 'reproduction' is always at the same time a matter of the production of social relations, of change. Having posed the problem, he fails to solve it; and at the critical moments dodges the issue, falling back on language that assumes we all know what it is ('the essentials', 'capitalism') that is getting reproduced. This is like Habermas, who at the equivalent point in *Legitimation Crisis*, pulls out of the hat an abstract 'principle of organisation of society' to express what it is that is normally reproduced—which really amounts to a name for the type of class relations that have already been taken to define the stage of capitalism being discussed.

Of course this is intended by all these authors just as a device of exposition, freezing a pattern, bracketing its historical dynamics, to allow an analytic treatment of the moment of its reproduction. But the effects go much deeper than simply aiding exposition. A crucial split is introduced into the theory of structure. If dynamics are recognised, we now have a theory divided, like the cycles and epicycles of Ptolemaic astronomy, between the big trajectory of the system winging its way through history (class dynamics), and the little orbits of the people and institutions within it (reproduction). If dynamics are not recognised, we have functionalism. Only Lefebvre partially escapes this dilemma, and that more by ambiguity than by argument. It is, I suggest, a problem embedded in the very language of 'social reproduction'.

Reproduction analysis, to put it in the most general way, is based methodologically on a bracketing of history which, unless the most strenuous efforts are made to prevent it, must suppress the agency of people in creating history, in creating the very structures whose reproduction is being examined. This is peculiarly dangerous when the bracketing marks out realms that come to be seen as qualitatively different: for instance, a realm of culture in which the reproduction of economic relations occurs; or (as in some of Mitchell's [1975] arguments) a realm of patriarchy in which the reproduction of capitalism occurs. Class is *from the start* a cultural fact. Cultural struggle (and for that matter patriarchal relations) is part of the process by which people constitute classes and class relations—as the historiography of Thompson (1968), Gutman (1976) and others reminds us, even when theory doesn't. It isn't good enough to say, even in the most abstract formulations, that symbolic force is 'added to' a pre–existing power relation, as Bourdieu and Passeron put it in their very first theoretical proposition. As they rightly observe later on (1977: 36), there is no such thing as naked power. Class relations which are not already cultural relations are as mythical as the bunyip, and an equally bad basis for theory.

This is not to imply that reproduction analyses are talking about a non–problem; it is certainly to criticise their approach. The methodological problem is broader than simply re–inserting culture into the concept of power. It is to formulate the whole set of issues in a way that acknowledges the intrinsic and integral historicity of class processes (crippled from birth by Bourdieu and Passeron's attempt to formulate à theory applicable to any society); and to formulate historicity in a way that gives full weight to the fact of structural constraint. We conduct class analysis, not because we have philosophic certainty that we live in a class world (the one proposition on which Althusser manages to agree with Sartre), but because as a matter of fact in the real world classes are constantly being constructed around us, people are constantly *doing* class. But we do not do so for the pure joy of it. We live, and die, under terrifying constraints, to which we always have to respond; we bear on our minds and bodies the huge weight of living history, which theorists try to capture with the Medusa's-head of structural theory. It is not just an error of taste to talk of people being 'acted by the structures' and 'spoken by the discourse'; it is a failure of humanity, a political flaw.

This 'doing' of class is impossible to formulate precisely as the 'reproduction' of a relationship. Bourdieu is half-way there with his characterisation of reproduced practice as 'invention within limits', an observation characteristically sharp and, within its own limits, completely justified. But it needs to be taken outside the world of the ethnographic present and the pre-existent power structure, back to the real world where the actions people improvise occur in real historical time, on such-and-such an occasion in year x at place y. Historical time itself forbids an identity between the practice (and the structure being constructed by it) of the 6th August and that of the 5th. The point holds even for the most repetitive job in the most tightly-controlled cannery, where the boredom itself seems to prove reproduction theory true. Each day does not come out of the same mould, it comes out of the day before. And if nothing else has happened, another batch of fish is in the can, the balance-sheet totals of Amalgamated Octopuses have crept up again, everyone is a bit more experienced, the working class has had another strategic defeat, and the workers and their bosses are one day nearer to dying.

The 'reproduction of social relations' is a chimera. In all strictness, it never occurs; it cannot occur. We cannot treat social structure as something persisting in its identity behind the backs of mortal people, who are inserted into their places by a cosmic cannery called Reproduction. And it is senseless to try to rescue the concept by loosening 'identity' to 'similarity', pointing to the resemblance between today and yesterday, and supposing that the resemblance contains 'the essentials' being reproduced. We cannot rescue a scientific concept from its difficulties by making it *less* precise. Rather, we have to shift standpoint. The continuity, the persistence through time, with which theory is concerned, does not have the ontological structure of a *reproduced identity*, but that of an *intelligible succession*. It is not a relation of similarity between the structure today and the structure yesterday that is the point, but a relation of practice between them, the way one was produced out of the other.

I make no apologies for introducing the epistemological idea of intelligibility into a statement about the nature of the subject-matter. As I have tried to show in Chapter 6, an effective theory of class is one that offers an intelligible account of a process of transformation in historical time, of the generation of one state of a structure out of a previous one. It is the process of generation, and the claim to have understood it, that is the core of class analysis. The concept of social structure refers to the constraints that operate in generative processes; themselves not abstract but a matter of real practices, things done by knowing people as they respond to situations that arise for them in a world of power, of strategies, of oppression, affluence and deprivation. If anything is 'reproduced' it is not a 'relation' or a 'structure' but a *situation*; and that is not strictly reproduced, but generated out of the situation before.

By 'knowing people' in the previous paragraph I do not mean simply informed or rational. It may be a question of a wholly emotional apprehension of a situation, structured by completely repressed conflicts—thus even unconscious as well as non-rational. (The point is significant in terms of my later criticism of the cognitive bias in Bourdieu's account of the 'habitus'.) The argument does imply active apprehension, and an intelligibility in what is apprehended; for the basis of such a view of knowledge see Piaget's *Biology and Knowledge*.

Of the reproduction theorists, Lefebvre comes much the closest to this view, especially when stressing that reproduction is a consequence of strategies. The trouble is that the ones he is thinking of are quite exceptional. Ruling-class pursuit of the coherence of the system is basically a phenomenon of crises—the conscious strategies of social reconstruction adopted in the wake of the 1930s depression being a classic example. If we are to talk of strategies we must be consistent, and talk also of those routine strategies of capitalists that are directed against each other; and most importantly, of the strategies of working class people in their own lives which may help to stabilise the power of capital.

Bourdieu and Althusser speak a good deal of 'misrecognition' as a crucial mechanism here. When 14-year-old Ellen Oldcastle adopts (with some misgivings) the view current in her milieu that the way for her to escape the factory job she fears is to stay longer in the school she dislikes, and distance herself from her peers; or when Mr and Mrs Bailey, coming from poverty in depression childhoods to modest comfort in the postwar boom, buy, redecorate, extend, and enjoy a suburban house; they are in fact doing things (breaking down solidarity, extending the property market) that in Australia in the 1970s tend to reinforce ruling-class power. But this is not because of 'misrecognition' or an 'ideological effect'. It is a question of the structure of possibilities in the actual situations they face. They could analyse their situations in the light of reproduction theory until they were blue in the face, and it would still be pointless for them to decide anything but what they have done. We need not only the concepts of strategy and of ideology, but also a way of talking about traps for praxis—and what is really involved in getting out of them.

How is it done?—the black box

This has already brought us to a second basic question about reproduction theory: how is the reproducing supposed to be done? Most accounts of social reproduction become rather gestural at this point. Lefebvre runs through a range of arguments about it, but is very much clearer about what won't work (e.g. any theory of a 'generative nucleus') than what will. Even his argument about space remains inexplicit. 'Analysis will show', he writes, 'how this [leisure] space *actively reproduces* the relations of production' (1976: 84); but it seems that the required analysis is just too obvious, for Lefebvre doesn't produce it. Nor does Althusser, in explaining that ideology calls to the person, get far in explaining how the voice is projected or how we get ears that can hear. Lacanian psychoanalysis is suggested in another essay as a route to an understanding of ideological misrecognition, but it all remains highly schematic. It is only Bourdieu who offers a serious treatment of the problem, through his concept of the habitus, 'the durably installed generative principle of regulated improvisations' (1977: 78).

Bourdieu's definitions of habitus are striking, because they are not simply statements in the language of personality formation (i.e. that such-and-such a disposition is formed); they are always accompanied by a specification about social effects. This is true of the passage just cited, and is succinctly put in *Reproduction*:

> Pedagogic Work tends to reproduce the social conditions of the production of that cultural arbitrary, i.e. the objective structures of which it is the product, through the mediation of the habitus, defined as *the principle generating practices which reproduce the objective structures*. (Bourdieu and Passeron, 1977: 32–3; my italics.)

In such definitions Bourdieu does not specify a particular thing or process, he specifies a conceptual space, a mechanism required by the theory of reproduction—a black box, in short, which produces certain effects. The same must be said for developments of the concept, such as the idea of 'cultural capital' which is the key to his analysis of the way class effects are produced by the interaction of children with an education system. When you look into it closely, the concept of cultural capital boils down to the kind of habitus that would be required to produce the class selectivity we know occurs, on the supposition that this is produced by the kind of mechanism (distance between the culture inculcated by the family and that inculcated by the school) that Bourdieu suggests. It is all done by definitional mirrors. Of course Bourdieu really does have some idea of what is inside the black box, though it doesn't come into his *definition* of habitus. His ideas are, in fact, strikingly traditional: they are about the gradual inculcation of information and habits of thought in children by instruction from adults delegated to do the job and given sufficient disciplinary powers for it. The talk is about 'pedagogic communication', 'pedagogic authority', 'information transmitted', 'irreversible inculcation', and so forth—oddly suggestive of Mr Chips running a behaviour modification programme. While this may not be a bad description of what a lot of teachers (especially in advanced education) think they are doing, it has two massive deficiencies which must strike anyone who has paid attention to the actual complexities of personality formation.

Firstly, it almost completely ignores conflict and contradiction in the forming of a person and within the person formed. Bourdieu presupposes a more or less homogeneous culture in each class defining the 'cultural arbitrary' which is inculcated by primary pedagogic action (a wildly inaccurate assumption for real working classes under capitalist domination). He assumes a more or less harmonious absorption of the child by the primary pedagogic work (ignoring the crises, resistance and discontinuities that child-rearing really encounters). And he ignores the significance of intra–personal conflict, of divided motives and purposes, in shaping practice in later life.

Secondly, Bourdieu's theory almost completely ignores emotional development, sexuality, unconscious motivation, and the crises and transformations of personality attendant thereon. It is an overwhelmingly cognitive account of growth and socialisation, and thus a seriously impoverished one. In this regard the old left–freudian tradition is richer, suggesting ways in which drives and emotions could be shaped by the social pressures of capitalist society and the integration of various groups thus accomplished. But this literature too played down contradiction within the personality (as in Reich's (1949) and Fromm's (1942) treatment of character types), or exaggerated the harmoniousness of its integration into society (as in Marcuse's *One Dimensional Man*); Bourdieu does not stand alone . . .

He and they are surely right in their strategy of arguing from the fact of structural persistence to the kind of people who make it happen, without getting bogged in psychological determinism of the pan–phallic or hereditarian kinds. We do need a social psychology, which must proceed from a realistic, historically–concrete, sociology

with none. His search for a way
became utopian. There is virtu
shatters the tyranny of the real
are done for. But it is also i
futures in mind, we must also tu
grounds of resistance.

At the beginning of the sectio
theory speaks about both relat
teristics of classes, and then has
the theorists being discussed, or
to say about it, and that—
educationally distinctive and
('cultural arbitrary')—is highl
concrete example offered, that
symbolic mastery because the w(
caused by material deprivation,
nonsense. As Bernstein argues (
usage does not mean a differe
speech is as packed with symbc
indeed, since literary gents regar
exhausted, and went to the wor

There is, nevertheless, an im|
theory assumes, without any p
duction of the characteristics of
reproduction of the relations bet'
view of classes, it is clear that th(
maybe even normally, in contrac
capitalist domination in the indus
social subordination between w
most situations I am familiar
construction of the working clas;
to the extent that it is politically
its 'social reproduction'. A great
about precisely that! And about t
Heath government failed; the Fr
succeeded.) While the general st
increase of class power and d
contradiction embedded in it is o1
in the capitalist social order. The
of recent history is not unified st1
fragmented struggles about the p

This is exactly what Gramsci
analyses that produced the conce
cook his scattered notes into a c

(not the bland abstractions that lie behind most socialisation theory), and must deal with people as makers of their own lives (not just sufferers of a trauma or bearers of a structure). This is why Bourdieu's work is exciting, as he is one of the very few systematic social theorists to have a way of talking about what living in the world is really like, its shadows and its sunlight, its langours and its teeth. If the criticisms above are sharp, it is because they ask for more—more realism, both about the person and the social order. A realistic social psychology (which will be both a historical psychology and a depth psychology, and in both respects will confront contradiction, and the open-endedness of a dialectic) must break out of the framework of a theory of reproduction.

That there is a persistent lack of realism in reproduction analysis is not hard to show. Althusser, Lefebvre, and Bourdieu all assume that the school system sorts people out quite firmly into their future class positions, giving them the appropriate attitudes and skills for the role they are 'destined' for (Althusser), or validating and devaluing what they already have (Bourdieu)—in either case, this being the crucial mechanism of the legitimation of class subordination. After reading a whole series of confident and unqualifed statements to this effect, it is somewhat startling to recall that there is abundant evidence that it is actually not true. Especially since American research on education and occupation in the 1960s, the main points of which have been confirmed in a number of other countries, it has been a familiar fact about postwar capitalist society that the correlation between the level of education a person rose to, and the economic position arrived at later in life, while positive, is modest. (See Blau and Duncan, 1967; Jencks, 1972; Boudon, 1974.) Bowles and Gintis' *Schooling in Capitalist America* is perhaps the most persuasive attempt to retrieve a reproduction analysis from this fact, but legitimation still can't work in the way our theorists suppose.

We might expect as much of course, reflecting on the dynamisms of capitalist society—changes in the labour market, individual and collective mobility, regional and technological transformations, the accumulation and devalorisation of capital (real capital, that is!), and so on. If this linkage is weak, it is futile to rest the legitimation of class society mainly upon it. This is not to deny that schooling is important to legitimation; but it does not produce either a class fate, or a justification of that fate, by itself. It has to be studied in a context of economic practices and expectations, of personal and family trajectories, and of struggles about the scope and meaning of education itself, before its ideological role in class relations can be well understood.

Structur
d

To summarise the argum
theories have to make unte
be able to talk about its
cannot) give an adequate
coherent and persuasive er
be summed up in a word:

The rise of reproduction
has been exactly matched
radical activity can do. A
oppose the dominant ideo
ineffective. Bourdieu and
carefully knock progressiv
inculcating a cultural arbi
only that, but

all these Utopias constitute
who seek, through denunc
themselves the monopoly

so they are equally nasty;

The 'soft approach' may b
of symbolic violence in a d

or in plain language, pro;
when conservative techn
reminded of the schoolt
bastards'; and, after the p
and put on their show,
bastards'.

Lefebvre, mercifully, is
tacitly accepting a syste
explicitly opposing it. It is
reproduction theorists wh
process of liberation. H
project, based on the reco
the political ambiguities
countries, and centred
admirable, and has useful
remains somewhat abstrac
found it difficult to base t
force; seeking out any so

have been various interpretations of them. In particular there has been a functionalist take-over of the term 'hegemony' in which it has come to mean very much what Parsons called 'pattern maintenance and system integration' (Parsons, Bales and Shils, 1953). This is completely at odds with what I would see as the main thrust of Gramsci's argument, his insistence on analysing a state of play rather than a concept. The idea of hegemony was a means of analysing a *situation*, and this is the way we must recompose 'reproduction' analyses—into analyses of the possibilities and the traps in the situations various groups face.

Seeing their imbalance of power, we perhaps over–estimate the freedom of the ruling class and the constraints upon workers in confronting their situations. Praxis traps (where people do things for good reasons and skilfully, in situations that turn out to make their original purpose impossible to achieve) are not the fate of the working class alone. Indeed the most elegant example of all must be the case of capitalists in a stock market boom, when the interlocking of thousands of individually correct and rational strategies for making and taking profits prepares, with Aeschylaean rigour, the downfall of the lot. (That corporate sharks like Slater Walker or Minsec sometimes swim in and devour investors before they devour themselves, doesn't invalidate this point. It merely shows that praxis is not a matter of mechanical logic, that some capitalists are smart enough to operate meta–strategies on the possibilities created by other peoples' strategies.) Many practices have destabilising, transformative consequences, even when quite unintended.

Further, mutations in the structure can occur in partial ways, without gigantic convulsions, that open up new situations and changed possibilities. We can see this in the history of education itself. (If 'ideology has no history', the ideological apparatus certainly does.) Its most important change in the last generation, in countries like Australia and the U.K., is undoubtedly the massive expansion of secondary education and the shift to comprehensive schools. This was a change pushed through with surprisingly little opposition—given its scale—by coalitions of progressive educators, educational bureaucrats, reforming politicians and technocratically–minded capitalists. It was made possible by the postwar boom and expansion of the state, and by a mass demand for more training and for mobility through education. Neither secondary pedagogy, nor its role in class processes, could be the same after this as before.

We now have a teaching force that forms a mass occupation (which is both highly unionised, and has a high turnover, in relation to the length of training involved). We have a plethora of new or newly-transformed high schools in working–class milieux (themselves often (not the bland abstractions that lie behind most socialisation theory), and must deal with people as makers of their own lives (not just sufferers of a trauma or bearers of a structure). This is why Bourdieu's work is exciting, as he is one of the very few systematic social theorists to have a way of talking about what living in the world is really like, its shadows and its sunlight, its langours and its teeth. If the criticisms above are sharp, it is because they ask for more—more realism, both about the person and the social order. A realistic social psychology (which will be both a historical psychology and a depth psychology, and in both respects will confront contradiction, and the open-endedness of a dialectic) must break out of the framework of a theory of reproduction.

That there is a persistent lack of realism in reproduction analysis is not hard to show. Althusser, Lefebvre, and Bourdieu all assume that the school system sorts people out quite firmly into their future class positions, giving them the appropriate attitudes and skills for the role they are 'destined' for (Althusser), or validating and devaluing what they already have (Bourdieu)—in either case, this being the crucial mechanism of the legitimation of class subordination. After reading a whole series of confident and unqualifed statements to this effect, it is somewhat startling to recall that there is abundant evidence that it is actually not true. Especially since American research on education and occupation in the 1960s, the main points of which have been confirmed in a number of other countries, it has been a familiar fact about postwar capitalist society that the correlation between the level of education a person rose to, and the economic position arrived at later in life, while positive, is modest. (See Blau and Duncan, 1967; Jencks, 1972; Boudon, 1974.) Bowles and Gintis' *Schooling in Capitalist America* is perhaps the most persuasive attempt to retrieve a reproduction analysis from this fact, but legitimation still can't work in the way our theorists suppose.

We might expect as much of course, reflecting on the dynamisms of capitalist society—changes in the labour market, individual and collective mobility, regional and technological transformations, the accumulation and devalorisation of capital (real capital, that is!), and so on. If this linkage is weak, it is futile to rest the legitimation of class society mainly upon it. This is not to deny that schooling is important to legitimation; but it does not produce either a class fate, or a justification of that fate, by itself. It has to be studied in a context of economic practices and expectations, of personal and family trajectories, and of struggles about the scope and meaning of education itself, before its ideological role in class relations can be well understood.

Structural change and historical
depth psychology

To summarise the argument so far, I have suggested that these theories have to make untenable assumptions about class structure to be able to talk about its reproduction, and do not (and probably cannot) give an adequate account of how it is done. Yet they are coherent and persuasive enough to have a political impact, which can be summed up in a word: pessimism.

The rise of reproduction theory in socialist discussions of education has been exactly matched by a loss of political confidence in what radical activity can do. Althusser notes that some heroic teachers oppose the dominant ideology, but they are rare, and—he implies—ineffective. Bourdieu and Passeron are clearer. They explicitly and carefully knock progressive educators, as being no less involved in inculcating a cultural arbitrary than are conservative educators. Not only that, but

> all these Utopias constitute an instrument of ideological struggle for groups who seek, through denunciation of a pedagogic legitimacy, to secure for themselves the monopoly of the legitimate mode of imposition

so they are equally nasty; moreover

> The 'soft approach' may be the only effective way of exercising the power of symbolic violence in a determinate state of power relations (1977: 12–17)

or in plain language, progressive education is what capitalism needs when conservative techniques are seen to be too crude. One is reminded of the schoolboy who wrote in an essay, 'Coppers is bastards'; and, after the police public–relations unit visited the school and put on their show, changed his mind: 'Coppers is cunning bastards'.

Lefebvre, mercifully, is able to see that there is a difference between tacitly accepting a system of domination and exploitation, and explicitly opposing it. It is not surprising that he is the only one among reproduction theorists who goes on to talk in any detail about the process of liberation. His general conception of a new socialist project, based on the recognition of the global scale of capitalism and the political ambiguities of the working class in advanced capitalist countries, and centred on the theme of self–management, is admirable, and has useful implications for educational practice. Yet it remains somewhat abstract. Like Marcuse in the same years, Lefebvre found it difficult to base the project of liberation in a definable social force; seeking out any source of opposition as a possibility, satisfied with none. His search for a way of transcending 'reproduction' in fact became utopian. There is virtue in this, of course. Utopian thought shatters the tyranny of the real, fires the imagination; without it, we are done for. But it is also incomplete. While bearing imaginary futures in mind, we must also turn back to an analysis of the practical grounds of resistance.

At the beginning of the section before last I noted that reproduction theory speaks about both relations between classes and the characteristics of classes, and then has almost entirely ignored the latter. Of the theorists being discussed, only Bourdieu and Passeron have much to say about it, and that—assuming that each class has an educationally distinctive and more or less homogeneous culture ('cultural arbitrary')—is highly implausible. Practically the only concrete example offered, that the ruling class specialise more in symbolic mastery because the workers are stuck in practical exigencies caused by material deprivation, is, not to put too fine a point on it, nonsense. As Bernstein argues (1971: 197–8), a different context and usage does not mean a different capacity; working–class life and speech is as packed with symbolism as any other. It is not so long, indeed, since literary gents regarded *bourgeois* culture as anaemic and exhausted, and went to the working class for new strength!

There is, nevertheless, an important problem here. Reproduction theory assumes, without any particular argument, that the reproduction of the characteristics of classes goes hand–in–hand with the reproduction of the relations between them. When we take a historical view of classes, it is clear that the processes thus referred to are often, maybe even normally, in contradiction. The care and maintenance of capitalist domination in the industrialised countries (i.e. the relation of social subordination between working class and ruling class) is, in most situations I am familiar with, best served by *preventing* the construction of the working class as a well–defined social entity, and, to the extent that it is politically and socially mobilised, by *sabotaging* its 'social reproduction'. A great deal of conservative political work is about precisely that! And about managing the resulting tensions. (The Heath government failed; the Fraser government has, until recently, succeeded.) While the general strategy of capital is the simultaneous increase of class power and decrease of class structuration, the contradiction embedded in it is one of the crucial sources of instability in the capitalist social order. The actual form of class politics in much of recent history is not unified struggle between mobilised classes, but fragmented struggles about the process of mobilisation.

This is exactly what Gramsci was trying to reckon with, in the analyses that produced the concept of hegemony. It is impossible to cook his scattered notes into a completely coherent theory, so there have been various interpretations of them. In particular there has been a functionalist take-over of the term 'hegemony' in which it has come to mean very much what Parsons called 'pattern maintenance and system integration' (Parsons, Bales and Shils, 1953). This is completely at odds with what I would see as the main thrust of Gramsci's argument, his insistence on analysing a state of play rather than a concept. The idea of hegemony was a means of analysing a *situation*, and this is the way we must recompose 'reproduction' analyses—into analyses of the possibilities and the traps in the situations various groups face.

Seeing their imbalance of power, we perhaps over–estimate the freedom of the ruling class and the constraints upon workers in confronting their situations. Praxis traps (where people do things for good reasons and skilfully, in situations that turn out to make their original purpose impossible to achieve) are not the fate of the working class alone. Indeed the most elegant example of all must be the case of capitalists in a stock market boom, when the interlocking of thousands of individually correct and rational strategies for making and taking profits prepares, with Aeschylaean rigour, the downfall of the lot. (That corporate sharks like Slater Walker or Minsec sometimes swim in and devour investors before they devour themselves, doesn't invalidate this point. It merely shows that praxis is not a matter of mechanical logic, that some capitalists are smart enough to operate meta–strategies on the possibilities created by other peoples' strategies.) Many practices have destabilising, transformative consequences, even when quite unintended.

Further, mutations in the structure can occur in partial ways, without gigantic convulsions, that open up new situations and changed possibilities. We can see this in the history of education itself. (If 'ideology has no history', the ideological apparatus certainly does.) Its most important change in the last generation, in countries like Australia and the U.K., is undoubtedly the massive expansion of secondary education and the shift to comprehensive schools. This was a change pushed through with surprisingly little opposition—given its scale—by coalitions of progressive educators, educational bureaucrats, reforming politicians and technocratically–minded capitalists. It was made possible by the postwar boom and expansion of the state, and by a mass demand for more training and for mobility through education. Neither secondary pedagogy, nor its role in class processes, could be the same after this as before.

We now have a teaching force that forms a mass occupation (which is both highly unionised, and has a high turnover, in relation to the length of training involved). We have a plethora of new or newly–transformed high schools in working–class milieux (themselves often new, notably the outer suburbs), facing a clientele largely drawn from families that have little previous experience of secondary education. Class differentiation of the state schools now takes the form not of an official hierarchy of types of high school (as they used to be: junior, technical, selective...), but of the effects, on the catchment areas of nominally equal schools, of the geographical class structuring of cities. The politics of secondary education is plainly very different now. However, as patiently shown by Ford (1969), this does *not* mean that class inequalities have been reduced or the purposes of the reformers achieved!

The real world of class relations, then, is a world where some kinds of possibilities are constantly being opened up, others closed down; where some kinds of practice lead into unexpected traps, and others to unexpected transformation; in sum, where structural mutation is the rule rather than the exception. This raises the interesting and important question of whether such changes can be traced not only in the institutions of education but also in the process of production of personality. Is there really ground on which the historical depth psychology suggested in the last section can stand?

Among the classics in this field there are two main lines of thought. One was suggested in Freud's later writings, and taken up by Marcuse in *Eros and Civilization*: that the advance of civilisation saw a growing weight of repression imposed upon instinct by the demands of social integration and class domination. Liberation in this argument meant abolishing the 'surplus repression' imposed by the requirements of a class society over and above the technical needs of civilized life. This thought remained in a rather abstract relation to history until Marcuse in *One Dimensional Man* inverted it, now arguing that the abundance created by postwar monopoly capitalism in the advanced countries allowed a reversal of the historic trend, and a solution to the problems of social control by controlled release of erotic energy, 'repressive desublimation'. Fascinating; but we do not know if it is true. (See Chapter 1 for a fuller discussion.)

The second line of thought stemmed from Freud's earlier work on fixation, descending via Reich and the early Frankfurt school to Fromm (1942) and Riesman (1950, 1952). This was the idea of a historical succession of character types, formed by the typical defence mechanisms or coping strategies that arose in response to a given set of social relations. Fromm's sequence was given by stages in the development of capitalism, Riesman's by a more or less mythical (as he later acknowledged) imperative of demographic change. Though his sociology was naive, it was Riesman's concepts that were the more closely tied to a concrete investigation of lives-in-their-historical-contexts; and there is still much that is very impressive about the studies in *Faces in the Crowd*. The trouble is, his notions about succession appear to have been mistaken in fact. It is difficult to see the hegemony of the other–directed among today's middle–aged (Riesman's youth—and the parents of today's teenagers). These ideas too remain intriguing speculations.

There have really been no effective successors to this generation of theorists (unless one takes Maslow, Roszak and their followers a good deal more seriously than I can). Historical depth psychology remains a gleam in the theoretical eye rather than an established branch of knowledge. But we can say that some lines of work are more or less promising. Specifically, the scheme of a succession of character types appears most unlikely, given both what we know about the importance of improvisation in social practice, and the dangers (already mentioned) of exaggerating the integration of personality and the harmony of socialisation processes. That there is inter–cultural variation in personality or in characteristic response styles is well enough established from the researches of Benedict, Kluckhohn and other cultural anthropologists. That these have to be explained by a concept of 'modal personality' or typical character structure is a quite unwarranted, though common, inference. That there is a historical succession of character types linked to the transformations of the structure of production, is even less plausible. (For a somewhat pedestrian but useful summary of the arguments back and forth, see Inkeles and Levinson, 1969.)

We have, however, new ground from which the analysis of lives–in–context can proceed, on which an adequate knowledge can be built: a much fuller recognition of what is involved in the interaction between capitalism and patriarchy (or, more generally, class structure and sexual power structure). I have already suggested that patriarchy cannot be analysed as an ideological realm which is the locus of reproduction of class relations. There is a patriarchal structuring of production, a class structuring of culture; the two are co–ordinate, not complementary. But they are also interwoven. Their dynamics interact, they help stabilise and destabilise each other, and their effects, in any real person's life, are condensed. For instance, there is no 'class situation' that is simply shared by working–class boys and girls. Even the capital/labour–power exchange is sexually structured, for girls and boys enter a segregated labour market, and they know it. And that segregation is in part created by capitalists' knowledge of their employees' practices of marriage and child rearing, and the economic dependence of women, and the sense of masculinity. And the sense and practice of masculinity is simultaneously dependent on the existence of an economy that valorises male labour, in conjunction with a family that valorises male children, and a sexual culture that valorises male genitalia, and devalues women while insisting on heterosexual object–choice. And so on.

The condensations of patriarchy and capitalism in individual lives need not be, often will not be, *functional* in the terms of reproduction theory—this is, I think, the basic theoretical error of Reich. At crucial moments they may be destabilising, if we are to believe the arguments of socialist feminism and the gay left. The essential point is that as a matter of fact the joint structure *is* the effective context of the formation of the person.

Note that, if this is generally correct, the criteria already suggested for analysing the stabilisation of class relations also apply—*mutatis mutandis*—to the analysis of patriarchal social relations. Again, we cannot take for granted a structure, bracket its history, and dissect the moment of its reproduction. We must, here too, attempt to grasp the role of the 'reproduction' processes in the construction of the groups and relations that make up the current situation in the patriarchal system. The oppression of women, and of homosexuals, is not simply a presupposition for the analysis of character formation. It is being accomplished in part through that process; and its contradictions open up their specific potentialities for change.

Liberation

In the last section I have been trying to sketch the ways in which discussions of reproduction can and must be extended to take account of historical mutation. In conclusion a brief reflection on one kind of mutation—liberation.

It is striking how reproduction theorists, dealing with the apparently placid course of daily life, are led to use the language of force. Althusser sets up his theory of ideology with the analogy of police hailing a suspect; Bourdieu and Passeron propound a theory of 'symbolic violence'; Lefebvre, in his book on everyday life, talks at length about the 'terrorism' to which ordinary people are subject. It is equally striking how two of the most peaceful radical movements in modern history (Women's Liberation and Gay Liberation) have adopted the style of third–world armed revolution—the very word 'liberation', to the generation that created them, conjures up a fist holding a rifle. The most influential psychology in the milieu they came from saw psychic violence as the essential structure of family life, and collective violence as the central fact of modern history. And its most influential sociologist was an old man who saw repression in permissiveness, a noose in toleration, a soft totalitarianism in the 'free world'. (See Laing, 1967; Cooper, 1968, 1971; Marcuse, 1964, 1969.)

What is significant here is not the systematic claim, but the intuition behind it—an intuition that I think is common to all the examples just cited. The perception of a violent truth behind a placid exterior was exactly the way the revolt against an oppressive world was lived and thought by the new left of the 1960s. That movement was largely made up of radicals who had never experienced material poverty, and little frustration of other kinds; who for the most part had never been shot at, bombed, tear–gassed or beaten up until they went out and asked for it; in short who had grown up in the most affluent, the most pacified, the most comfortable milieu that the world has yet conceived. For them, almost alone in the world, going into opposition was a gratuitous choice.

In aligning themselves with people whose situation was almost the total opposite—the Vietnamese resistance, ghetto blacks, outback aborigines—it is perhaps not surprising that the order of their reality was inverted. They had to live the arbitrariness of their own actions, the violence (psychic and otherwise) they applied to free themselves from an enclosing culture. (Of course there is a great deal of real violence in patriarchy and capitalism—rape, marital violence, neo–colonial war, prisons and police, as well as the huge shadow of nuclear weaponry; but not, in all strictness, in many of the things most vehemently attacked at the time by the new left.)

The new left is buried, and a little whiffy;

> Now that my ladder's gone,
> I must lie down where all the ladders start,
> In the foul rag–and–bone shop of the heart.
>
> Yeats, 'The Circus Animals' Desertion'

The prospect of liberation indeed looks longer, messier, more mundane: more gritting of teeth, washing of dishes and sitting through committees; and rather less in the way of manifesto and satori. It is good to be reminded from time to time that liberation truly is a qualitative leap, a disjunction in the intelligible succession of social life. Even so innocent and amicable a scheme as self–management in the workplace in practice involves a formidable disruption of habits, self–conceptions, expectations and evaluations. Liberation is an astonishing event, that even when prepared by the most favourable circumstances still storms in like a beast from space, printing its bloody marks in the minds of all who dare to come close.

In the final analysis, it is the lack of any picture of this leap, the lack of a way of talking helpfully about a *liberating practice*, that is the fundamental flaw in reproduction theory. It is politically dangerous precisely because it occupies the ground of cultural politics with a message of defeat. Writing at just the same time, Marcuse noted the strategic point:

> At present, only a small part of this huge, truly underlying population is moving and is aware. To help extend this movement and this awareness is the constant task of the still isolated radical groups.
>
> To prepare the ground for this development makes the emancipation of *consciousness* still the primary task. (1972b: 132)

It is no use waiting around until the balance of class forces changes, the patriarchy collapses of its own weight, the day of revolution dawns, and the cultural arbitrary swings around in response.

But can social theory say anything about 'the emancipation of consciousness' anyway? Is it not so sharp a break, so astonishing an event, that the plodding feet of analysis can never catch up with it, let alone get ahead to direct the traffic? That was, in effect, the view taken by the groups in the new left who wandered off on the path of irrationalism and ended up in the bog of solipsism. The key argument against it is surely one that all students of Zen would recognise. Illumination is in no sense an exotic event, to be achieved only by the arcane. It arises in the midst of the everyday, and that is part of what is astonishing. So with culture, no realm separate from one of power; and so with the breaks and reconfigurations, large and small, that we are gesturing towards with a clumsy word like 'liberation'. And as liberation—inter alia, the transition to socialism, the destruction of patriarchy—is a surge within the structures of the everyday (not an irresistible one—emphatically resisted!), so it must be talked about within the theoretical language we use for them. If the language is not rich enough to cope, the language too has to be liberated.

9
Class formation on a world scale

In 1979 I had tried to pull my whirling thoughts about the problems of class analysis together in the shape of a systematic treatise on the theory of class. The result was too embarrassing to show to anyone except trusted friends, but at least it showed me a lot of things I didn't know and didn't understand. Among them how to grasp, in the context of a practice–based theory of class, the international dimension of class relations. When I was asked to speak at a conference on 'Organisation, Economy and Society' in Brisbane it seemed a good moment to try to work this out. The paper was given to a dazzling multinational audience of sociologists and potted palms in July 1981. It proved to be too cryptic, so has been expanded, and I hope clarified, here.

The problem

Things will improve. Sure they will.
There's no point in grumbling.
Life isn't meant to be easy;
not that it ever was.
We're not too badly off.
The family has all it needs,
a house, and a car,
they can't complain.
The kids are doing well at school;
the girl's in high school, the boy's at university.

> We've got a colour T.V., orchids
> and air–conditioning. Pray together sometimes.
> Yes, you could say we've made it.
> No use making a fuss,
> could get you into trouble.
> Only fools protest, it doesn't do any good.
> A man could even lose his job.

It could be Australia; the third line was our recent Prime Minister's most–quoted saying. It could be Reagan's North America, which certainly has the largest concentration of cars and air–conditioning in the world. Apart from the orchids it could be Europe, west or east. In fact it is Indonesia. This is a passage from the 'Song of a Family Photograph' by W.S. Rendra, that country's best–known poet and dramatist. It was written in 1975, between arrests: Rendra, a critic of the local urban elite as well as multinational capital and its 'development', was arrested by the Indonesian government in 1970 and 1973 and imprisoned for six months in 1978. His work has repeatedly been banned, and he is currently prevented from travelling to take part in productions of his works abroad.

Both the circumstances of Rendra's work, and its content, show how far class relations are international, not only in terms of the objective situations but also the ways they are experienced. His description of a particular class experience and sensibility, quoted above, is instantly recognisable to Anglo–Saxon readers. In the poem as a whole, which shows that family's life through the eyes of four of its members, the sense of familiarity becomes uncanny.

In one way or another, the fact that class relations are international has been recognized from the early days of socialism. Bakunin and Marx both proclaimed it; socialist organisations, from the time of the First International, have acknowledged it; and working people very often have acted on it. Without that real sense of international solidarity the Comintern, and all its devastating effects on twentieth–century socialism, could never have happened.

So it is a matter of some importance for socialists to get a clear understanding of the international dimension of class relations. That has not proved easy. Marxist theories of imperialism have typically got along with grossly simplified and mechanical models of class, while the question of the class structure of the Soviet–bloc countries has become so bitterly entangled with factional politics that many people on the left just refuse to think about it. Nevertheless, in the revival of socialist theory in the past fifteen years there has been a growing interest in these problems.

This paper is a reflection on some of the problems, both conceptual

and political, that come up in this enterprise. By way of brief introduction, I will try to show how difficulties about class emerge in two
of the most fruitful contributions to the new literature: Amin's
account of the social formations of peripheral capitalism, and Wallerstein's account of class formation in the capitalist world–economy.

In *Accumulation on a World Scale* Amin criticises orthodox
economics for separating itself from sociology, and defends marxism
as the one basis for a unified science of society. Nevertheless, when he
deals with classes on the ground the division reasserts itself. The basis
of the argument is an economic category, and the sociology is invoked
mainly to explain how the economic category got there, or why it is
absent or small, in a particular instance.

A notable case in point is his argument about the emergence of rural
bourgeoisies in Black Africa (1974: 366–7). Social hierarchies in the
pre–existing societies, ethnically distinctive labour forces, and rural
mobilisation against colonial forced–labour systems, all figure among
the preconditions. But it is notable that Amin makes no comparable
analysis of the social structure and dynamics of the rural bourgeoisie
as a living entity, once it has been untimely ripped from the womb of
history. Nor, indeed, does he offer any demonstration that there is a
class at all, in any sense other than a set of individuals performing a
particular economic function.

At several points in discussing the social order of third–world
countries, Amin uses the striking image of a 'mutilated society', a
body with a missing limb. While this vividly conveys the point that
there are different class structures, it is, on reflection, a curious image.
For it doesn't just make the point that there are parts of the class
structure that are located overseas, which is Amin's intention. (As, for
instance, we might point out that studies of the distribution of income
and wealth in Australia are hopelessly inadequate unless they include
the income and wealth of overseas investors—which no study of the
distribution of income and wealth in Australia has yet done.) The
image also, and powerfully, conveys the sense that there is such a
thing as a *well–formed* class structure, one with all its limbs present in
good order and in the correct number.

Here we touch on a key feature of Amin's method. For there is
indeed, in his reasoning, a definition of such a well–formed structure:
the theoretical model of *Capital*. Though Amin persuasively argues
that Marx's analysis of the accumulation process was time–bound and
Eurocentric, his own version of the drama still draws its actors
exclusively from the cast–list supplied by *Capital*. And this leads to
some very curious doctrines. One is the belief that the class structure
of the countries of the capitalist centre is marked by a deepening
bipolarisation, a reduction to the two basic classes. This makes his

analysis quite unreal in relation to the political problems actually faced by socialists in these countries. Another, perhaps more damaging, is his unwillingness to acknowledge that there may be classes in formation that simply have no name in the classical theory, even when he can see the class dynamic going on. The casual poor of third–world cities is one important example (recognised by Amin, 1974: 387; for the debate about their class identity see the useful summary by Lloyd, 1982).

In the final analysis, I think, this flows from the way Amin has set up the analysis of 'accumulation on a world scale' as a problem of *transfers of value* from periphery to centre. To use a phrase from debates about the theory of the state, this is a 'capital–logic' approach. That is, everything is analysed from the point of view of an overriding logic of capital accumulation. The mechanisms of this accumulation are taken to be those spelt out in *Capital*—the extraction of surplus–value, the changing organic composition of capital, and the sacred tendency of the rate of profit to fall. The world is analysed as a sort of domain onto which the algebra of value–theory is mapped; much as Marx mapped it onto his type–case of industrialising England, though here on a new scale.

There can be no doubt that Amin's account of class dynamics in the periphery rests on the notion of an overriding logic of accumulation (e.g. 1974: 360, 364). This is the rationale behind his thesis of the increasing homogenisation of third–world social structures (378ff.), a claim that seems increasingly implausible in the light of the dependent industrialisation of places like Korea, Taiwan, Singapore. And it leads directly to a functionalist account of class formation and class action (e.g. 385, 387), which is not so very different from Parsonian arguments about stratification, except that the functions are defined with respect to capital accumulation rather than social integration.

The approach serves Amin best, perhaps, in providing a rationale for one of his main claims: that the centre and periphery have *divergent* dynamics and tend to produce fundamentally different class structures. This is an important principle, a corrective not only to the ethnocentrism of 'development' theory in the North American style, but also to the characteristic ethnocentrism of the left which consists in trying to export one's own model of politics.

But because his capital–logic approach treats world capitalism as a single domain for the production of surplus–value, Amin slips easily from the sound observation that class struggle has world–wide dimensions to the much more dubious idea that there are *world classes*. He poses what from any other point of view is the distinctly odd question 'who are the world bourgeoisie, and who are the world proletariat?'. And he comes to the equally odd conclusion that the *'central nucleus of the proletariat'* (1974: 25, his italics) has shifted to the periphery, a pronouncement I have pondered for some days, and still find Delphic.

In such passages Amin is obviously grappling with real and basic issues: the nature of the class relation between the capitalists of the leading powers and the mass of the population in the third world, and the dynamic of the world system of class relations as a whole. But the kind of theory he is using allows him to formulate these problems only in obscure and stilted ways.

In Wallerstein, who sets out explicitly to analyse the dynamics of the world system, we find much greater clarity and sophistication about the concept of class. He recognises that classes have no fixed reality, but are constantly being formed and re–formed; that they exist in tension with other ways of organising social relations, such as ethnicity, and that class struggle is partly about the definition of social reality along class lines.

Yet when we look into the detail of Wallerstein's major work, *The Modern World-System*, we find something not too different from Amin. The cast–list is much the same: capitalists, proletarians, landlords, peasants, etc., are present together from the first act of the drama. What these terms signify, in Wallerstein's actual usage (e.g. 1974: 86–7, 124–5) is in each case a category of economic actors. Sometimes these categories are assigned a power of collective action, by means of personification. More usually their behaviour is taken to be the aggregate effect of the pursuit of individual interests.

The categories are ordered and interrelated, as in Amin's argument, by an external logic, in this case the world division of labour in the production and accumulation of surpluses. It is this that settles the ability of some classes to flourish (e.g. the Polish landowners) and the inability of others (e.g. the Polish bourgeoisie), by affecting the profitability of different kinds of enterprises in any given place. What was called in my undergraduate history courses 'the expansion of Europe'—that is, early imperialism—appears principally as a reconstruction of that division of labour. Classes and class relations form in the 'periphery' according to the way in which their particular region is subordinated within the structure of the whole, and form in the 'core' areas according to the opportunities the international division of labour opens up.

In a number of theoretical essays written more recently, Wallerstein has moved away from the capital–logic approach of his first formulations. He has, for instance, stressed that 'classes' are not in themselves basic realities, but are one way of ordering and under-standing the facts of the capitalist world–economy, in constant tension with other principles, notably that of division on ethnic/

national lines (Wallerstein, 1975). He has spelt out some of the internal differentiation of bourgeoisie and proletariat: three varieties of bourgeois, eight of proletarians (Wallerstein, 1979). And a critique has been made of the tendency to think of classes just as the categories of political economy, rather than as the products of a dynamic of struggle and the creation of consciousness (Arrighi, Hopkins and Wallerstein, 1982).

This work is helpful in pointing to the difficulties in theorising the international dimension of class; but it has not yet gone very far towards their solution. For all of Wallerstein's stress on classes coming into existence by a claim to class membership, the places that are available to be claimed are still those defined in advance by the structure of the whole. Wallerstein escapes functionalism, but he does so repeatedly by calling on the creaky old distinction between a class 'in itself' and a class 'for itself'—a formula that is always a sign that the underlying conception is one of class as category rather than class as practice. (The 1979 typology of bourgeois and proletarians is a striking example of categorical thinking.) And with it goes an underlying notion of a well-formed system which is able to impose its logic on all the constituent parts (see Arrighi *et al.*, 20). Wallerstein repeatedly speaks of struggle and practice, but it is hard to *feel* them in his more general formulations.

World–systems approaches to theorising the international dimension of class thus confront us with characteristic problems: a tendency to treat classes as categories of economic actors; an *a priori* cast list of classes; the appeal to a logic–of–the–system which carries a presupposition that there *is* a well–formed, coherent system; and difficulty in grasping class formation other than through functionalism or through the distinction of class–in–itself from class–for–itself.

Developments in the theory of class

These are problems that are familiar in other contexts. The image of classes as ghosts in an economic equation has been clarified, and contested, in the debates about marxist structuralism. The snarls about class formation within a categorical approach to class are familiar from critiques of stratificationist sociology (see Chapter 6). And, in general, the ways in which these problems can be resolved are known.

Baldly, class has to be understood consistently in terms of the politics of everyday life: in terms of the way social practices are organised, and the way they embody, and reconstitute, relations of

power. Class has to be seen as a form of structuring that enters into all
spheres of life, not as a special kind of relationship based on just one
(i.e. economic life). Relationships between adults and children,
relationships between men and women, domestic life, cultural
practices, sexual practices, are all essential parts of the picture of
class.

Classes have to be understood as historical agents emergent in this
field of practice, not as passively–constituted elements in a dynamic
which is external to them. A class structure is a structure in which
classes act—however unexpected and uncanonical the ways they do.
And in doing so they constitute themselves as classes, and make and
remake the structure.

'The structure' has no epistemological priority; it is to be
understood in terms of the processes that constitute its parts. (We
need a constructivism rather than a structuralism.) Yet those parts
always have to be understood in terms of the whole structure they are
making, not just a part. The field of reference now is planetary.

Two academic developments have converged to produce this view
of class. One is the set of developments in theoretical sociology that
can loosely be described as the development of a theory of practice. In
the later work of Sartre (1976), and in the writings of Bourdieu (1977)
and Giddens (1979), a good deal of attention has been given to the
knotty business of understanding a social structure in terms of the
processes that constitute its parts: the interplay of practice and
structure, the constituting of different kinds of groups, and so on. I
would not for a moment suggest the difficulties have all softly and
suddenly vanished away. Nevertheless this work does seem to offer
real ways of overcoming *a priori* categoricalism without falling into
methodological individualism.

The other development is the transformation that the last twenty
years has brought in writing histories of classes. In the work of
historians like Thompson (1968) and the *History Workshop* group in
the UK, Gutman (1976) in the US, and—I hope—Connell and Irving
(1980) in Australia, there is a shift away from both traditional labour
history and from the ballet of categories that was 'history' in historical
materialism. This work has moved to an investigation of class as both
lived reality and structuring process, the interplay of experience and
action, and the interplay of local with national dynamic.

No theoretical work on class is innocent, unconnected with the
contemporary politics of class. Nor is this. The growth of a concern
with the nature of practice, and with the history of practices, has
coincided with a period of rethinking and regrouping in western
socialism after the catastrophes of the Cold War. It has coincided with
a new concern among labour parties with the practical politics of
transition to socialism (of which the 1974 platform of the British

Labour Party is paradigmatic). And with a renewed concern among socialist theorists with the practical problems of labour movements (of which Gorz's *Strategy for Labor* is paradigmatic).

Marriages of theory and practice are not made in heaven, and there have been other theoretical currents jostling this for the allegiance of radical intellectuals—neo–marxist dogmatism and 'post-marxist' gauchisme among them. I would however suggest that there is a close enough connection for us to see the intellectual developments just sketched not as just another fad, but as an aspect of a profound transition in world socialism. They may in time be superseded, but they cannot be bypassed. And in one way or another, this perspective has to be built into our understanding of the international dimension of class.

Yet here we find an immediate difficulty. It is, like much else, writ large in the work of Thompson, the most distinguished representative of the new labour history. In his controversy with marxist structuralism (Thompson, 1978: 35ff, 229ff), there is a vigorous insistence on the uniqueness of the English experience as well as the uniqueness of the historian's methods.

That is understandable in response to attempts to liquidate history as an enterprise, or to declare English history deficient (mutilated?) in relation to some ideal European model. But it does seem to rule out any hope of grasping the dynamic of class on a world scale through a properly historical approach. The new labour history has indeed been reluctant to move beyond the national scale. Once we move beyond the home ground of which a historian can have tacit knowledge, it seems, all we can do is mutter and gesture. There must be something big out there; but we don't *know*, and perhaps cannot know, just what it is.

But couldn't the same difficulty be urged against the intelligibility of national class dynamics, from the point of view of the properly–studied region? And against the intelligibility of the region, from the point of view of the properly–studied local duckpond? There are studies of class formation that do make a reasonable fist of connecting the duckpond with national class dynamics, and, if rather more thinly, international: studies both historical (e.g. Foster, 1974) and contemporary (Eipper, 1980).

So this approach isn't incapable of doing the job. It certainly needs developing before it can do it often and well. We have to be prepared for structures at the larger scale that are very different from those familiar in local contexts. Amin's question 'Who are the world bourgeoisie...?' may strictly have no meaning, if things at the planetary scale do shape up in a radically different way. Only historical analysis can tell.

In the following three sections I will take small bites at three large problems that arise in trying to do this: how class relations spread around the globe; how we might think about the structure of the contemporary world in class–analytic terms; and what classes look like, as actual social groups, on a world scale. The final section will return to the problem of what kind of 'system' is in question.

How class relations spread

One of the most striking things about capitalism is how much better it has been than other social systems in actually taking over ground. Amin is quite right when he remarks

> Apart from a few 'ethnographical reserves' such as that of the Orinoco Indians, all contemporary societies are integrated into a world system. (1974: 3)

For the bulk of the world's population, that integration was remarkably fast—a matter of a hundred years or so, from the early nineteenth to the early twentieth century; a mere eye–blink in the perspective of human history.

There has naturally been much discussion of the conditions of that takeover, and its precursor in the 'expansion of Europe' in the sixteenth century. The importance of superior arms and transport is obvious enough, though that was not the whole story. As cases like the Spanish invasion of Mexico show, it was also a matter of the superior bloody–mindedness, military organisation and brutality of the Europeans. Of late there has been rather more attention to the social circumstances of the advent of capitalism. And here a paradox arises.

For one argument is that capitalism develops on the periphery by seizing hold of those aspects of the pre–existing social structures which in some sense create a predisposition to class formation. Good notes how

> Capitalism and the colonial state established themselves unevenly upon *the existing hierarchical elements and tendencies* within Papua New Guinea societies. (1979: 105)

The formation of a 'rich peasantry', an emerging class of rural capitalists, is an important case in point. Good observes that in several parts of that country, clan heads and 'big men' had been able to draw on customary rights to land and labour to get a start as cash–cropping entrepreneurs. Thereafter they engrossed the land with the aid of the state, and became employers in a more orthodox capitalist sense.

Yet in some other colonial situations, in Africa, Good (1976) has also spoken of an exactly opposite process. In these cases im-perialism did not elaborate on the local social structure but smashed it by violence, 'pulverised' it, and then constituted colonial class relations out of the dismembered wreckage. I am not suggesting that there is any inconsistency in Good's arguments. Both observations seem correct, given the different histories; and there is no reason why both processes could not go on at the same time and place. What the Americans and their client regimes were trying to do in Vietnam in the 1960s, shattering the old rural society by bombardment and resettlement, but also trying to base a regime on landowners and urban wealth, would seem to be exactly such a combination.

The point of interest is that the same kind of result—the constitution of capitalist class relations—can come from such diametrically opposed processes.

This gives extra force to a familiar observation about the colonies of settlement such as the USA, Canada, South Africa and Australia. Class relations are not exported there *en bloc*. They are transported in rather limited and specific forms, and then grow autonomously. In *Class Structure in Australian History* we had occasion to stress this point in relation to the emergence of trade unionism in the odd context of a convict settlement. This has usually been treated as a straight import, arriving from the metropole in the baggage of skilled workers in the 1830s. On the contrary, we argue, while the form may have been imported, the fact depended on something else. There had been a generation of informal, and mostly illegal, resistance by colonial working people (both convict and 'free') to exploitation by colonial capitalists. Resistance, and working–class organisation, were generated in the colonial situation itself.

Individual cases are no more than straws in the wind, but I believe these ones are blowing in a generalisation of some force. Indeed the spread of capitalist class relations involves an *invasion* of older social structures, as Thompson has stressed for the industrial revolution in England, and Amin for the periphery since. But that invasion could not have succeeded as a revolutionary transformation of social structures—revolutionary both in depth and speed—were it not for the extraordinary generative powers which nuclei of capitalist relations have, once established.

Capitalism is more like a cancer than like a machine. Each little fragment is capable of penetrating the surrounding tissues, and growing and multiplying with frightening speed. This is much more than an economic process, as classes are much more than economic categories. I have quoted a poet from the periphery, now let me quote one from a nascent core state—a famous passage from a love poem by John Donne, probably from the 1590s:

> Licence my roaving hands, and let them go,
> Before, behind, between, above, below.

O my America! my new-found-land,
My kingdome, safeliest when with one man man'd,
My Myne of precious stones, My Emperie,
How blest am I in this discovering thee!

'Elegie XIX: Going to Bed'

It is hard to imagine a clearer example of the way early capitalism penetrated the innermost recesses of English culture than this gorgeous imagery, where sexuality and imperialism are so completely fused. (Even the opening phrase is an image that fuses erotic preliminaries with the arrangements where monarchs licensed entrepreneurs to explore and exploit the new territories.) It is important always to think of the structuring power of the–system–as–a–whole in the light of these intimate local transformations that are the system's condition of existence.

Among other things, they introduce a turbulence into capitalist civilisation at a very fundamental level. One of its signs is the extraordinary shifting of the capitalist 'centre' or 'core', from northern Italy to the Low Countries, England, Germany, the eastern USA, the western USA and Japan... The rise of 'Silicon Valley' in California and its micro–colonies in South–East Asia, the microprocessor assembly plants, is a dramatic current example of a process with a very long history. This mobility is the more notable given the economic and strategic advantages that analyses of the world–system usually assign to the core.

The force with which the generative processes operate, and the different ways in which they can be set in motion and class constructed, are the kinds of things that make people think capitalism really is the expression of basic 'human nature'. I would suggest, rather, that capitalism makes unusually efficient use of some possibilities that are permanently present in social life. These are the possibility of making use of other human beings as means rather than ends; and the possibility of detaching the results of labour from its cultural and social conditions. In short, capitalism institutionalises the element of calculative ferocity in human life.

It might perhaps be argued that two of the more sinister political forms that have grown out of capitalism, bureaucratic dictatorship and fascism, each exaggerate one side of that amalgam—tortuous calculation on one side, and on the other, atrocity as a way of life. Stalin and Hitler, Pol Pot and Pinochet, are authentic products of a capitalist world system. If that sounds odd, bear in mind that its 'moderate' political forms, the liberal democracies, have also been capable of the bombings of Dresden, Hiroshima, and Kampuchea.

It is only at the level of generative processes, not that of realised class structures, that we can seek what is common in the societies produced by the historical spread of capitalism. There is no reason to assume a common structure, let alone an increasing homogenisation, either at the core or on the periphery. As the wandering 'centre' suggests, there is in fact systematic reason to assume diversity. In some cases we can see in detail why this must be so. Ram (1981), for instance, shows that the conditions of labour and politics in Indian cities are often such that a drive by local capitalists for profit, almost the definition of capitalist activity ('Accumulate! Accumulate! That is Moses and the Prophets'), actually *rules out* a replication of the western pattern of the concentration of labour in factories and the organisation of permanent wage–labour. For that would provoke both union organisation and state intervention, which would make the nominal legal rights of the workers a reality. And there is so vast a difference in India between the costs of labour organised in different ways as to make that option one that profit–seeking capitalists must avoid.

The capitalist world–system, then, is not an already homogenised unit, but the field of action of common structuring or generative processes. In plain English, the same kinds of things go on, though they produce very different structures, or states of play, in different circumstances. The most important processes set in train in the advent of capitalism, I would suggest, are three.

Firstly, a reconstruction of gender relations, sexuality, and domestic life. It is no mean feat to produce the kind of people who can actually operate a capitalist system. The new labour history has documented the assault on pre–industrial work habits and household organisation that was involved. The new feminist history has been filling in the picture of the related transformations in domestic labour and relations between the sexes. That the changes go to the very constitution of sexuality is strongly implied by the historical work on the development of homosexuality (see Plummer, 1981).

A major part of this is producing wage–labourers who work apart from, but are continuously supported by, households which are the scene of most of the remaining unwaged work in the society, and which provide the emotional life that wage labour destroys. Accounts of male industrial workers, such as the Detroit car workers described by Lippert (1977) and the Queensland coal miners described by Williams (1981), dramatically show how this works through the subordination of, and sometimes a fierce antagonism to, women. The record of the third world seems to show that the impact of capitalism usually, though not universally, means an increasing subordination of women as their position progressively approximates that of western wives (Schlegel, 1977). The Muslim world would seem to be the major exception, where westernisation has meant emancipation and the

recent upsurge of fundamentalism has seen a strong reassertion of the
patriarchal subordination of women.

The second key process is the concentration of the social surplus in
forms that allow a rapid and continuing reinvestment; and hence, with
luck, 'extended reproduction'. I hesitate to call this simply 'capital
accumulation', as I have yet to be convinced that the reproduction
schemas familiar under that heading since Volume II of *Capital* really
do cover the major ways in which the surplus is concentrated and the
economic dynamic of capitalism sustained.

In particular I would want to leave open the possibility that the
major part of this concentration is achieved, not by unequal exchange
(either of the labour–market kind analysed in Marx's account of the
extraction of surplus–value, or of the inter–regional kind stressed by
Emmanuel and Amin), but by force. I am very much impressed by the
redistribution of world income achieved since 1973 by the political
alliance of the OPEC countries. And I wonder if this is a clue to more
general questions. Could the political and military apparatus of
imperialism be seen, not as the guarantor of an economic mechanism
(as in Amin's value–theory), but as the economic mechanism itself?
Along this line of thought we might arrive at a picture of world
capitalism that acknowledges the coexistence of a number of different
ways of concentrating a social surplus, and seeks whatever logic the
system has in the way the elements of that surplus are brought into
relation with each other, once concentrated. At all events, it does
imply the systemic importance of the state.

The third key process, consequently, is the rationalisation and
expansion of the state. Frankly I don't believe the periodisations
found in a good many theories of the state: the minimal liberal state of
competitive   capitalism,   the   expanded   interventionist   state   of
monopoly capitalism, and so on. Seen in a world perspective, the state
has always been a crucial actor in the expansion of capitalism and the
constitution of class relations; Wallerstein's position on this issue is
incontrovertible. More, the state has always been 'interventionist'
(what else is imperialism?); and has fairly consistently increased in
scale, sophistication, and powers. These growing powers have equally
consistently been directed to the reconstruction of social life; though
by no means always in the same direction, as there is unending social
struggle in and about the state.

These processes could be expected to lead to different class
structures even if there were a homogeneous starting–point, not only
because of the complexity of their interaction, but because each of
them is internally contradictory. It would take too much space to
develop this argument here, so I will have to take it as read; but it is
important if we are really to grasp the relationship between local event

and global structure without falling into a kind of functionalism. Contradiction and transformation are found at every level.

The class structuring of the international order

It is striking that Amin could publish a massive monograph on *Accumulation on a World Scale* without any attempt to analyse the world's second industrial power, or its relations with the rest of the world economy. He has more recently (1980) turned to discuss the USSR, but the question remains marginal in his thought, as it does in most socialist analyses of advanced capitalism. The communist countries figure mainly in a discussion of whether, or how far, they have broken out of the capitalist logic. How their course presently *interacts* with that of the rest of the world is a problem given over to the right.

Yet the question has been picked up in some analyses, notably by Marcuse. In *One Dimensional Man* he observed how the cold war had been internalised on both sides:

> For the Enemy is permanent. He is not in the emergency situation but in the normal state of affairs. He threatens in peace as much as in war (and perhaps more than in war); he is thus being built into the system as a cohesive power. (1964: 54)

The relation between the systems, in short, had become part of the ordering of class relations within each. Marcuse was writing of a particular historical moment, but we can accept more generally that the presence of the communist regimes has profound significance for the capitalist two–thirds of the globe, just as capitalism massively influences the evolution of class relations on their side.

We don't have to settle for either of the cold–war versions of this, i.e. that the communist systems represent socialist internationalism and a transcendence of capitalism, or that they represent a new class despotism and a new imperialism. The peculiar thing about them is that in some respects they have been both. It is the combination that accounts for the kind of pressure that they put on the capitalist order—and its limits. Soviet aid in the late 1960s was vital in supporting the Vietnamese national–revolutionary effort that finally got rid of American imperialism from Indochina; but at the same time the Soviets supressed by force a popular progressive movement and government in Czechoslovakia. In Poland recently an overwhelmingly popular resistance movement has been suppressed by force. The western working classes know about this.

The dualism here is familiar from the earliest days of the Russian regime, when it faced the first contradictions between consolidating Bolshevik power in Russia and fanning the flames of revolution in Europe. Arthur Koestler, when a journalist visiting Russia in 1932, literally embodied it, carrying his papers of accreditation as a respectable bourgeois correspondent in his right–hand pockets, and papers of accreditation as an agent of the Comintern in his left (1954: 61–3).

It seems likely that there has been a historical shift in this relationship, dating from about the middle of World War II. Before this the USSR put pressure on the capitalist world mainly as an encouragement to militancy on the part of the western working class. After this it was mainly as a military power and a rival imperialism, rapidly losing any grip on the imaginations of workers. The moment in early 1943 when Stalin introduced epaulettes for officers in the Red Army (Rokossovsky, 1968) may serve as a symbolic marker.

The imperial rivalry between the Russian ruling class and the western ruling classes was seen by Goebbels and Hitler, with the clarity of the doomed, even while the grand alliance of World War II was in full swing (Goebbels 1948: 347–9, 398–402). From this point of view it makes sense for each to encourage popular resistance movements in the territory controlled by the other, though their ability to do so is very limited. More important is the way that the external threat created by the imperial rivalry has been a means by which each power has sought to stabilise class relations within its own territory. This was done most successfully by the western ruling classes in their anti–communist campaigns of 1947–55, a key element in the blocking of socialist movements in the west. Fraser, Reagan and Thatcher seem to believe that there is still life in the same old horse, and they may be right in principle, though a good many of the details have changed.

The main change is very familiar: the increasing 'pluralism' of both the camps that seemed so solid in the 1950s. The huge preponderance of American capital in the immediate postwar years has not lasted, with the regeneration of advanced capitalist economies in western Europe and Japan. Any account of the bourgeoisie of the core must therefore now deal with the integration of these three regions. The Rockefellers have kindly provided a word for this, with the founding in 1973 of the 'Trilateral Commission' as an inter–regional think–tank. (More of this later.) Yet even the Rockefeller way with words may be overtaken by events, given the economic dynamism of new candidates like Brazil, where the world's worst continuing genocide is helping fuel a drive into the front rank of international capitalism.

It is, as the last section noted, difficult to see the international order of capitalism as being organized around a stable 'core'. We see this in the Australian economy since the war, in the shifting balance of foreign investment. This country was first a field for British capital, then American, then Japanese and European, and now south–east Asian as well. Indeed some of the major investors in Australia, including the second largest corporate empire in the country (the Rio Tinto Zinc group, including Conzinc Riotinto of Australia, Comalco, Hamersley iron, Bougainville copper, Mary Kathleen uranium), hardly seem to have any particular nationality at all. What else can be said of operations like the mobilisation of Eurodollars by British businessmen to ship Australian iron ore on long–term contracts to Japanese mills? (See West, 1972.) The same kind of story can be told for the big developments in aluminium and coal that provide the main thrust of the 'resources boom' sponsored by the Liberal federal government.

Rather than a stable core, what we see is a continuing effort to create one, a continuing *process* of centralisation and subordination. This process is turbulent and unpredictable because it is contested on several sides. Any particular strategy of concentration is liable to be contested by rival groups of capitalists. It usually is contested by the workers out of whose hide the surplus–to–be–concentrated is taken. And it can be contested by the controllers of particular states in pursuit of their own strategies. At the same time the process of subordination finds many local allies, not only among local elites, as is notorious, but also among groups of workers. In Port Moresby, for instance, the waterside workers favour foreign investment, for the very simple reason that it creates jobs for them (Good, 1979: 149).

The main developments in the institutional structure of international capitalism since World War II, I would suggest, are essentially responses to this turbulence and contestation. We can see this in three major cases: multinational corporations, global capital markets, and the international police mechanism.

Though socialist discussions of multinational corporations have dwelt heavily on the way they allow capitalists to dominate local workers and governments (e.g. Wheelwright, 1974), it is important to remember they have real disadvantages as well. As they grow larger, they suffer problems of communication and coordination. Different units within one multinational, and different multinationals based in the one country, can pursue contradictory strategies. They create political antagonism almost everywhere they step. Williams (1981) gives us the striking case of a workforce in open–cut coal mining in Queensland who might be expected to be entirely bought off by their very high wages, but who, largely because it is a multinational they work for, are radicalised and militant.

It is clear from the accounts we have of particular multinational companies (e.g. Sampson, 1973, on ITT) that these difficulties can at times be severe. That the tendency has still been strongly in their direction is a measure of the importance of a mechanism that offers simultaneously a counter to political mobilisation by labour, a means of evading state regulation, and a means of dampening the rivalry of national capitals by amalgamating them.

As a means of evading state regulation, however, the multinational company is left for dead by another mechanism that has emerged on a huge scale in the last decade, the global market in stateless capital. The growth of the Eurodollar market in the 1960s is perhaps the most discussed case, but the phenomenon is much wider. Some of its flavour is nicely caught by the Commonwealth Bank's recent ad showing a snappily dressed young executive grasping his phone and barking: 'What's your best price for a million US dollars?'. Only the amount is piddling, in a market whose Eurocurrency component was estimated by *Business Week* in 1978 at above $400,000 million.

There have been some attempts to use the international capital market as a conscious policy instrument, through development banks and the IMF (see Wachtel, 1980). But the more striking fact is the way it has evolved *outside* state control (and *a fortiori* outside the control of labour movements). Indeed, each time governments have moved to regulate international money flows, the system of stateless currency has been given a new fillip. Even the *possibility* of state controls does this, it seems. American companies moved into the Eurocurrency market to forestall capital controls rumoured to be under consideration by the Carter administration.

The most direct response to contestation and turbulence, however, has been a dramatic growth in the state's capabilities for exercising control, the creation of an international police and surveillance mechanism. Its importance is sufficiently indicated by the fact that the pruning knives of neo–conservative governments bent on cutting back the growth of the state in the early 1980s have regularly stopped short of the military, the police, and the spies. Fraser's knife spared the Australian Security Intelligence Organization (ASIO); the Reaganites campaigned actively to restore the morale, funds, and secrecy of the CIA. Blind Freddy can see that most of the build–up of military force around the world in the past thirty years is for the purpose, not of defence against external aggressors, but of controlling the local populations. That is how it mostly has been used in fact. We should be very familiar with that fact in Australia, as half a million people have died on our doorstep recently in two sustained massacres carried out by the Indonesian army, in Java and Timor.

The United States government has been the key coordinator of the global intelligence and military networks, repeatedly stepping in when a local regime seemed to be falling down on the job: Iran, Guatemala, the Dominican Republic, Vietnam, and so on. Once again, however, it could not begin to do this job if its agencies were not able to mesh with local ones attempting to perform similar functions, from Ngo Dinh Nhu's secret police and special forces to the killer squads of the El Salvadorean military.

Over this scene of internal policing and resistance still hangs the prospect of the larger external violence, the nuclear confrontation between the superpowers. For all the internal pluralism of the capitalist world, and the fissuring of the 'socialist camp' of 1950 by the Sino-Soviet feud and the development of 'national communisms', the military polarisation remains a crucial feature of the world. The dominant powers on either side will not tolerate certain kinds of breaks that threaten the stability of their alliance systems. That is the basic reason for the military overthrow of socialist movements in Czechoslovakia in 1968 (see Fejtö, 1974: 212ff) and Chile in 1973.

It would exaggerate the matter to think that the nuclear confrontation and arms race, mad and dangerous as it is, has become the central dynamic in the world system, as Thompson (1980) seems to think. There is, nevertheless, a case for regarding it as incomparably the most immediate issue, and it plainly has a large effect on other practices and processes. Among them are the development of an international capitalist power industry with heavy reliance on nuclear reactors; uranium mining in places like northern Australia and southern Africa; and the increased policing and high-technology surveillance that follow both (see Jungk, 1979). It is nice to see that ASIO, according to its leaked annual report (Plunkett, 1981), has decided that anti-nuclear protestors, like people trying to organise the unemployed, are subversives. ASIO is right.

These cases may give us some feel for the way class practices work to constitute a particular international order, and conversely how the structure of the global whole enters into local practice. But it is another step from the notion of class structuring in a global order to the notion of the world-system as a structure of global classes. Let us therefore turn to the question, strictly defined, of class formation on a world scale.

Global classes

Phrases like the 'world bourgeoisie' and the 'world proletariat' have a fine round ring to them. They can be a useful way of dramatising the fundamental fact that there is a minority of the world's population

who do very well out of the social system we have now, and a large
majority who do badly. Not just in terms of money income, but also
in terms of nutrition, housing, education, health, the very term of life.
Yet such phrases may also be profoundly misleading. Their terms
have embedded in them a whole battery of theoretical implications
derived from the analysis of class relations on a national scale. If we
loosely let those implications carry over, with the terms themselves,
to the global scale, gross errors of understanding may result. A
simple, but important, example is this. The terms 'bourgeoisie' and
'proletariat' carry the theoretical implication of a smaller privileged
group whose income is extracted from the labour of a larger one. It is
clear on Amin's own figures (1974: 66ff) that this cannot describe the
relationship between the capitalists of the centre and the masses of the
periphery. Transactions with the periphery make up only a small
fraction of the economic activity of the USA, EEC, and Japan.
However profitable, they cannot be the main source of income of their
capitalist classes.

At the same time it is obvious that there are interests that the
capitalists of the rich countries do have in common with each other,
and with bureaucrats, businessmen and planters in the third world.
There are even interests that the ruling classes of the Soviet bloc have
in common with those of the West, which combine with the nuclear
stand–off to set real limits to their mutual rivalry. For all the puff and
bluster, it is notable that the Americans made no attempt to stop the
Soviet strangulation of reform in Czechoslovakia, nor did the Soviets
do anything in particular about the corresponding American
operation a few years later in Chile. In December 1981 when General
Jaruzelski staged his *putsch* and suppressed the most popular
resistance movement ever to emerge in the Soviet bloc, the EEC
foreign ministers were discreetly sympathetic to the move, and western
businessmen were openly pleased. 'One West German banker was
quoted . . . as saying that some military discipline would be good for
the Poles' (*National Times*, 20 December 1981). One can see why:
about $23 billion of capitalist loans is riding on the continued health
of the communist regime in Poland.

This remains, nevertheless, at the level of specific deals, and fear of
mutual destabilisation. The international camaraderie of the rich does
not yet reach across to embrace the communist bosses in its social
network.

The common interests of the rich of the capitalist world are firm
enough to provide bases for some forms of global integration. One is
the network of economic institutions already noticed, the
multinational corporation and the global capital market. Another is
the intermeshing of the state structures controlled by bureaucrats or

political entrepreneurs sympathetic to capitalism. The elaboration of regional planning structures like the EEC, and the dovetailing of military and intelligence apparatuses, would seem to be the most important aspects. (It is notable that where formally under parliamentary control, the 'intelligence community' takes pains to keep its operations well clear of the political influence of working–class movements; even the very moderate Whitlam government was regarded as dangerous.)

Yet these structures are far from organising the world's rich and powerful *as a class*, in the sense in which we speak of 'class formation' locally or nationally. The international economic structures in practice are the vehicles of antagonism as well as solidarity, as the bitterness surrounding the current trade dispute between the US and Japan demonstrates. The meshing of state structures is usually done by people marginal to the owning classes as such; far from mobilising them as a collectivity, it is often clandestine, as it runs a real risk of offending the nationalist sentiments that right–wing politics trades on. Something closer to a class identity for the world's rich is provided by cultural institutions such as Rotary International, businessmen's conventions, Hilton hotels, and the America's Cup yachting final. But there are limits to this too. One does not find David Rockefeller or Daniel K. Ludwig lining up for the warm Riesling and the cold Chicken à la King at their local Rotary on Tuesday nights.

Nevertheless people like these do sometimes take a statesmanlike interest in the collective welfare of the rich. We then find them concerning themselves, not with growing a class identity, but with the organisation and management of culture as a whole and with elite political and economic planning institutions. The international programmes of the Ford Foundation and Carnegie Foundation are the kind of vehicles they use for the former; the US Business Advisory Council and the Trilateral Commission, vehicles for the latter.

The body of 'outstanding citizens' that makes up the Trilateral Commission has come in for a good deal of critical attention as an organising body for international capitalism (Sklar, 1980). It is interesting on a number of counts. One is that not all the criticism has come from the left. Launched by David Rockefeller and mainly funded by the Ford Foundation, it has appeared to the ideologues of the American right to be a creature of the Eastern Establishment, and dangerously liberal. Another is that it is trilateral, not multilateral. The elites of the third world and of the new capitalist powers are not drawn into its planning process. A third is that it has a rule that when its members become part of a government, they have to resign. One presumes this is because their credibility in national politics would be destroyed by seeming to be part of a supra–national party.

These points lead me to two conclusions. One is the extreme difficulty even the richest and most powerful men in the world have in moving towards international organisation in characteristically class forms. The other is that perhaps they do not really need to. As their intervention in culture shows, they are able to act in ways directed more towards hegemonising a field than towards corporate class-formation.

There seems to be a parallel here between cultural and economic processes. One of Amin's more important points is that the peripheral economies are constructed in an 'extraverted' rather than an 'autocratic' form (1974: 286ff). That is to say, each of the sectors of a dependent economy is directed towards exchange with the countries of the centre, rather than with each other. This point also applies to the underdeveloped world as a whole. This economic disarticulation resembles the cultural disarticulation that is the principal mechanism of hegemony. Hegemony works not so much by suppressing or obliterating the culture of the oppressed, which is probably impossible to do anyway; rather by fragmenting it, by preventing the crystallisation of a coherent cultural base for resistance. What counts most, it would seem, is not getting a world ruling class organised, but keeping the world's workers safely separated.

There have been times when it was the workers who seemed to be better-organised on a global scale. We have had, after all, a series of Internationals that set themselves just that task. How far does labour-movement internationalism represent a process of class formation on a world scale?

The period when the association of socialist parties seemed practically closest to being the united mobilisation of an international working class was the 1890s and 1900s. Wage labourers then were much more homogeneous ethnically, and much more concentrated geographically, than they are now. Even so, the association smashed beyond repair in the first days of war. There is a familiar argument that the smash-up flowed from doctrinal error, from the reformism of the Second International. This is highly implausible. Even the pure-line revolutionaries of the Third, in the much more favourable circumstances of the years around 1920, could not put together the means of an effective international class mobilisation. All they could do was split the world's labour movements in the name of inter-national solidarity.

The Bolsheviks did eventually put together a disciplined inter-national party from the products of that split, a mechanism perfected by Stalin. But when it had reached this stage the communist movement was not so much a means of class mobilisation as parasitic upon it. In a number of important episodes, including Greece and

France at the end of World War II, the communists' international party was a means of *preventing* class mobilisation, in the interests of the Russian foreign policy of the day (Claudin, 1975). Where communist parties have been central in a popular mobilisation, notably in China and Vietnam, has been where they committed themselves to an independent national strategy. The various 'Internationals' that remain are clandestine, or sectarian, or gutless; and in none of these cases serve as a means of class mobilisation.

The conscious attempt to organise political solidarity of an international working class, then, has collapsed. Its place has to some extent been taken by the much more limited apparatus of international cooperation created, with very little fanfare, by the unions. The roots of this go back to the late nineteenth century; it had its heady days too with Industrial Workers of the World, then subsided into bureaucracy and the International Labour Organisation. With the growth of multinational companies in the most recent decades, new forms of cooperation between unions were also evolved. It is clear, however, that they still face immense difficulties, and are very vulnerable to political attack. In 1978–79, for instance, the International Transport Workers' Federation (ITF) organised industrial action in support of the workers of the Malaysian Airlines System, who were making a wage claim. In February 1979 the Malaysian government arrested twenty–two members of the airline union under internal security laws, as well as the Asian area representative of the ITF. In April they threw thirteen of the arrested members into prison, without trial, for two years, and disbanded the union. In general, the weakness of international union organisation is shown by the fact that effective international strikes are still almost unknown.

The difficulty of organising internationally in characteristically class forms is not only a question of sectarianism and repression. There have also been profound changes in the labour force on which capitalism draws. In the advanced capitalist countries we have seen a massive importation of labour, and ethnic differentiation of the workforce, which have created severe difficulties for the union movement. Each union faces them as a question of how to make contact with its own 'ethnic' members, and it is clear that there are vast differences in the energy and goodwill with which different unions have tackled that question. But it is also clear from comparative research (notably Castles and Kosack, 1973) that a wider transformation of the working class is going on herè, which means that the unions cannot rely to the same extent on traditional social bases of class solidarity. A migratory work force, and an ethnically divided one, is likely to lack the kinds of neighbourhood and kinship networks on which class politics has informally but heavily relied.

In the postwar boom, further, there was a fundamental change in the sexual composition of the capitalist labour force. The workforce participation rates of married women in Australia, for instance, rose from about 5% to about 40%. Labour movements almost totally controlled by men, and oriented to the expectations, ambitions, and career patterns of male workers, have been very slow to reorganise themselves around the needs of women workers.

In third–world cities, and to some extent in the countryside as well, there has grown a massive workforce which is neither working class in the ordinary sense, nor peasantry, though it survives partly by casual wage–labour and partly by its ties to village society (Ram, 1981). Here too the traditional forms of working–class organisation seem to have little grip. Nevertheless the labour these people perform contributes to the surplus appropriated eventually by capital.

The conclusion to which all this seems to point is that while international class relations are real and important, and class exploitation and class struggle are global, it is empty rhetoric to speak of *global classes*. And it may be politically disastrous to act as if they existed. The international solidarity of exploited groups and progressive movements has to be constructed in a more piecemeal and painful way.

This does not for a moment imply that there are structural reasons why solidarity cannot be built. The global mobilisation in support of the Vietnamese shows that a powerful and effective movement can be built from very disparate elements. But the total collapse of that alliance since 1975 also shows how little we can take for granted. Solidarity is always an achievement, not a given.

The capitalist 'system' and socialism

In a good deal of current socialist thought there is a pessimistic preoccupation with the determination of local situations by an over–riding international structure. Sometimes this reflects an accurate judgment of the facts, the balance of forces in play. But sometimes, too, it is the result of a theoretical habit of mind that systematically exaggerates the coherence of the capitalist system.

This takes various forms. There are economistic versions, for instance those that paint pictures of the world centering on the multinational companies. There are structuralist versions, which interpret anything whatever in terms of a formalisation of how capitalism in general must work. In either form, the characteristic of this approach is to discover some mechanism which is taken to be the key to the whole, and then interpret the world as if it formed a coherent system around this mechanism.

When this system–building is in full swing, it is also characteristic that it virtually ignores the communist states; they simply have no place in the model of capitalism–as–a–system. Or, perhaps more sinister, it reads them in, but in the only place that is left unfilled: the place of the negation, the transcendence, the place of socialism. The pessimism of the structural intellect is then matched by a most terrifying optimism of the will, if all that the negating of capitalism can lead to is the paradise offered us by Stalin's children.

I think it is a historical as well as a strategic error to assume that the powers that grew up in the space opened by the October Revolution now have anything at all to do with socialism. (They may at times, and for their own purposes, offer support to socialist movements in other countries; always with the intention of corrupting them.) But it is not enough just to say that. It is necessary also to offer an alternative to the account of world capitalism that leads to that assumption.

There have been some developments in modern socialist thought which seem to be compatible with the class–practice approach argued in this paper, and which do offer the possibility of such an approach to the structure of capitalism as a whole. I will briefly note two.

In his messy but stimulating book *The Survival of Capitalism* Lefebvre remarks on the question of its coherence. In actual practice, he observes, capitalism is decidedly incoherent. What systematicity it has is *an achievement of its ruling class*. A political achievement, in fact. Systematicity is an object of strategy, not a theoretical given.

In a series of books and articles that have been the main theoretical contribution of the Italian 'Autonomisti', Negri develops an argument that has a very different starting–point but some similar conclusions. In *Crisis of the Planning–State*, Negri argues that the law of value, long taken as the centrepiece of marxist analysis of the capitalist system (as it is by Amin), now no longer operates autonomously; it operates only so far as the intervention of the state *makes* it operate. The workers' struggle has *de–structured* capitalism, to the point where its nature is simply contentless command, a mere apparatus of force. In *The State–Form* and *Domination and Sabotage*, Negri develops the analysis of working-class action as a project of 'proletarian self–valorisation'. Rather than its labour acquiring value only through the mechanisms of capitalist employment and the exchange of commodities in the marketplace, the working class makes direct claims based on human needs, a refusal of conventionally–determined work, and new forms of political mobilisation.

Negri's argument is far more complex and sophisticated than this suggests; and I don't want to suggest that I agree with all, or even most, of it. But it seems to me particularly important in offering some bases for a dialectic of structuration and de–structuration, which sees socialism not as a passive opposite of capitalism, nor as the opposing monolith, but as a ferment actively at work in the belly of the monster, an aspect of daily life and daily politics.

Negri was arrested on 7 April 1979, in a wave of arrests of Italian radicals, and as far as I know remains in gaol at present under security laws, accused of being a leader of the 'Red Brigades'.

None of this is to deny that a capitalist international order exists, and has real and terrible effects. It is to stress that it exists as a state of play, not as an object or essence. A state of play that is always contested, in the imagination if no other way is available. I started by quoting one poem by Rendra. Here are parts of another, 'Song of the Condors':

> The mountain wind moves softly through the forest,
> sweeps across the wide river,
> and finally comes to rest among the tobacco leaves.
> Sadly it watches
> the weary pace of the farm labourers
> as they march across the rich earth,
> which offers them only poverty ...
>
> They live in shanties without windows
> and harvest for landlords
> who live in palaces.
> Their sweat falls like gold
> for those who run cigar factories in Europe.
> When they demand their share of the profits,
> the economists straighten their ties,
> and send them condoms ...
>
> By sunset, their bodies are pulp.
> They lie down, exhausted,
> and their souls turn into condors.
> Thousands of condors, millions of condors,
> moving to the high mountains
> where they can rest in silence.
> Only in silence
> can they savour their pain and bitterness.
>
> The condors scream. They scream with rage
> as they escape to the lonely mountains.
> The condors scream,
> and their screams echo among the rocks
> and the silent mountains.
> Millions of condors clawing at rocks,
> pecking at rocks, pecking at the air.
> In town, men are preparing to shoot them.

PART THREE

10
The concept of role and
what to do with it

Though it was published in 1979, this essay includes the oldest
work in the collection. I first came across role theory while doing
courses on social psychology as an undergraduate; and had
another dose while doing a PhD on 'political socialisation', since
a lot of the American literature on this topic presented itself as
an analysis of role learning (the 'citizen role' and so forth). By
the end of that, I felt it was time to get systematically to grips
with the underlying theory, so spent part of 1970 sitting in the
University of Chicago library reading through Goffman, Mead
(who turned out to be massively misrepresented in most of the
'role' literature), Sartre and a host of others, and arguing about
it with Pam Benton. That argument continued for the next eight
years or so, as she worked on 'sex–role' ideas in social
psychology, welfare and the women's movement, and I struggled
to get clear what was wrong with role notions as social theory. It
became more and more obvious that, for all the powerful
criticisms that had been made of role concepts, they remained
extremely influential. The criticisms were just ignored. I now
think that role theory has to be regarded, not as scientific theory
at all, but as part of the practical ideology of academic social
science. Its significance is mainly in the conservative influence it
exerts in the welfare semi–professions and other arenas of that
kind. It can't be destroyed by rational criticism, since role
theorists take no account of criticism. But it can, perhaps, be
laughed out of court, and displaced by better ways of doing
social science.

The idea of 'role' is one of those domesticated concepts that rarely call attention to themselves, but are constantly to be found in the background when you look for them. Role is part of the furniture in the social sciences. Just how much it is taken for granted can be seen in the common response to proffered criticism: surprise, even astonishment, as to why anyone should raise doubts, or what offence could possibly be taken at so helpful and so obvious an idea. No doubt this is why the penetrating criticisms of role theory that appeared in the first half of the decade (Urry, 1970; Coulson, 1972; Pfohl, 1975) have failed either to provoke a theoretical debate, or to dampen the flow of role literature in the journals and applied text-books. Practitioners, it seems, do not take criticism seriously. To them the concept of role is practically unquestionable.

Yet it is questionable, very. In this paper I will try to set out a brief but reasonably systematic case for rejecting 'role' as a theoretical paradigm in social science; hoping to provide grounds for understanding its ideological effect as a practical concept.

The role paradigm

Social life as a play, with people as actors performing according to some script, is an old metaphor. Every text on roles reliably quotes Jacques' speech from *As You Like It*—

> All the world's a stage,
> And all the men and men, meerely Players;
> They have their *Exits* and their Entrances,
> And one man in his time playes many parts ...

—though I have not yet seen one which noted that this speech, in its context, is a comic reflection on the *universality* of human fate (a constant theme in Shakespeare) rather than a discussion of social differentiation. (For a typical misinterpretation see Dahrendorf, 1973: 11–13).

The metaphor became a formal social-scientific concept at a time and place that can be specified much more exactly than is usual in the history of ideas: the United States in the 1930s. The person who was mainly responsible for it was the anthropologist Linton, who in *The Study of Man* (1936) wrote a chapter called 'Status and rôle' which is the point of departure for most of the sociological literature. It is interesting that the concept was first formulated in an introductory textbook, and significant that it was a strongly functionalist one. Linton constructed the role concept via an argument that patterns for behaviour between people or classes of people, based on reciprocity,

are required for a society to function. The role concept provided his
way of thinking these functionally-required reciprocities. In the light
of the later uses of role theory in social work and other realms of
social control, it is striking to find, in this first formalisation, the
argument

> It is obvious that . . . the more perfectly the members of any society are
> adjusted to their statuses and rôles the more smoothly the society will
> function. (114–15)

Obvious! And it soon becomes obvious too that it is useful for a
society to have social class distinctions: for this limits competition, and
makes social interaction easy. . . (131)

The conservative political implications of functionalism, its
ideological usefulness in disguising the reality of a capitalist society
rent by class struggle and economic crisis, are familiar (see Gouldner,
1971). As the functionalist perspective was absorbed from anthropology into American sociology and political science and became
dominant there, the role concept also rose to prominence. The 1950s
and early 1960s were indeed the golden age of role theory. It became
the building-block in several attempts to state a general framework for
structural sociology (Parsons, 1951; Dahrendorf, 1973 [1958]) and
anthropology (Nadel, 1957). Role research burgeoned in experimental
social psychology (Bales and Slater, 1955) and field sociology
(Goffman, 1972). It began to acquire a technical literature of its own
with titles like *Explorations in Role Analysis* (Gross, Mason and
McEachern, 1958), exploring questions such as that of conflict in role
definitions. By the time Biddle and Thomas brought out their reader
Role Theory: Concepts and Research, one might well feel, as they did,
that 'role' was on its way to maturity as a scientific field, and already
the nearest thing to a *'lingua franca* of the behavioral sciences' (Biddle
and Thomas, 1966: 8).

Ironically, that was about the end of the boom. With the retreat of
functionalism and the rising criticism of consensus perspectives in
academic social science, role *theory* stagnated. There have been no
significant developments in ideas about role since the early 1960s.
When Komarovsky (1973) came to give her presidential address to the
American Sociological Association on 'problems in role analysis', it
was essentially the theorists and the problems of the 1950s with which
she was wrestling. Some strongly dissident voices had been heard in
the meantime. Andreski (1964) commented that role theory 'consists
of pompous, nebulous and incredibly lengthy re-statements of what
has been common knowledge for a very long time'. And there had
been a sharp critical reaction to Dahrendorf's attempt to introduce the
role paradigm into German sociology (Popitz, 1972). Role concepts

quietly dropped out of mainstream theoretical debate in western sociology.

But the role *literature* flowed on. Something like 200 papers specifically concerned with role are published each year in psychological and sociological journals around the world. It was, to give one example, the undefined and uncriticised language for a symposium of papers on 'sex-roles and sexuality' in the *Australian and New Zealand Journal of Sociology* (Fenwick, Novitz, and Waghorne, 1977). Further, role concepts remain a taken-for-granted teaching framework, not only in some of the duller introductory sociology and social psychology textbooks (e.g. Light and Keller, 1975; Kando, 1977); but more importantly in a wide range of textbooks in *applied* social science, for students in fields from social work (e.g. Berry, 1974) and management theory (e.g. Miner,'1971) to teaching (see the excellent criticism of this literature in Coulson, 1972). The significance of this lies not only in the nature of the audience, i.e. people who are active and have power in the systems of social control, but also in the fact that they are rarely likely to encounter an alternative—despite the fact that role theory is no longer currency in sociological theory.

Role research has further been boosted by the impact of the women's movement in the 1970s. Social scientists have responded to contemporary feminism mainly by launching a great deal of research on 'sex roles', which has now become the largest single field in role research. And reciprocally, the language of role has been absorbed into the discourse of feminism (see Franzway and Lowe, 1978).

As even this short sketch might have suggested, there is a good deal of diversity in the role literature. And there is, of course, no simple agreed definition of 'role'. Biddle and Thomas gravely note a 'lack of denotative clarity' in the role literature; to translate, much of it is hopelessly vague. There are also genuine differences in purpose and conception among role theorists. Some locate the concept of 'role' in what people actually do, and some only in what they are expected to do; some regard role performance in the light of a rational calculation of rewards and benefits, others as the irrational working-out of motives and social pressures; and so on.

Despite this variety, there is a common conception underlying almost all of the social-scientific role literature. It is with this, rather than with the individual versions of particular role theorists, that my argument will be concerned. The core of it can be spelt out in five points. The first two state the essential metaphor, a *dramatis persona* and a script:

1 An analytic distinction between the *person* and the social *position* (or place, office, or status) which she 'occupies'; and

2 a set of *actions* (role behaviours, tasks, etc.) which are assigned to the position.

The next three state the means by which the social drama is set in motion and held to its script:

3 The assignment of actions to positions is specified by *expectations* (rules, prescriptions, norms, etc.);
4 which are held by the occupants of *counter-positions* (ego and alter, role senders, reference groups, etc.);
5 and enforced by the *sanctions* (positive and negative reinforcements, rewards, etc.) which they apply to correct or incorrect performance by the occupant of the position.

Though there is infinite variety in the terms used, these are the basic ideas on which role theory is built, and which underlie its claim to provide a general analysis of social interaction. To put it in a sentence: role theory is the approach to social structure which locates its basic constraints in stereotyped interpersonal expectations.

It appears, on the face of it, hard to quarrel with the five points just listed. They are broadly applicable, to many different cultures and to many different social situations. At the same time they relate well to everyday experiences, such as moving into a new job or a new school class, being told what to do, and being praised or blamed, paid or punished, according to performance. Indeed role theorists, when expounding role concepts, constantly appeal to us with familiar examples. They take us gently by the elbow and introduce us to that amiable (and familiar) fellow Herr Doktor Schmidt the teacher, with his fifteen positions and roles from 'man' and 'adult' down to 'card player' and 'driver' (Dahrendorf, 1973: 14ff). To which we easily answer 'yes, I recognise that'; and accept the rest of their sociology in the same spirit.

The concept also appears to have substantial theoretical virtues. Dahrendorf remarks that 'the category of role ... falls on the borderline of sociology and psychology' (1973: 38). More exactly, it offers a framework of social analysis which allows a simple and straightforward account of the insertion of people into social relations. How to link person and society is of course a traditional, and difficult, theoretical problem of the social sciences.

Further, when approached from the angle of role acquisition, it offers a way of analysing social learning in substantial units, escaping the atomism that used to plague learning theory. As Goffman says, 'we do not take on items of conduct one at a time but rather a whole harness load of them ... Role, then, is the basic unit of socialization. It is through roles that tasks in society are allocated and arrangements made to enforce their performance' (1961: 77).

Yet, I will argue, these are illusory gains, and the obviousness of role theory is the obviousness of ideology, not of truth. A full demonstration of this would require not only a conceptual critique, but an exploration of the way the role perspective operates in various fields of social practice. The present paper attempts only the first step in this, the task of conceptual criticism. Even so, it is necessary to approach role theory at several levels. First, the paper considers the tangles and absurdities that arise in trying to generalise the elements of the role paradigm (position, prescription, counter-position, and sanction); in the course of this, it will emerge that role theory is not genuinely a sociological theory at all. Second, it raises the substantive inadequacies of role-theoretic argument (even in the fields to which it is usually applied) as a framework for the understanding of social learning; and the logical circularity that arises when one attempts to give the concept of 'role' a concrete, socially-determined meaning. Thirdly, it sketches the ideological effects that arise from the use of the role paradigm as social theory, the nature of the misrepresentations that occur, and their political implications.

The attempt to generalise role concepts

The role paradigm obviously does fit some social situations fairly well—such as acting in a play, or consciously 'acting a part' for a definite purpose. But this is trivial. The ambition of role theory is to be a social theory of some scope and power. To achieve this it must generalise the 'role' concept far beyond dramatics. In doing so it must generalise each of the sub-concepts that make up the role paradigm. Many of the difficulties in role theory become apparent when one considers in turn what is involved in generalising each of the elements of the paradigm.

Position. If someone asks you to think quickly of a role name, the chances are you will come out with a job title: chicken-farmer, journalist, commercial artist, etc. The position indicated by a job title is usually well-defined in various ways. A person enters it at a definite time (when she 'takes the job'); the prescribed actions are often laid down (in a sense to be discussed later) formally, by the employer or by an award; and the principal reward for performance, the wage, is also clear. But of course the ambition of role theory is to be much more general than a sociology of occupations. Role theorists never tire of telling us that the man who is a chicken-farmer in the realm of necessity is also, in private life, a husband and a father, a friend, a citizen, etc.

These are not 'positions' that are, on the face of it, very like the 'position' involved in an occupational role. One of the important differences is that they have greatly different breadth and bases. If we look over the set of fifteen positions occupied by Dahrendorf's Herr Schmidt, for instance, we find a range from 'card player' and 'driver' and 'treasurer of the local soccer club' up to 'professional man', 'citizen', 'married', 'adult', and 'man' (Dahrendorf, 1973: 19ff). The range is typical of the role literature; though some other authors do a bit better at the fringes. Linton (1936: 121) has, as one of his ascribed social statuses (= positions), alongside sex and age statuses, the status 'dead'. Bauman (1969: 5) manages 'members of society in their role of no-role-performers'. While Sarbin (1954: 235) has it that people fucking are enacting a role, though admittedly at an unusually high level of involvement on the 'organismic dimension' (*sic*). (Social psychology, however, seems to have retreated from even this modest level of liberation. In the second edition of this work (Sarbin and Allen, 1968: 494) the example of 'participants in sexual congress' is quietly dropped. Beatlemania, however, is allowed.) Here and there in the role literature one encounters the ultimate role, 'the role of person' (and perish all who unkindly ask what the relevant counter-position is).

Now consider the bases of such 'positions' even in a single list such as Herr Schmidt's. There is a physiological fact ('man'—compare 'the sick role' in Parsons); a favourite recreation ('card player'); the operation of a machine ('driver'); the geographical area where one was born ('citizen'); the passage of time ('adult'); the vicissitudes of emotional life ('married'). Some of the 'positions' are lifelong, some are momentary (Goffman, 1971, gives classic analyses of transitory encounters). Some have potential reference to most of a person's activities; some refer to a very narrow range. Some are very broadly defined, such that almost anyone could be one; others very closely specified, such that hardly anyone is (compare Goffman's example of 'principal surgeon in a cardiac surgery team').

What I am getting at here is that these are very dissimilar facts about people, and refer to very dissimilar aspects of social process. To lump them all together under the role paradigm—i.e. to construe the relationship between what people do, and all these 'positions' they occupy, under the one formula of expectations and sanctions—is to create a false unity. It is to attribute a kind of homogeneity to social life that it does not in fact possess. This is not for a moment to deny that there are *links* between these different areas of life—there is indeed a structure of society as a whole. But you cannot arrive at an understanding of links and relationships by throwing all the different parts into a blender and homogenising them into a soup.

Prescription. In the usual presentation of role theory a given position has a definite set of actions attached (the role behaviours, tasks, etc.) whose performance constitutes the enactment of the role. The idea that a set of actions is set down as if by a script is central to the role metaphor; and in a more technical sense it is central to the notion of role acquisition (via the sanctioning of specific performances or non-performances) as the basis of social learning and personality formation.

Now a little reflection will show that the prescription of actual behaviours *cannot* be the basis of some quite familiar roles. There may be a loose prescription that doctors shall heal the sick, or at least be seen to be trying to. But there is no way in the world that a role prescription can say what specific behaviours the doctor must produce in any given interaction, for then the role definer would have to know in advance what was wrong with the patient. A stronger example can be given, based on a familiar philosophical argument against determinism. It is impossible to lay down as a role prescription what exactly is to be enacted by a scientist, because if one could do that, one must already know the course of the research, i.e. have prior knowledge of the scientific knowledge that is in process of being produced.

I would argue that these are not peculiarities of professional or scientific roles, but are general conditions of social life. It is useful to go behind the idea of a 'script' to the language in which it is written. As Chomsky (1959) argued in his famous review of Skinner, it is impossible to analyse the development of a rule-governed (i.e. socially orderly) but creative activity, like speech, as the learning of a definite series of actions which are later reproduced or simply generalised. The laws of grammar do not lay down in advance what shall be said; rather they describe the framework within which one can improvise. Practically all speech *is* improvisation; if it were not possible for speakers to improvise and hearers to understand improvisations, human communication would be either drastically limited or hopelessly cumbersome.

The point applies very widely to social behaviour, as both Urry (1970) and Pfohl (1975) argue in critiques of role theory. Social behaviour is improvised—though in definite situations and under definite constraints. ('Men make their own history, but they are not free to make it just as they choose: they make it under conditions given to them and transmitted from the past . . .' [Marx, 1852]). What governs the improvisation certainly has to be explained in terms of a *social* theory (here I disagree with Pfohl), but it cannot be accounted for in terms of the usual concept of behavioural expectations and sanctions in role theory. Even the most strictly-defined 'occupational role', governed by wads of regulations and reams of job specifications, does not and can not exactly specify what behaviours are to be emitted. The regulations and specifications state, strictly speaking, *criteria* to be met by some performance improvised by the worker: for instance, times for a given operation, and tolerances for the dimensions of a product. Indeed, when workers *do* take the specifications of criteria to be statements of expected behaviours, as role theorists would have them do, it is universally recognised that we have, not correct routine role performance, but a strike—the 'work to regulations' strike.

This problem can be solved by making the role concept *vaguer*—by saying, for instance, that role expectations prescribe only general features of actions, e.g. some generalised healingness about the behaviour of doctors, or motherliness in mothers, or some metallic quality in the behaviour of metalworkers. But this rapidly reduces the idea of role expectations to little more than another way of naming the positions. And in any case it seems profoundly unsatisfactory that a scientific concept should have to be rescued from its difficulties by a resort to vagueness. The direction of argument should be towards more precision, not the reverse.

Counter-position (role frames). In the previous section I argued, in effect, that 'role' is not an apt metaphor for most of the situations it is applied to. I now want to suggest that even if it were, it does not provide a means of building up a coherent social theory. This can be seen by considering what happens when we generalise the notion of a counter-position into the idea of a role frame or a structure of roles.

A role is, in role theory, never defined by itself (except in those eccentric examples of the 'role of person' or 'the role of no-role-performer'). It is defined in relation to other possible roles—mother and father in relation to daughter and son, merchant in relation to customer and artisan—which can be designated counter-positions. (In most versions of role theory the occupants of the counter-positions are the sources of sanctions that enforce role performance—e.g. Parsons and Shils, 1951: 15ff.) A set of positions and counter-positions defined in relation to a specific criterion (e.g. kinship, age) can be called, following Nadel (1957: 74) a role frame. This is the basis on which the analysis of *a* role can be extended towards an analysis of social structure, of social relations at large, and not just a single situation.

As Nadel forcibly points out, there are severe limits inherent in this approach, which flow from the disparate logical bases on which 'roles' are defined. We may define, for a given society, a set of age roles in which an old woman does the right things *vis-à-vis* a young woman; and also a set of economic roles, in which a landowner does the right things towards a tenant. But role theory in itself does not provide a way of relating the age role to the economic role:

> A great many actors never can 'play their roles relative to one another', simply because the roles have no common locus, logically or empirically. The absence of a common logical locus precludes the assumption of a unitary, coherent system; indeed, there seem to be as many separate systems as there are logical role frames. (Nadel, 1957: 97)

Though one can, moving out along the chain of positions and counter-positions in any one role frame, get an analysis that includes all the *members* of a given society (e.g. assigning them all 'age roles'), one cannot get a coherent account of all their *activities*. For to give an account of their economic activity involves the definition of another role frame, which cuts across the age frame; and to give an account of their kinship behaviour requires a third, which cuts across the first and second; and so with religious activity, recreational, political, cultural, and so on and on, until the brain reels. The vagueness of the role paradigm allows an indefinite proliferation of role frames. And as the role frames proliferate, the possibility of a consistent account of the social structure as an organised whole steadily recedes. In short, role theory as a model of society cannot achieve both coherence and comprehensiveness. Like a happy drunk, the more it tries to take in, the more incoherent it becomes.

Nadel, who defined this problem most carefully, also worried away at possible solutions. It is, I think, striking that the partial solution he came up with (1957: 114ff) involved a move to another level of abstraction where actors in roles are compared with respect to their 'command over one another's actions' and 'command over existing benefits and resources'—or, to put it more bluntly, power and wealth. This is, *pace* Nadel, not really a higher order of abstraction within role theory. It is a set of very concrete issues (as the powerless and the poor well know), whose analysis provides the basis for a very different understanding of social structure. More of this later.

Sanction. Role theory is constantly presented to us as distinctively *social* theory. It is presented as the means of setting personality in its social context; of thinking the social aspects of human learning; of understanding the social sources of intra-psychic conflict; and so forth. It is presented as a framework for sociology and social anthropology. It is seen, both by opponents (Wrong, 1961) and supporters (Dahrendorf, 1973), as the classic illustration of social determinism: 'Homo sociologicus', the-man-who-is-his-roles, the over-socialised model of man.

It may be surprising to people familiar with these arguments to be told that role theory does not involve a social determinism at all. Yet that is quite readily shown. What is it that sticks the components of a role, the position and the actions, together? Unless the role exists wholly and solely in the head of the theorist, it is the expectations of people in counter-positions to the said role. What gives their role-definition its force? It is, and can only be (within role theory), the application of sanctions by those people to enforce their expectations. What determines the application of the sanctions? This cannot, logically, be regarded generally as a role-prescription for the holder of the counter-position; for that way we get into an infinite regress. (Who enforces *this* role-expectation? If another role-incumbent, who enforces *her* role-expectation? etc. etc.) Somewhere, and hopefully not too far along the chain (for sanity's sake), the application of sanctions must be rested on the will of the incumbent of a counter-position, on her personal willingness to apply the sanctions. The ultimate determinism in role theory, that is to say, is psychological, not social. (For clear illustrations of this in a classic of role theory see Gross *et al.*, 1958: 4-5, 289.) The ultimate constraints lie in the willingness of members of the system to impose sanctions, and this is not explicable in terms of role theory itself.

This very basic point about role theory is disguised, rather than overcome, by the many formulations of role in which the definition of role-performance is referred to abstract obligations or norms. (One need only ask what exactly these 'norms' *are*, and how the 'obligations' are made obligatory.) And it is not escaped by the idea that role expectations in due course are internalised by the role performer—which is probably untrue most of the time, and where it is true merely pushes the willingness-to-sanction back in time to the process of initial role learning.

This line of thought gives some grip on why role theorists insistently miss, or misrepresent, questions of power. Take, for example, the role-theoretic account, in a recent textbook on adult development (Kimmel, 1974: 66), of a shopper in a department store. According to this account, the shopper pays the price demanded by the salesperson because that is part of the role-expectation of a 'customer'. The idea is that the salesperson applies sanctions to incorrect performance such as offering too little or too much, with 'social constraint' applied by the store's security guard. This manages to miss almost everything of interest about such a transaction and its determination: that the department store is a capitalist enterprise engaged in extracting profits from its customers, which has succeeded in squeezing most other types of retail outlets so it is often the only convenient place for the shopper to go; that the salesperson is a wage-worker constrained (usually imperfectly) by the threat of unemployment and loss of income to police the property relations between the store's owners and customers; and that many customers do cheerfully steal when they think they can get away with it, while police and magistrates exist to try to see that they don't ... Of course there is social determination here, very strong social determination; and it is not reducible to the will of the sales person, or the policeman, to enforce sanctions; nor even the will of Mr Myer or Mr Woolworth to make their profits. Nor is the social determination acting on the housewife reducible to the expectations or the will of husband, or children, or the editors of *Family Circle*. (As proof, see what happens to women who try to leave. Documentation is abundant in women's shelters: see Johnson, 1981.)

These four lines of thought hardly exhaust the problems of generalising the elements of the role paradigm, but they are perhaps sufficient to establish the formidable—and often unrecognised—barriers to erecting it into a generalised social theory. It is only fair to note that there are a few role theorists whose work escapes most of these criticisms. In his essay on role distance Goffman talks about the limitations of the role framework, and decides to confine his attention to the roles that operate within 'situated activity systems'—such as the performance of a surgical operation, the playing-through of a game, the getting and giving of a haircut (1972: 85). This may seem to be simply evading the question of the extension of role concepts, but it is a legitimate if tacit answer to it. Goffman is, in effect, confining his usage to that rather limited class of situations which the 'role' metaphor does not have to be extended very far to cover.

This is not to say that role theory provides a *good* account of these situations—merely that it doesn't provide a *strained* account of them. One might well argue (and Goffman would probably not object) that most of what the principal surgeon does during the operation is governed by her actual technical knowledge of surgery, not by her enactment of a performance sanctioned by other members of the team. Let us now turn to this question of the substantive merits of role theory as an account of the situations to which it may be supposed relevant.

What the role paradigm can't do

One of role theory's major claims to significance is that through the concept of internalisation of role prescriptions it can give an account of social learning and personality formation. Role, in Goffman's words, is claimed to be 'the basic unit of socialization'; and personality, in the words of a paper on the subject by Brim (1960:

137), consists basically of 'learned roles and role components'.

There are two main options open to the role theorist in giving an account of personality formation. The first is to offer role as an *alternative* to a trait conception of personality, stressing the situational specificity of behaviour, and the well-known failure of personality research to find very convincing evidence of the generality of traits across situations. This is the option taken by Brim: 'The learned repertoire of roles is the personality. There is nothing else.' The other is to accept some conception of stable traits or lasting features of personality (perhaps along the lines of the charming defence of trait theory by Bem and Allen, 1974), and to offer role acquisition as a means of explaining their formation. This is the option taken by most of the literature on femininity, which explains the formation of traits such as nurturance, lack of aggressiveness and fear of success in terms of the role-learning pressures on the growing girl.

The first of these options is not easy to refute, but it is also not very interesting. It assumes away the problem of how social structure gets embedded in the person, or it simply translates it into a more abstract language. The question of social motivation is not really greatly clarified by suggesting that the development of motivation consists of learning that correct role performance is desirable! (Brim, 1960: 148.)

The second line of thought is more important, not only because it is the more widely argued, but also because it has more theoretical power. The notion that role prescriptions are internalised in a process that establishes a certain kind of performance as a lasting feature or trait of personality offers both a perspective on personality and a perspective on social stability—whose explanation is the central task of functionalist sociology. The *match* which is produced between societal need (as specified in the role prescriptions) and personality (as developed in the relevant traits) guarantees the stability of the system as a whole. Role learning becomes the psychological moment in the explanation of the reproduction of the social order.

As an account of the formation of the person, or even of traits and characteristics of the kind referred to in discussions of 'sex-role' (e.g. Hartley, 1964) this has some fairly marked deficiencies. Firstly, it fails to give any grip on the *force* with which constraints are established within the person. It is difficult to see, for instance, how such a trait as heterosexual object-choice could be established by the process of role learning via sanctioning and the internalisation of expectations. That is, established in its *reality* as a structure of violent passions and revulsions, with those contradictions and tensions that are familiar not only in psychotherapy but in the experience and writings of the sexual liberation movements. Yet object-choice is without any doubt a socially shaped aspect of personality, which is central to the social patterns talked about in sex role literature. It is interesting that Hartley's 'Developmental View of Female Sex-Role Identification' simply did not mention object-choice. And it is no accident that recent discussions of the formation of femininity, which do, have begun to draw much more heavily on psychoanalytic conceptions of repression and identification Chodorow, 1974; Mitchell, 1975) which go far beyond the boundaries of role theory.

On the other hand, role theory cannot account for the opposition with which social pressure is met: the girls who become tomboys, the women who become lesbians, the shoppers who become shoplifters, the citizens who become revolutionaries. There is, of course, a role-theoretic literature on 'deviance', which is the usual way these unarguable facts are met and absorbed. 'Deviance' is typically explained via imperfect socialisation, or better still by role conflicts, produced by tensions between the different roles a given person has to perform or disputes about the definition of a given role. But this will not do. Both these explanations precisely ignore the element of *resistance* to power and social pressure as such. This resistance is a fundamental fact of social life, of human history, and of the forms of social organisation that arise in history. Whether it is embedded in human biology, as Marcuse (1955) and Chomsky (1976) in different spheres suggest, or is a necessary feature of social relations, does not matter much for the present argument. The fact of systematic resistance to social control is enough. (It is interesting that the revolutionary Italian 'Il Manifesto' group (1972) used the phrase 'role-contestation'—not to refer to 'role conflict' as understood in role theory, but to refer precisely to the refusal of workers to accept unexamined the division of labour in production, i.e. the 'roles' laid down by the exigencies of management.)

Finally, both conceptions of personality formation as role acquisition rest on an assumption in role theory which we have already examined—the idea that role expectations set out a definite series of actions to be performed, which are duly learned over a large number of trials:

> ...the individual learns the behavior appropriate to his position in a group through interaction with others who hold normative beliefs about what his role should be, and who reward or punish him for correct or incorrect actions. (Brim, 1966: 9)

That this is not a *possible* account of social behaviour in general (nor, *a fortiori*, of its formation) has already been shown.

All of the foregoing has assumed that role theory, if not very apt or accurate, was at least a definite, determinate way of representing social transactions. A given action could generally be explained as a case of role enactment, as a performance in role by someone occupying the relevant position. But when we begin to probe into this kind of explanation, difficulties arise. There are, for instance, some 'positions' which are hardly to be distinguished from a set of performances as such—for instance, the position of 'driver' in Dahrendorf's list of fifteen, which is hardly to be distinguished from the fact that Herr Schmidt drives a car. It is stretching logic and language to suggest that we can explain his driving a car by his occupying the social position of 'driver' and thereupon enacting the expectations. Even when the position is well defined in advance, it is difficult in any unequivocal way to explain the relevant action, when it occurs, as due to role constraints. In doing the 'right' action one may, for instance, be lying; or pretending; or wishing to give the impression of being X or Y; or doing one action as a disguise for another. (For a witty exploration of these possibilities, see Austin, 1961; and for their prevalence in situations familiar to psychologists, Szasz, 1972.) In all of these cases the *explanation* of the action via the role fails, even though the action is the right one for the given role.

But there is something more basic here. How do we know that a given action *is* the right one for a given role? Most expositions of role concepts don't raise this question, because they approach it from the other direction, describing a position and listing a set of actions which are tacitly defined as belonging to it (cf. Pfohl, 1975). But if we start simply with the flux of social events in reality, this isn't so easy. Role theory explains an action by assigning it to the role connected with a certain position; but what *guarantees* that the assignment is correct? Smith shoots Jones: was it in role as a jealous husband, or in role as a defrauded partner, or in role as a quarrelling drunk? (The ambiguity of this sort of knowledge, with a slight twist, is the basis of the classic Whodunit, where several people have rival and equally good reasons for shooting Jones.)

Role theory answers, as it must, that the assignment is guaranteed by the existence of a social definition of the role, a set of expectations enforced by sanctions. It is this that guarantees the role is a *social* construct, not an arbitrary invention of the theorist. Unfortunately, this does not escape the problem. For how do we know that we have got the right expectations and sanctions? As role theorists constantly insist, each person has quite a number of positions, each with its counter-positions or reference groups; i.e. each person is inserted in a number of role frames. That counter-position whose attached expectations and sanctions provide the guarantee-from-outside in the specification of a given role can only be defined by starting from that role itself. The multiplicity of role frames, of possible constructions of role, itself guarantees that there is no universal criterion of relevance. To establish the social construction of the role, we first have to postulate the role in its fullness. There is thus a fundamental logical circularity in role theory.

This circularity can be escaped; but only by shifting to another method of thinking about social relations, a historical method.

The ideological working of role theory

The date and context of the main waves of interest in role theory is significant. The first arose at a time when western capitalism was facing economic and political crises, and a working-class revolt that embodied a profound crisis of legitimation. As part of a much broader spectrum of cultural responses, the behavioural sciences responded by producing a sociology of occupational roles, a theory of their stratification, and a general sociology that attempted to show the functional necessity (for social survival) of role performance. The apogee of role theory in the 1950s corresponded to the triumph of conservative ideology in western social science at large. As this hegemony broke down, role theory became impossible to maintain as a general theory of society, but could and did retreat to fields such as educational sociology, social work, and personnel work in management theory—precisely those fields which are concerned with the management of the integration of people into the social order. (Role theory, indeed, may usefully be thought of as the spontaneous ideology of professionals working in such fields.) Finally, when faced with a new legitimation crisis caused by the rise of sexual liberation movements, the behavioural sciences responded by developing a sociology of 'sex roles' and a descriptive account of supposed changes in their norms.

It now becomes clearer why role theory is unable to deal with the theoretical problems of resistance. This is so because role theory is, in effect, a theoretical ideology developed to cope with the stresses in the cultural order *created* by movements of resistance. At a less abstract level, it is the practical ideology embedded in the daily work of counsellors, social workers, teachers, and personnel officers so far as they are concerned with shaping people and their activity to the requirements of the system, i.e. forestalling resistance. The association of role theory with concepts of 'deviance' and pro-grammes of therapy is thus not accidental at all. The link works both ways. Studies of deviance give a spurious air of reality to role theory; and role theory gives a spurious legitimation to repressive therapies.

(Startling, but true, example: Glasser's (1965: 69ff) 'reality therapy' for a houseful of delinquent girls, who are made to learn, *inter alia*, hair-dressing and cosmetology as the 'reality' they have to come to face. Psychological 'normality' or 'recovery' for women frequently is taken to mean developing an interest in clothes, makeup, men, and sometimes housework (compare Reik, 1948: 148; Rapoport and Rosow, 1957: 234: Chesler, 1973.)

Here the fact that role theory purports to be, but really is not, a *social* theory, becomes important. Just as the ultimate determinism in role theory is an individual one, so the problems of 'role performance' and deviance are represented, ultimately, as individual problems. It is a question of mismatch of personality and role expectation, or inadequate socialisation, or disagreements between the opinions of 'role definers' about the proper expectations of a role (e.g. Gross *et al*.), or the inability of a person to resolve conflicting roles she is in, or the sheer bloody-mindedness of the confirmed deviant. Role theory rests on a contradiction, that between the recognition of social constraints, and an individualist mode of theorising them—a mode that reads social processes as inter-individual transactions, and grounds them in individual wills. That the things which obscurely register in the role literature—class conflict in industry, revolt against sexual oppression, resistance to social control—might be *collective* problems, capable of solution only by the transformation of society, is a truth that it is, in effect, the business of role theory to conceal.

Many critics have noted the affinity of the role literature and social conservatism (Coulson, 1972, is the wittiest and best). To some extent this is not a necessary connection. The over-socialised conception of man doesn't strictly follow from role concepts (merely from one reading of them); ideas of value-consensus in society are not strictly necessary in role theory; and so on. It is possible to produce a role-theory with the value-signs reversed, which is exactly what feminist sex-role theory has done. But it is still the case that role-theory *works* as conservative ideology. At the least, it offers no resistance to a dominated image of people and a consensual theory of society. Most role-theorists talk as if these *were* correct, and most role applications argue as if they *ought to be* correct. Role theory plainly appeals to those who like to think that the social order works by mutual agreement; that people ought to do what they are told, and there is something wrong with people who don't; that force, oppression, and exploitation aren't very important in the everyday working of society; and that the constraints that do operate on people reflect some kind of wisdom, whether of the older generation (socialisation) or of the society as a whole (function). These may not be logically necessary links, but they are plainly very pervasive.

That role theory has succeeded, even to a certain extent, illustrates the supremacy of what people want to hear, of the apt metaphor, over considerations of logic. For most of the inadequacies and absurdities summarised in this paper are by no means new discoveries. Most have been known, in one form or another, for a good many years. Considered by the ordinary canons of scientific argument, the role literature is really rock-bottom, simultaneously muddled and pedantic, usually impervious to criticism, and most of it stupefyingly dull. To say that theoretical writings on role rarely have original ideas is a serious understatement. Most of them are statements of utter banality, puffed out by endless distinctions and definitional refinements. Even a sympathetic reviewer (Morris, 1971: 408) was driven 'to admit a certain bafflement at the tautological nature of many of the conceptual elaborations reviewed above ...' The empirical literature on role for the most part is equally bad, being abstracted empiricism of the most arid kind. In such company, a fairly ordinary writer like Goffman appears a miracle of acuity and wit.

I am, indeed, tempted to suspect some dark purpose in all this, that the idea of role literature is to bore people so badly that they never enquire too deeply into the concept. But, on reflection, it isn't needed. As an element of practical ideology, the role metaphor can and does appeal regardless of the role theorists. The concept picks up features of everyday experience which people can easily recognise as their own, and reflects this experience back as 'science'.

Hegel has a phrase, 'the objectivity of appearance', which sums up what I am trying to get at. Some of the conservative undertones of the role concept may be optional, as I have suggested, capable of being filtered out. But in its basic structure, its taking inter-individual transactions in their immediacy as the content of social theory, and the method of cross-situational generalisation as its framework, role theory is irrevocably tied to conservatism. No inversion of the value-judgements can change this. Role theory paralyses the social (and sociological) imagination by taking the given as the real, the immediately accessible as the fundamental structure of society. It is, in this regard, an authentic member of the positivist family of social-scientific ideologies, and is subject in full to the criticisms of that family offered, among others, by Marcuse (1964).

In my view the most important point of this criticism is that the structure of positivist theory is ahistorical. It is unable to theorise the constant coming-into-being, transformation, and supersession of social forms. If an example is wanted for role theory, there is no better one than the case where role theory does explicitly try to reckon with class conflict (Dahrendorf, 1959). It does so (as it must) by postulating an ahistorical, eternal conflict between the occupants of the roles at the bottom and those at the top.

To reject role analysis is not, as it may seem to some psychologists, to reject a social analysis. It does not imply a resort to simple voluntarism. (Indeed I think I have shown, albeit sketchily, that role analysis itself is built on a kind of voluntarism.) Rather it is to insist on the need for a more authentic social theory. From the critique already developed we can specify some of the features such a theory must show. It must deal, centrally, with those issues of power and wealth, oppression and exploitation, that emerged as the keys to an understanding of the overall structural coherence of society at the point where role frame analysis gave out. It must offer a more powerful account of the constraints that operate in personality and in social structure, and of the way the two levels are linked in the process of being produced. And, to be capable of doing this, it must obey a fully historical logic. It will not *be* anything like role theory, though it will *deal with* popular role concepts as cases of ideology and myth, along the lines of Janeway's (1971) excellent discussion of the mythology of 'woman's place'.

Those criteria are difficult, but not impossible of achievement. There is at present—largely growing out of the women's movement and the labour movement, but with some presence in academic social science—an intellectual development along these lines. It is, I think, the direction that an authentic social science and an authentic psychology must take. In the end, role theory will come to be seen as a particularly sterile diversion. The sooner it is buried, the better.

I would like to end, like the role theorists, with a homely example, intended to register the difference between a historical and an ahistorical social science. Think of three occupational roles: say, chicken-farmer, journalist, and commercial artist. Role theory might have something to say about how the incumbents of those positions would interact if they came together, though I suspect not very much. It might even, via socialisation theory, have something to say about an ex-chicken farmer, an ex-journalist, and an ex-commercial artist. But think of how much more we begin to understand what they actually do if we throw in even the small historical detail of their names. They came together in 1929; their names were Heinrich Himmler, Joseph Goebbels, and Adolf Hitler.

11
'The glory of God and the permissible delectation of the spirit': J.S. Bach—some sociological notes

Everyone who has seen the plan of this book agrees that this essay seems a little isolated, and so it is. But there is a theoretical point to including it, beyond the fact that I like it.

I had been teaching courses on the sociology of culture from time to time; and the question always came up as to how the analysis of ideology, as an account of the way social structure affected thought and belief in everyday life, could give any grip on that unpredictable and almost–by–definition exceptional activity that we call 'art'. If it could not, then a social analysis of culture condemned itself by being unable to talk about the most interesting aspects of culture, creativity and innovation.

There were, of course, some classics which brought it off—notably Lucien Goldmann's magnificent book on Racine, *The Hidden God*. But one always wondered if these worked mainly because of some peculiarity in the subject–matter. I wanted to try the approach on a new topic, one I knew a little about, since Bach is my favourite composer. I soon discovered that, as the opening of the essay notes, this was a strenuous test indeed. One problem I did not have to tackle, though, was the old chestnut of the relationship between 'high' art and 'popular' culture. In the circumstances Bach was working in, there was no institutionalised division between them.

A first sketch of this paper, called 'Bach and his bachground', was made in 1975. The more developed version, 'J.S. Bach—some sociological notes', was composed for a sociology of art seminar at Macquarie University in August 1976. I wouldn't have been game to publish it without the interest shown by David Rumsey of the NSW Conservatorium of Music, whom I commend to all readers both for his skill at the organ and his excellent taste in sociology.

Johann Sebastian Bach poses a severe test for a sociological approach to art. A figure of such importance can hardly be ignored; yet, on the face of it, he defies commonsense linkages between the nature of his art and the pattern of his life and social relations. His music is often passionate and turbulent, even his solo instrumental works being renowned for their emotional impact. In his own day he was criticised for his florid style, and the contract of employment drawn up when he took the important post of Cantor in Leipzig stipulated that his church music should not be 'too theatrical' (Geiringer, 1967: 57).

Yet there is nothing florid in his life. He seems the complete antithesis of the romantic notion of the artist, having a systematic and industrious approach to the craft of music, and leading a private life of blameless, even cosy, domesticity. Apart from some disputes with employers, the only touch of colour is when, as a young church organist at Arnstadt, Bach was summoned before the Consistory to explain the presence of a 'strange maiden' making music in the choir loft. It was his cousin, and he shortly married her.

To complicate the task of seeing Bach in his social context, it is often remarked that he seems to be out of his period. He wrote the Reformation's music, including magnificent versions of Luther's hymns, but wrote it two centuries after Luther in the age of Pope, Linnaeus, and Voltaire. In producing an oeuvre that is widely regarded as the culmination of Baroque art, he moved in a direction contrary to that of the musical taste of the eighteenth century. While still at a height of creative power he was severely criticised by aesthetic theorists, and at his death left no influential school. The two most successful of his carefully-trained sons, Carl Philipp Emanuel and Johann Christian, developed markedly different styles from his. It seems odd to say it, but the conclusion seems to be that the greatest musician of the century was an anachronism, an aesthetic hangover.

The few surviving documents from Bach's hand tell us little directly about his music. We learn from them that he contracted to do this job and that, and kept up contact with his relatives. We learn that as a young man he was in a brawl with a student whose bassoon–playing he had insulted, and that in middle–age he fought some bureaucratic battles with censorious town councillors and a reform–minded headmaster. We learn that, like all artists of consequence at the time, he attempted to win the patronage of various princes. But there is little in the documents about the purposes or reasons of his musical work. His rules for thorough–bass accompaniment, the nearest thing to a guide to musical practice that we have from him, are of the most bald and technical kind. Even his 'Short but Most Necessary Draft for a Well–Appointed Church Music; with Certain Modest Reflections on the Decline of the Same', is almost entirely about the recruitment, training and pay of musicians for his choir and orchestra. It says nothing directly about the principles of his church music. (See translations of these documents in David and Mendel, 1966.)

Nor do the main biographical facts immediately suggest much more. He was born in 1685 into a family whose hereditary trade was music. Apart from a spell of secondary education in an ancient town near Hamburg, and various travels to inspect organs and hear other players, he lived all his life in an area of central Germany only a hundred miles long by fifty miles wide. He had two jobs as church organist, three in the court orchestras of petty local princes, and in 1723 became director of church music for the important trading town of Leipzig, a post that he held till he died after a bungled eye operation in 1750. He was famous as a keyboard player and particularly as an organist, was much in demand to inspect and test newly-built organs, and was especially celebrated for his organ improvisations.

This was probably the form in which his composing was best known. Some of his keyboard works were published in his lifetime, but little of his choral music and none of the cycles of church cantatas and oratorios that were his main work at Leipzig. These compositions themselves aroused little response from the burghers. The first performance of the *St Matthew Passion* (probably in 1729) seems to have passed without notice in the town. The manuscripts were little used after the composer's death, probably a third of the cantatas being lost. A small group of enthusiasts preserved the memory of his work and collected his manuscripts, and thus some of his music became known to Mozart and Beethoven. But it was not until well into the nineteenth century that his compositions became widely known. (More detail is available in a fascinating, although rather elitist, history (Blume, 1950) of the reception of Bach's work in his own day and thereafter.)

The difficulty of finding a key to the music in facts like these is so plain that the most famous book about Bach, a long appreciation by Albert Schweitzer, opens with a resounding declaration of the independence of his art from his life:

> Bach belongs to the order of objective artists... Their art not coming solely from the stimulus of their outer experience, we need not seek the roots of their work in the fortunes of its creator. In them the artistic personality exists independently of the human, the latter remaining in the background

as if it were something almost accidental. Bach's works would have been the same even if his existence had run quite another course. (1911, vol. 1: 1)

But this will not do. All kinds of details of the works, scoring, level of difficulty, themes chosen, and so on, do reflect the conditions under which they were to be performed and the occasions and people for whom they were written. If this is not the 'roots' of the music, then something fairly close to it must be involved in the marked periodisation of Bach's output, and its link with the patrons for whom he was producing. As court organist at the Lutheran court of Weimar (1708-17) he composed, or began, the bulk of his works for the organ, including many well-known preludes and fugues, the *Passacaglia in C Minor*, and the chorales of the 'Little Organ Book'. As Kapellmeister to the prince at Cöthen (1717-23), a Calvinist state where Lutheran music was literally out of court, he shifted to the field of secular music for entertainment, composing among other things the *Brandenburg Concertos*, the cello suites, *The Well-Tempered Clavier*, and the three violin concertos. As Cantor at Leipzig (1723-50) he produced the great choral liturgical works, including most of the cantatas, the *Passions*, and the *B Minor Mass*. Of course the periodisation is not absolute; but even qualifications to it can be related to Bach's social situation, such as the keyboard concertos he wrote at Leipzig for himself and his sons to perform to a definite audience that existed outside the church context.

We have, then, many indications of links between the music and what might be called its conditions of production: the audience, the performers, the occasions, all the contours of the composer's job.

Bach came, as already remarked, from a family of professional musicians. His father was one, his first father–in–law was one, the elder brother with whom he stayed after being orphaned was another; while a second cousin, Johann Christoph, was an eminent organist and composer of the previous generation. Bach absorbed a craft–like approach to the production of music. One aspect of this was his attention to apprentices. He saw to it that his sons and other students got a broad and deep musical training, and he composed many works, some very fine, for teaching purposes. His first great collection of organ preludes, for instance, is entitled 'A Little Organ Book, wherein the beginner may learn Chorales of every kind and also acquire skill in the use of the Pedal...' (see the discussion in Taylor, 1971). This attitude was abandoned by later masters as the craft–like economics of music broke down and a more thoroughly entrepreneurial pattern succeeded it.

Another indication of the links was his use of other composers' works. The conditions of Bach's work required him to produce a stream of melody for at least weekly performances. Much of this he supplied himself, but much also he quarried from the works of other composers, which he collected energetically throughout his life. Some of this was simply transcribed (leading to problems for historians, as works known from Bach's personal copy have been wrongly attributed to him), some was adapted, some was used as the starting–point for an elaborate new work.

Bach took the same attitude to his own work, quarrying pieces already written for sections that could be used in a new production, often of a very different kind. Thus the cantatas produced in enormous number, and sometimes great haste, in his early years at Leipzig, more often than not contain melodies and arrangements from his earlier 'secular' works. A musicologist has estimated that 'of the 250-275 known cantatas, both sacred and secular, no less than 163 or about 65 per cent, show traces of borrowing to a greater or lesser extent' (Carrell, 1967: 118). This has led to a certain amount of learned speculation about the interpenetration of the divine and the secular in Bach's vision of the world, but can be understood much more mundanely as a consequence of the pressures under which he produced. It was only with a change in the relation of the artist to the audience, with the creation, in effect, of a market for performances, that the work as such was to become a commodity. Then the aesthetic notion of the uniqueness and indissolubility of a work, and the legalistic notion of the composer's copyright in his or her product, and the complementary notion of plagiarism, could become dominant.

The significance of the conditions of production, of the social structure of the practice of music, goes even deeper into Bach's work than this. When a journalist and musician named Scheibe in 1737 published a sharp criticism of Bach's music in the name of modern aesthetics, among his complaints (along with the music's being too turgid and sophisticated) was that 'all his parts, too, are equally melodic so that one cannot distinguish the principal tune among them' (quoted in Geiringer, 1967: 89-90). A Bach polyphonic piece is indeed a kind of democracy of several melodic lines. That this was a conscious principle with him is shown by his teaching. In teaching harmony to his pupils he laid down that the series of notes in each 'voice' (in orchestral music, each instrument or group) should make musical sense in itself.

The vocal character of Bach's instrumental writing has often been noted. Here too there is a profound contrast with the music of the nineteenth century, already foreshadowed by Scheibe. The tendency increasingly was to let the ensemble dominate, and the division of labour become so marked that individual instrumentalists no longer had a recognisable piece of music to play. Bach's compositions, rather, insist on the craft–like character of the work of each member of the ensemble. A notable example is the harpsichord, typically used to provide a harmonic base, but converted by Bach to an equal partner, and sometimes (e.g. in the first movement of *Brandenburg Concerto No.5*) given brilliant passages in the lead. We have here in music an intriguing analogue of a very general process in European society over this period, the replacement of simple commodity production under craft or craft–like conditions by industrial production processes with an increasingly elaborate division of labour and more and more marked alienation of the worker. Under these conditions each individual worker was left with a more or less meaningless fragment of activity, sense being made only when they were all fitted together by the rationality of the capitalist at a higher level. In Bach, music had not yet become part of the world of alienation; though in his lifetime, it was beginning the transition.

This is not to deny that there was a market situation in Bach's time. He, like other musicians of the time, shopped around for jobs, and entered quasi-contractual relations with his employers. (Telemann, for instance, was another applicant for the post of Cantor at St Thomas' in Leipzig, and was actually offered the post before Bach; he got very good terms, then went back and used the offer to extract a higher salary from his current employer, the town of Hamburg). The social relations of the time were by no means strictly feudal, taking feudal society to be one in which social obligations are essentially customary rather than contractual. Yet the transition was slow. Kinship was still a leading principle of social organisation in the central–German society of the time, and the extended kinship network was very important in Bach's own life. As an established musician he took his own younger relations as pupils and supported them in their search for posts, just as he had been trained and supported earlier. He passed his first organist's job on to a cousin, married another, and lost a promotion to Kapellmeister at Weimar because of the Duke's sense of obligation to the kin of the late incumbent.

The employment relations that musicians entered still had elements of the lifelong obligations of feudal society. Once employed, one was not expected to move elsewhere without the permission of the employer, and this was not always readily given. Bach's father had been obliged to stay on against his will as a town musician at Eisenach, where Johann Sebastian was born. In 1717 Bach was actually arrested and imprisoned for being too importunate about getting a release from his post at Weimar in order to take up the offer from Cöthen. The patronage relationship that leading musicians attempted to establish with princes also had strong traditional status elements. Bach was conscious of the drop in his own status from being concert–master to a prince, to being Cantor at Leipzig. He later applied for the official title of Court Composer to the Elector of Saxony, which, when eventually granted in 1736, appears to have strengthened his hand in conflicts with the local authorities. The musical homage offered in exchange for patronage could be quite personal. The six *Brandenburg Concertos* which Bach sent in the hope of gaining the patronage of the Margrave of Brandenburg seem to have been based on the current Cöthen repertoire; but the *Musical Offering*, an elaborate set of contrapuntal variations composed for Frederick the Great, was actually based on a theme of Frederick's.

In a variety of ways, then, we can see the social conditions in which Bach lived affecting not only the reception, but also the substance of his music. But the argument does not yet seem to have got close to the specific quality of his music, to the sustained drive and inventiveness evident in his work, and the scale and magnificence of his musical conceptions. In Bach's mature polyphony we do not have just a set of voices which harmonise, but a tightly-knit structure of extraordinary complexity, governed by principles of melody, harmony, ornamentation, and an architectonic conception of overall form. The mathematical problems alone that Bach had to solve in constructing something like the *Art of Fugue* are daunting, even though he seems to have solved them rapidly and intuitively, if we are to believe contemporary evidence about his ability to improvise complex variations for hours on end at the organ. Certainly he was intrigued by number games and acrostics, building obscure number symbolism into several of his later works. The point will be taken up again later.

We need, then, something that will give us a grip on what Sartre called the 'project' of the artist (see his development of this concept and its application to Flaubert in Sartre, 1968). In an interesting book that is well worth considering as a study in method, Chiapusso (1968) attempts to do this in terms of Bach's religious commitment. He attempts to fill in the thin documentation of Bach's own life from the much richer documentation of the society around him: the kind of schooling he must have had, the uses of music in the towns and courts of Germany, and the ideas and controversies of the intellectuals with whom he came into contact in the churches and the university city of Leipzig. Chiapusso reconstructs the lines of Bach's religious thought as a conservative, orthodox Lutheran in a somewhat embattled position with the rise of the subjectivist, sentimental 'pietist' movement in the church, and the enlightenment outside. (Bach's theological library, catalogued in the inventory of his estate, included two complete editions of Luther.)

Chiapusso goes beyond this statement of context to make the essential link with the work. Put very briefly, his view is that Bach's life and work revolved around the 'goal of a well–regulated church music', as Bach himself put it in resigning from his second post as organist (see document in David and Mendel, 1966: 60). Music was for Bach a form of worship, the form that employed his particular God–given talent; and his basic project was to achieve the reform and reconstruction of the entire musical service: practically, to recreate a Reformation in music. To this end he sought not just posts as a church musician, but full control over the church's music. When he finally got it, at Leipzig, he wrote an entire liturgy in music: a prodigious series of cantatas, amounting to five year–cycles; harmonisations of the Lutheran hymns and a set of magnificent organ works based on them; a series of sacred oratorios for feast days; and a variety of other devotional works including the *Magnificat* and five masses (though the last were probably not intended for ordinary Lutheran church performance). All of this was in music that was no mere decoration, but a closely–worked realisation of the theological ideas and liturgical practices.

> Bach fulfilled his mission. Every detail of the elaborate Lutheran liturgy was now properly introduced, ornamented, illustrated, and closed with fitting music... No composer has integrated the entire yearly service with such absolute devotion and such a profoundly mystic spirit as Bach. (Chiapusso, 1968: 228).

In many ways Chiapusso presents a persuasive account of Bach. It integrates many of the odd facts about his life that have come down in the documents. Details of his conflicts with authority, for instance, become intelligible in the light of his attempt to establish control over the church music for this grand aim, and to defend it once established. It is also subjectively fitting. The grandeur and passion of the music make sense when seen in the context of the over–arching religious purpose and the stately liturgical practice.

But there are some inconsistencies. Why did he stay so long in his early manhood, from 1708 to 1723, in court positions where he did not have the control of church music? Why was he not only willing to move, but insistent on moving, from the Lutheran stronghold of Weimar to a thoroughly secular job at Cöthen, and then had grave misgivings about going on to Leipzig? Why, when it was written, did he not try to have his liturgical work preserved or circulated more widely, and if that was because he expected other musicians to make their own, why did he not at least set down and circulate the principles on which his own work was based? In the final analysis, the idea of this solid, practical man, this careful teacher, inspector of organs, and seeker of princely patronage, as a religious mystic, is incongruous.

There has been some controversy among Bach specialists over the extent of his personal dedication to religion. Blume (1963), for instance, has gathered a number of pieces of evidence, including new datings of Bach's compositions, that undermine the image of Bach as an earnest and dedicated Christian labouring away year in and year out for the glory of God alone. Blume proposes, in fact, 'a new picture of Bach' which stresses the volume of his secular composing and the extent to which the church works were simply part of a job; a picture of Bach as a musician rather than a theologian, and a somewhat testy and difficult character to boot. Perhaps this can be taken too far. I do not doubt that he was a serious Lutheran, well-versed in the literature of his church and well able to interpret it, as will be shown shortly. But in trying to construct a coherent life-project, Chiapusso seems to have gone a good deal further than the evidence will actually take us.

Further, this kind of interpretation, to the extent that it gives a valid account of the artist's life project or intent, gives us little purchase on the specific way in which the project is realised and its effects achieved. For this involves questions of communication, of the symbol system in which the work is done; and this must take us beyond questions that can be formulated in terms of the individual life. Artistic symbol systems are collective products, decidedly so in a very public art such as Bach's. (Some counter-examples can be found, such as the highly personal symbolic languages of Blake's prophetic books and of Joyce's *Finnegans Wake*, but even here there is discoverable meaning and a basis in shared knowledge.) There are of course esoteric elements in Bach, especially in his later work, but even these had their audience of musical cognoscenti. As already stressed, Bach worked in a well-established tradition of musical thought and practice. He adapted and developed forms such as the fugue and the suite of dances, rather than attempting to create his own. The very complex structure he achieves in works like the organ fugues and chorale preludes is a result of the fact that he is drawing out the logic of a well-understood form.

Such remarks on the formal complexity of Bach's work might seem to sit oddly with the observations at the beginning of this paper on the emotional character of the music and the contemporary criticisms of its theatricality. The two points can be reconciled (at least in part) by a consideration of what might be called the second-order symbol system in baroque music. As the tradition developed in the seventeenth century, a number of rhetorical conventions became established by which particular motifs and types of harmony came to represent ideas and images.

Such symbolism abounds in Bach's choral and organ music. For example, in the cantata *Ein feste Burg ist unser Gott* (BWV 80), based on a famous hymn of Luther's, it ranges from a grand representation in the opening chorale of a struggle between the forces of evil and the divine fortress, full of battle motifs, down to small touches such as the twisted chromatic figure that occurs in the second duo at the mention of death. Schweitzer (1911, vol. 2: 56–122) offers quite a long list of the motifs Bach uses. There are characteristic methods of expressing such emotional states as confidence and hesitation through an imitation of different kinds of steps, and characteristic ways of expressing peace and tumult, joy and grief. Motions, objects and spiritual states are represented, and also spiritual beings such as angels and Satan (who typically gets a writhing, serpentine motif evidently based on his snakish activities in the Garden of Eden). At times there are combinations of two or three motifs to represent a complex idea or event. The symbolism works through characteristic rhythms and harmonies as well as through melodies. It is constantly present in the choral works, where it emphasises the meaning of the text. But it is also common in works such as the chorale preludes, where it represents and recalls the absent text of the chorale from which the theme originated.

This motif–symbolism was based on conventions that were probably well understood by most hearers. Bach went further, where probably most of his congregation could not follow him. Not only motifs, but also musical forms, appear to have been symbols. Thus the canon (a contrapuntal piece where each voice repeats the identical theme, though displaced in time or pitch) was in itself a symbol for divine law. (The term 'canon' comes from the Greek word for 'rule'.) In the last years of his life Bach seems to have gone more and more deeply into the abstruse field of form, writing a series of elaborate canons and a systematic treatise (in music) on the fugue. It is possible that he was in this attempting to reach and explore another order of symbolism beyond that of the liturgical work, the realm where music meets mathematics and leads to speculations about implicit harmonies governing the universe. Bach's interest in number symbolism has already been noted. In this part of his work he was moving sharply against the general drift of taste in the mid–eighteenth century towards 'naturalness' and what was taken to be simple emotional expressiveness.

The motif–symbolism in the church music itself has an internal structure. Many of the symbols fall quite naturally into a system of oppositions: peace vs tumult, joy vs grief, God vs devil, faith vs hesitation, and so on. Bach does not jump suddenly from one to the other, but he certainly uses the contrasts in his larger works, building emotion by moving through a series of expressive devices, alternating moods as he alternates performers. The basis of this vocabulary of symbols is easy to find: it is grounded in the structure of the religion which the music expressed. Bach and his audiences (apart from the Cöthen period) were steeped in Luther's writings, his interpretations of the Bible, and the vigorous hymns that the German reformation produced. That literature is intensely dramatic; Luther's own theology and rhetoric are full of struggle images and sharp contrasts. His central theological idea of justification by faith, of the accusation of sinners by the law and their salvation by imputed righteousness, is itself a dramaturgical concept of interaction between person and God. Both the images in Bach and the system of links and oppositions between them thus derive from central features of Lutheran religion. As Goldmann (1964) suggests, great art can crystallise and clarify what is confused or merely latent in the world–vision of the social groups from which it arises. Bach's art drew out a structure that had become obscured and crusted over in the institutional religion of his day. It is no wonder that he repeatedly came in conflict with modernising elements in church and intellectual life.

We can see, here, a more general basis of Bach's music: it is linked to social structure through the ideology in which it is grounded. But to make this argument concrete, it is necessary to show how this ideology worked in its social context. Here my arguments become more speculative; plainly, a great deal of detailed work would be required to establish them. But I will at least suggest some hypotheses.

Throughout his career, Bach was a functionary, the holder of an official post, and drew a salary from official revenues. Part of his income as Cantor came from customary fees from weddings, funerals, and the like (he once complained humorously about the shortfall in his income caused by an unusually healthy year in Leipzig); but even these fees were legally enforcible. The church was part of the state organisation; it was actually the Leipzig town council, not the minister, that appointed him as Cantor. So whether he was in a court post or a church post, he and his family were living off the social surplus extracted from Thuringian peasants, artisans and traders by the state. It is interesting that in the inventory of his estate taken when he died, the first item listed is 'one share in a mine called Ursula Erbstolln'; but this was only valued at a small fraction of the estate, and there is no other sign that he was a rentier, no land being listed in the inventory (see David and Mendel, 1966: 191). He lived by his art, as a craftsman employed by the state, on a comfortable salary. In exploring the ideological roots of his art, our attention must go to the role of the state and its connection with religion.

Lutheranism had not always been an official state religion. Luther himself had provoked a sharp split in the ruling class of renaissance Germany, and his religious revolt was one of the important stimuli to peasant risings (which he brutally condemned) and some urban revolutions in the sixteenth century. A dramatised, earthy religion with an appeal to private conscience and a vigorous contempt for corrupt authority retained some revolutionary potential as long as its original texts were read. But by and large it was tamed, and by the late seventeenth century, after the hideous experience of the Thirty Years' War, had settled down as the institutional religion of half the German principalities, closely analogous in its social role to Anglicanism in England.

Meanwhile the nature of the state itself was changing from the ad hoc personal power structures of late feudalism, acquiring a more rationalised and bureaucratic organisation. The connections of this development with a changing economy and social structure are exceedingly complex and controversial, but the general direction of movement is clear. It was of course more advanced in the large centralised monarchies such as France and Prussia, but even in the central–German principalities a bureaucratic and secularised state apparatus had emerged by the eighteenth century. And as this developed, its relation with religion changed, from what had once been an interpenetration, to one where religion became subordinate and supportive. The ideological function of Lutheran religious art similarly changed, from dramatising and leading a religious and social upheaval, to one of embellishing and justifying a status quo. It was then easy for its practitioners, like Bach, to alternate between religious art and a secular art which directly celebrated the rulers and their way of life. There was no fundamental conflict between music that embellished the church service and music that embellished the communal life of the courts or the almost equally hierarchical governments of the towns. The religious works for state occasions sometimes composed by Bach (such as the cantatas for the Leipzig council elections, and pieces celebrating royal visits) nicely combine the two.

Yet Lutheranism had once been revolutionary religion; and it contained potentialities at odds with this social function. Its appeal to individual conscience and to the personal experience of justification contained the seeds of a subjective and psychological religion, and this was picked up in Bach's time by the pietist movement. Bach opposed this solution; but he too responded to some of the concealed potentialities of the Lutheran tradition. In particular he responded to its dramaturgical, almost Manichaean, vision of the world. In a sense this too was a psychological interpretation, but not an individual one. It was a response in terms of a public drama elaborately representing the cosmic drama of fall and redemption.

But cosmic drama was not what the ruling classes of an agricultural province and modest trading cities wanted. They wanted a tamer, celebratory public art. The criticisms of the operatic character and emotional lushness of Bach's music have already been mentioned. Intellectuals who were aligned with the forces producing the secular bureaucratic state wanted a more rational art and a more straightforward technique. From their point of view Bach's intricate formal structures were 'contrary to reason'. In a sense, his superb technical equipment, the culmination of two centuries of musical development, was itself what unfitted him to meet the ideological demands created by these political and economic changes. In terms of the social functions of official music of the time, he could be acclaimed as a virtuoso performer and regarded as a competent organiser of ceremonial music, but could not be accepted as a significant composer: and that is exactly what happened to him.

I am in no sense suggesting that Bach was a revolutionary figure, even in the sense in which Luther was. It is abundantly clear that he accepted without question the hierarchical society of his day, and though he saw himself at times as a musical innovator it was within a firmly–established framework. Yet for the reasons I have suggested, his art was increasingly at odds with the ideological demands of his environment. A growing perception of this may well have given urgency to his liturgical work at Leipzig. The failure of the liturgical work to win the response and support he expected may further have led him to explore other possibilities in the Baroque tradition he had mastered.

For there is a significant shift in his work towards the end. It can be seen in two famous works of his later years, the *Mass in B Minor* and the *Art of Fugue*, as well as others connected with them. *The Mass*, though a profound religious work, is not one that could be performed as part of the regular Lutheran liturgy (nor the Roman, though it has sometimes been seen as a Catholic mass). Geiringer (1967: 207) aptly describes it as 'an abstract composition of monumental dimensions'. The *Art of Fugue*, even more, has moved very far from the mellifluous and elegant style of Bach's early days. It is an exposition of fugal technique of a strongly intellectual character, almost harsh at times, developing simple elements into patterns of extraordinary complexity but remaining under complete formal control. This body of work does not seem explicable in terms of the symbol structure based on Lutheranism.

As already suggested, Bach seems to be moving here into a realm governed by an aesthetic of abstract form. My hypothesis is that this move resulted from his failure to overcome the antinomies of the ideological field within which his main liturgical work was constructed. It was a move only available to a composer with an exhaustive knowledge of the Baroque tradition; as far as I know it had no parallels at the time; and it remained for a long time—perhaps until the later works of Beethoven—without successors.

Bach's work, then, is profoundly influenced by the social relations in which he lived and the historical situations that he faced. This is in no sense a simple determination, and to that extent I can agree with Schweitzer's view. But it is sheer mythologising to separate the music from its performers, its audiences, its occasions, its purposes, the ideological ground from which it arose, and Bach's changing responses to all these conditions. To understand it in this context is not only an exercise in cultural analysis. It is also, I think, to enrich the musical experience of this extraordinary work.

12
The porpoise and the elephant: Birmingham on class, culture and education.

This essay was first written in April 1980, as a working paper for the School, Home and Work project, in an attempt to get to grips with what was currently the most influential account of the relations among adolescence, class, culture and schooling. The researchers at the University of Birmingham's Centre for Contemporary Cultural Studies (CCCS) had, in the second half of the 1970s, published a series of books which had virtually revolutionised discussions of this set of issues. In analysing our interviews, we found ourselves increasingly at odds with their approach. This is an attempt to set out the basic reasons why.

The focus is on the argument about youth subcultures and education, the main texts for which are *Resistance Through Rituals* (1975), *Learning to Labour* (1977), *Women Take Issue* (1978), and *Working Class Culture* (1979). This doesn't exhaust the concerns of the Birmingham Centre, but is perhaps the most influential part of its work, and displays what I think are its underlying difficulties. I perhaps unfairly ignore the differences between different authors (e.g. McRobbie and Willis on sexism), and the shifts in focus over the years, in order to concentrate on what seem to be the most basic arguments.

In 1975 *Resistance Through Rituals* performed the very important task of exploding the undifferentiated concept of 'youth culture' that had been common in postwar discussions of adolescence. By dipping into a number of different youth groups around England, the

Birmingham researchers were able to document convincingly both the variety and liveliness of what they called 'subcultures', and also to show that these were in vital ways related to the ways of life of the social classes from which they emerged.

Reciprocally, *Resistance Through Rituals* used the material on youth to argue a case about classes. It was able to demonstrate vividly, at least for the case of the English working class, the cultural complexity of a class, its internal differentiation, incoherencies, disjunctions. And it argued for the importance of a notion of cultural struggle. Factory and parliament are not the only sites of class conflict. Class struggle can, and does, happen as different social forces produce, contest, and transform cultural forms—styles of dress, speech and recreation, among other things.

Especially in the case studies, both in *Resistance Through Rituals* and later works like Willis's *Learning to Labour* and *Profane Culture*, this grew into a deliberate stress on the creativity, inventiveness and resourcefulness of groups of people like delinquent boys. In older traditions of cultural analysis (classically, in the second part of Hoggart's *The Uses of Literacy*) such groups had been virtually written off, seen as practically culture–less, and certainly incapable of significant cultural creation.

This in turn changed the terms of the argument about culture and working–class education. The school system now is not seen as the (more or less inadequate) purveyor of good culture to the unenlightened, who respond (more or less inadequately) to it. It has to be seen as a field of cultural struggle between various groups, all of whom are in possession of their own cultures.

In this way the CCCS not only reconfigured some traditional debates, but achieved an impressive intellectual synthesis. As the 1970s wore on it embraced not only youth studies and class analysis but also feminism and structuralist tendencies in the analysis of subjectivity. Both its energies and its limitations sprang from the implausible encounter, in the Birmingham Centre of the early 1970s, of a strongly Althusserian marxism with the tradition of field observation that had been around in youth research since Whyte's *Street Corner Society* thirty years before. Like the offspring of the porpoise and the elephant, the product was intelligent and frisky. But it also showed a tendency, weighed down by gigantic tusks, to sink to the bottom of the sea.

The Birmingham researchers tended to call their research approach 'ethnography' and their field procedure 'participant observation'. (There is a long technical appendix to *Resistance Through Rituals* on the latter.) By comparison with the abstracted empiricism of most survey research on adolescence, there was good point in stressing the importance of close–up observation. But what the researchers actually did in the field fell a long way short of the methods of ethnography as they are understood in field anthropology, the attempt at a total description of a way of life after total immersion in it for considerable periods. The Birmingham researches never seem to have been anything like as intensive as that, depending rather on a mixture of open–ended interviewing and field observation for limited periods. The term 'ethnography' implicitly makes an inflated claim.

It was a claim that allowed them to evade two problems on the borderland of methodology and theory. First, they were enabled to ignore problems of *representativeness*, which would have had to be confronted if it was a question of plain old survey research. Some really startling over–generalisations of findings from very small numbers of people resulted, aided by a feature of the Birmingham approach to class analysis which I will mention in a moment. Second, they were led, by a tacit belief that they *had* written ethnographies, to adopt the concept of 'culture' that is traditional in ethnographic reporting, without in fact having made a real test of its applicability. More of this, too, shortly.

The approach to class which underlay the cultural analysis was firmly in the structuralist tradition. Every good Althusserian, including Althusser, repudiates Althusserianism, and the Birmingham researchers are no exceptions. Willis gets in some shrewd blows against the old boy towards the end of *Learning to Labour*; and Johnson announces a 'settling of accounts with our erstwhile Althusserianism' in *Working Class Culture*. (...The first time as tragedy, the second as farce?) Without doubting that these statements are wholly sincere, it is still the case that some features of the Althusserian approach are central to the work of the CCCS in ways that may not be obvious to the writers. Four seem to be of particular importance.

The first is the conception of class itself. There is no need to repeat the observations on this from chapter 7, but it is worth noting some consequences. The structuralist conception of class translates into the CCCS analyses as an assumption that behind the superficial complexity of everyday life, there is a fundamental class situation which is the same for everyone in that class. At the level of fundamental structure, that is to say, classes are homogeneous. It is this assumption, along with the idea of 'ethnography', that lies behind the massive over–generalisations of some of the arguments about the working class in books like *Learning to Labour*.

Closely associated with this assumption is the idea that there is an inner core to class relations, a central reality, which is known to the knowing theorist, but not known (except in partial or distorted ways) to ordinary social actors. The treatment of 'labour power' in *Learning to Labour* is an important case in point. And it is characteristic of the approach that the main concern in the political and ideological analyses, and even sometimes economic arguments, is with the *reproduction* of that inner core, rather than with its dynamics.

The second consequence of the structuralist approach to class is a characteristic way of reckoning with ideology and culture. The key move is 'decoding'—that is, finding a hidden meaning in what is immediately apparent. Of course this style of thing goes back long before Althusser. There is, for instance, a whole library of sub–Freudian cultural analyses in which every cultural phenomenon from hair–styles to Hitler has been decoded to reveal its unconscious significance. It was, nevertheless, the Althusserian school who gave this approach an enormous boost in the 1960s and 1970s, elaborating a theory of ideology in which mis–recognition of social reality was supposed to be well–nigh universal. This validated, indeed demanded, a habit of 'reading' cultural forms as if they were texts, to discover their underlying, and normally unrecognised, meanings and functions. How could this escape the classic problem of the sociology of knowledge, total relativism? By postulation. 'Reality' was counter-posed to 'ideology' (e.g. *Learning to Labour*: 189), the 'reality' being given us by the structural theory of class. (Which in turn validated this theory of ideology, which in turn validated this procedure of decoding, and so on round the circle.)

Thirdly, the legacy of this approach to class was a way of thinking about people and social structures in which the people are distinctly secondary. This is the point at which the Althusserian heritage is most plainly at odds with the field research tradition. However well or ill you do your fieldwork, there is no way that you can escape the faces and accents of particular people.

The tension is in many respects creative. Some of the best things to have come out of the CCCS work are just at this intersection: the lively portraits of particular peer groups in Willis's *Learning to Labour* and *Profane Culture*, and McRobbie's papers on girls, strongly informed by a sense of their location on the maps of class and patriarchy. But it remains an intersection, not an interaction; the fieldwork doesn't react on the conceptions of social structure. Indeed, in the gradual elaboration of an analysis of patriarchy, we can see the structuralist approach taking over the new material as it arrives. The eventual result is an abstract theory of social reproduction (see *Women Take Issue*, and Willis, 1981), not a theory of what the field material so beautifully demonstrates, sexual power structure.

Finally, the meeting of the two traditions produces, of all things, a deep confusion about the concept of 'culture' itself.

In the long theoretical paper that introduces *Resistance Through Rituals* and sets out the main lines of the CCCS approach to cultures and sub–cultures, there is a striking passage where the concept of culture is defined. The one paragraph (on pages 10–11) weaves together no less than five different definitions, all of which are endorsed, with no signalling of possible conflict between them. They are:

1 A distinctive way of life, a 'shape', a pattern of consociation.
2 How the 'raw material' of social and material existence is symbolically handled, understood or expressed.
3 The practices that objectivate meanings, or that objectivate group life in meaningful forms.
4 The set of values, meanings and ideas embodied in institutions, customs, and so on.
5 The patterns of relationship through which the individual is socialised, given an identity.

Each of these is a reasonable meaning to attach to the word 'culture', and each is duly applied in CCCS analyses. The trouble is that there *are* potential conflicts between them; and there are very certainly different implications and uses. Because they are not stated or explored, the subsequent arguments slip and slide among them. Of the resulting inconsistencies and incoherences, two seem particularly important.

Both the Althusserian and the 'ethnographic' traditions lean towards a total conception of culture and ideology, that is, identifying culture with the totality of a way of life, or at least of its subjective side. This leads the CCCS researchers, as soon as they have identified a group, to start talking about its culture.

But the word also carries the implication of a *distinctive* way of life or pattern of experience, that is, a way in which groups are divided from each other. Because the two conceptions are blurred in the same set of terms, the CCCS arguments constantly assume, as soon as any group is named, that it must have a distinctive way of life and subjective experience. 'Culture' becomes 'cultures', and cultures, it seems, can be found everywhere. We find not only 'working–class culture' and 'middle–class culture' but also 'teeny–bopper culture', 'the culture of femininity', 'shop–floor culture' and so on. (Though for some reason the notion of ethnic cultures hardly figures in the CCCS work.)

One result of this is that the concept of a separate culture becomes simply a necessary part of the concept of class. The approach obliterates the question of whether there actually *is* a distinctive culture possessed by the working class at a given time and place—surely one of the most important questions to be asked in any analysis of hegemony. Indeed, at some points the concept of culture is so reified that it has virtually become a place which people inhabit, rather than an aspect of what they do. Willis, for instance, finds no difficulty in talking about 'members of a culture', or talking about a shop–floor culture that his boys aren't in yet but are mostly 'destined for' (*Learning to Labour*: 52); nor does McRobbie in talking about girls 'inhabiting a culture of femininity' (*Women Take Issue*: 101).

Further, cultural struggle, of which the CCCS group are very conscious, becomes struggle between cultures. Cultures are taken to be dominant over each other. Hegemony, in this account, becomes not the domination of one group of people over another through cultural techniques, but the relation of domination/subordination between cultures (see *Resistance Through Rituals*: 12). The people seem, as usual, a bit epiphenomenal.

Possibly this tendency in their theorising is a matter of geography as much as anything else. The corporatism that British intellectuals have traditionally detected in the British working class, and their tendency until very recently to ignore questions of race and region, translate easily into assumptions about a distinctive class culture. Whatever its origins, it has important consequences. In most situations it reinforces the political pessimism that came with the structuralist heritage.

In the case of education, for instance, it construes the relation between working–class kids and their schools as, at the root, a culture clash. And that is a picture that gives teachers, practically speaking, no purchase. I think it is important in understanding schools to see the possibility of cultural struggle which is *not* the clash of fully–formed cultures. It is less dramatic, and perhaps harder to grasp, but it is a pattern which can give teacher politics some purchase.

The second problem in the conception of culture has to do with the antinomy of creating and being created. The CCCS analyses take from Althusser the notion that ideology interpellates individuals as subjects (e.g. McRobbie, 1978: 100); more plainly, that culture is about the way people are *given* an identity and *positioned* in a structure of social relationships. It is this notion that lies behind Willis's otherwise strange claim that the school/work transition and the way it is negotiated is what settles the fate of his boys—strange, that is, in the light of the rest of his account of class, where the fates available seem to be pretty thoroughly settled by much larger structural determinations. Culture acts as the secret police of the social structure, arresting the suspects and shoving them into the correct cells.

At the same time, the Birmingham authors hold a view of culture as creative activity, as the process of 'working up' raw materials of experience into symbolic form, giving meanings, and transforming already existing elements of culture. As I have already mentioned, this was a key point of departure from Hoggart. It is central to the treatment of subcultures in *Resistance Through Rituals* (for instance the discussion of the way the 'teddy boys' seized an abortive *haute couture* fashion trend and turned it to their own account); it is important in *Learning to Labour*, and has been reiterated in Willis's more recent writing (1981). At times, indeed, they seem quite pleased, and a little surprised, to have discovered all this creativity among the workers. It might not have been so strange if they had been reading a bit of anarchist literature as well as the heavy marxism.

The trouble is, you can't have it both ways. If you are serious about the creativity of social practice, then you must recognize that the structures themselves are constantly created and re-created by creative practice; and that means the idea of 'interpellation' *can't* work. Yet some such notion is imperatively demanded by the theory of social structure inherited from Althusserian marxism. Because of this bind, the notion of a practice of cultural politics becomes very difficult indeed to get clear. Willis ends *Learning to Labour* at this point, swaying gently back and forth in a net of antinomies.

I now want to try to pull these observations together by formulating what seems to me the most characteristic move in Birmingham–style cultural analysis. One of its great strengths is its recognition of diversity, incoherence, and contradiction in a cultural field (see *Working Class Culture*: 235, 253). And one of its great ambitions has been to tie the phenomenal complexity discovered by field techniques to a sophisticated and powerful analysis of social structure.

It seems to me that this is characteristically done by a move exactly analogous to the field distinction in Poulantzas, discussed in chapter 7. Complexity is assigned to a surface level, simplicity and determining power to a deep level of structural determination; the porpoise and the elephant again.

The prime case of this is class. Here the elephant is very familiar. The deep structure, 'the real' (as it is called in various formulations that pit a realm of interpretation, culture, against a realm of real material relations or experiences), is the conventional marxist machinery of relations of production, sale of labour–power, extraction of surplus value. CCCS works with a dead simple political economy; they hardly ever refer to any text of economic analysis later than 1867. Culture is layered on top of that, though as Johnson explains, it is not a case of reflection:

> It follows that there can be no simple or 'expressive' relation between *economic classes* [my italics] and cultural forms, and that we should start

any such analysis by looking for contradictions, displacements in a culture, as well as unities. (*Working Class Culture*: 235)

As in Althusserian class theory, the field distinction means that we get no effective relation between the two levels: merely a superimposition in which the one (complexity) signifies the presence of the other (unity). In brief, it's a metaphor; and that's why the main procedure of analysis is a literary one, a decoding.

There are further examples of this pattern of a complexity superimposed on a simplicity. For instance, Willis's notably tendentious treatment of the 'teaching paradigm' (*Learning to Labour*: 63ff, esp. 72), where every pattern of teacher–pupil relations is pre–judged as being a superficial variation on an underlying structure of teacher domination and an exchange of knowledge for respect. The treatment of patriarchy is similar, with a structure of domination/subordination presupposed, and the phenomenal complexities analysed as the process of social reproduction of this structure. (It is only fair to say that this is also true of most other theories of patriarchy.)

The problem this creates for the reader of their work is that there is no criterion of proof for the 'reading' that discovers the footprints of the underlying structure in the superficial complexity. If we think we already know what is to be found there, there is no problem—but also little interest in the quest. Otherwise, as in literary criticism, we simply have to rely on the authority of the critic. And in that case it might be more honest, as well as a great saving of time, to scrap the heavy machinery and get right on with the interpretative commentary. Winship's paper on the magazine 'Woman', in *Women Take Issue*, is a fine example of good criticism labouring to escape a ponderous theoretical machinery.

The theoretical problem created is perhaps more important. The general procedure suppresses the role of culture in the *constitution* of the basic categories of social structure. In the passage quoted above Johnson contrasts cultural forms with economic classes. There are no such things as 'economic classes', there never have been, and it is very depressing to find such an expression in what is presumably a carefully–worded theoretical text of 1979. Yet it is not surprising, in view of the general methods of the CCCS group throughout.

Everything comes to a head in politics. The constant implication of the CCCS is that things *are not really as they seem*, at least, not as they seem to the benighted masses. Youth culture is really a differential response to class situation, progressive education is really a new form of social control, sexism is really (or also) an assertion of opposition and a valorisation of the repressed. Ideology involves misrecognition, youth cultures involve a distorted, indirect and imperfect (imaginary) handling of real problems. Delinquent working–class kids may be able to 'penetrate' some of their conditions of existence, but they don't really understand it, there are all these limitations deflecting the penetrations. The contraceptive theory of youth culture . . .

So much for Them. On the other hand there is Us, the marxist intellectuals, who do understand about $\frac{s}{v}$, and social democracy, and the teaching paradigm, and ideology and conjunctures and things like that. We know, even if they don't, that they really need the revolution; and in the light of our science we can tell what is Good in their culture (the penetrations) from what is Bad (the limitations). We have the secret knowledge that enables us to decode their culture (though we don't do much to help them decode ours), and to work out the ideas they *ought* to have (the 'proper logic' of their discontent—*Learning to Labour*: 150).

It's all depressingly familiar. Of course some of these problems are acknowledged in the CCCS literature, nowhere more clearly than at the end of *Learning to Labour*. But the structure of the CCCS approach prevents Willis from moving towards a solution; he is simply immobilised in the face of problems such as the educational rôle of radical intellectuals. As, indeed, are other structuralist marxists who have written about education—compare Sharp (1980) and Harris (1982).

To overcome these problems doesn't just need a better epistemology. It needs a different understanding of the relationship between the working class and intellectuals, and ultimately, a different practice. I'll try to suggest something of what this might be, in the final chapter.

13
Intellectuals and intellectual work

This chapter is an attempt to give perspective to the essays collected in this book, not by trying to synthesise them, but by trying to clarify the project for which they are intended. Some of its themes I have been concerned with for twenty years, others have come into focus quite recently. I have found it difficult, but illuminating, to bring them together.

Why theory?

The essays in this book, and the drafts and working papers behind them, represent a fair proportion of my working life over half a dozen years. On the face of it, writing about social processes at several removes of abstraction from any actual events is a bizarre way to spend one's life. I have had my share of doubts about the exercise, compared with policy research, or compared with straightforward political action.

It is not particularly helpful to say that practice needs theory, that wrong ideas lead people astray and have to be combatted, or that right ideas are needed for effective practice. Often what needs to be done is crystal clear, and needs no more than determination and energy to get started. You don't need a profound grasp of the practico–inert when someone comes at you with a knife, or targets you with a nuclear missile.

Worse, it is clear that *wrong* ideas can also lead to effective practice. People often think that if the statement of a strategy is followed by something like the intended result, the strategy must have been correct. This was why the Bolsheviks gained such terrific prestige in the world socialist movement around 1919–20. Yet that case is itself one of the clearest proofs of the contrary. There can be little doubt in retrospect that their very successful practice in Russia in the years of revolution and civil war was based on monumentally wrong views about the dynamics of world capitalism and the imminence of an international revolutionary crisis. And what are we to think of the theory that guided Hitler's rise, only a few years later, from almost nothing to total power in a major state—one of the most stunning political triumphs in modern history?

Yet it is also possible to find clear cases of the pernicious effects of wrong ideas. The influence of monetarist and other new–right doctrines on conservative governments is far from being the only cause, but is certainly one of the influences deepening the impact of the current recession on the western working classes. Perhaps the most common problem on the progressive side of politics is ideas that are not so much wrong as muddled, unclear, or insufficiently thought through. A case could be made that a good many of the problems encountered by the rather moderate reform programme of the Whitlam government had this kind of source.

Perhaps the mere possibility that theoretical work will sometimes help practice is enough justification for doing it. But my main conclusion from years of pounding around this particular track is that there really is no general pragmatic justification for theory. (Nor, for that matter, is there a general pragmatic justification for ignoring theory or denouncing theorists.) Theory commends itself, or fails to, mainly on its own ground—as a project of enlightenment. I value theory because I want to understand the way the world works, and to help other people to. I *hope* that as people's understanding deepens, the world will become a better place, or at least a safer one (for plants, fish and animals as well as us). But I don't *expect* that any piece of theoretical work that I, or anyone else, can do will make a measurable impact on the next election. Indeed, theory would still be worth doing if we could be sure that it didn't have a practical effect in politics, provided that it contributes to the long, often–threatened but always–renewed effort at understanding the world, ourselves, and the relationship between the two.

So this essay isn't another attempt to produce a general doctrine of theory and practice. The interesting questions seem to me those about the people who do them, about theorists and practitioners. The main concerns of what follows are how intellectuals are to be understood in social terms, what we are to make of their politics, how we should understand the production and consumption of social theory; and, ultimately, what are the directions for theoretical work that might be found in reflection on these questions.

Intellectuals

When Freud was a very old man, weakened by long illness and almost unable to work, Hitler staged his invasion of Austria and merged it into the Third Reich. The Nazi Party and Himmler's secret police promptly got to work in Vienna. As a Jew, Freud was in danger; his house was twice invaded by Nazi search–parties. His friends and disciples in other countries moved heaven and earth to get him out. Eventually the authorities agreed to let him go, after signing a document declaring he had no complaints against the Gestapo. There is a harrowing photograph (Jones, 1957, vol.3, facing page 241) of his arrival in London, exhausted and ill after a train trip across half Europe. The following year he died in exile.

I have always found this a very moving episode, perhaps because it seems to symbolise something larger. For all the unorthodoxy of his psychology, Freud was a classic, almost archetypal, figure as an intellectual. And he too, like ordinary people, was reduced to flight by the impact of power politics.

The Nazi movement was almost as anti–intellectual as it was anti–semitic. Hitler had a withering contempt for the 'gentlemen with diplomas'; and it was a Nazi playwright, perhaps unsure of his own footing, who coined the famous phrase 'Whenever I hear the word "culture"', I release the safety catch of my revolver'. When it came to the war, the Nazis did as they had said. The extermination programme for the conquered lands of the East explicitly included the local intelligentsia as well as Communists and Jews.

It would not be hard to fill a book with tales of the impotence of intellectuals: Marx in exile, Gramsci in prison, Galileo before the Inquisition, Servetus at the stake. In the Age of Information, the 'technetronic society' when intellect seems all the rage, it is sobering to reflect on just what did happen to many of the leading figures of Western intellectual history. And if all that seems past history, reflect on what has been happening to intellectuals in the last ten years in places like Chile, Kampuchea, Iran and El Salvador. With murderous regimes, being a fountain of knowledge is no protection; it may indeed invite attention.

There is a whole genre of writing about intellectuals which starts off from the notion that they are alienated outsiders, that there is a necessary distance between 'the intellectual' and 'society'. Pushed any distance, this implies a picture of intellectuals as occupants of a kind of ethnographic reserve, licensed oddities, perverts, clowns and grotesques. The image goes right to the roots of the modern European tradition. It is nowhere better expressed than in the 'Confession' of the anonymous twelfth–century Archpoet:

> I am of one element,
> Levity my matter,
> Like enough a withered leaf
> For the winds to scatter.
> Since it is the property
> Of the sapient
> To sit firm upon a rock
> It is evident
> That I am a fool, since I
> Am a flowing river,
> Never under the same sky,
> Transient for ever ...

The whole of this marvellous poem is too long to quote, but even this short passage may give the flavour of what Waddell (1954: 175) called 'the first defiance by the artist of that society which it is his thankless business to amuse'.

It is not surprising that this image of an alienated intelligentsia should arise among the Latin–speaking wandering scholars. But it is also worth noting that the same generations, and even the same people (such as Peter Abelard, famous as a versifier as well as a disputant), were involved in the creation of the universities, the institutions which were long to represent the other, stable side of intellectual life. And in them we see displayed numerous ways in which intellectuals are tied in to the social order: their recruitment, their pecking order, their funding, their fights. Even the publish–or–perish syndrome is not characteristic of academic life as such—it arises as a peculiar form of academic life produced in an intensely unequal and competitive social milieu.

This is a key case, because of the historical importance of universities; in colonial milieux like Australia they have been by far the most important basis for the formation of an intelligentsia. But the point has much wider application. The notion that intellectuals are people who are somehow freed from the hurly–burly of economic pressures has simply not been true of most intellectuals in our lifetime. Indeed one of the major developments in the recent history of occupations has been the dramatic growth of categories of workers who do intellectual work to earn their living, and depend on certified intellectual skills (in the form of educational qualifications) for their rights to jobs. The 'semi-professions', as these groups are sometimes called, are an extremely important phenomenon in understanding the intelligentsia, and I'll discuss them in more detail in a later section.

The growth of these groups, and the expansion of higher education throughout the industrialised world, has been so dramatic that it has suggested an equally dramatic thesis to a number of sociologists. I must admit that I blink a bit when, in a world quite likely to be destroyed by capitalist developers if the military don't get to it first, I am confronted by a book explaining that intellectuals are already, or are about to become, the new ruling class. Yet doctrines of that sort are now quite influential.

It seems to me that the notion of the intellectuals as an ascendant class, both in the Communist states (as in Konrád and Szelényi's *The Intellectuals on the Road to Class Power*) and the capitalist (as in Gouldner's *The Future of Intellectuals and the Rise of the New Class*), is based on a sound insight into the dynamic character of both regimes, and a stark misconception of the relations between knowledge and social force.

No-one can seriously deny the importance of technical knowledge and rare skills. The current drama of micro–electronics confirms it, if proof is wanted. But it is another matter altogether to argue, or imply, that the *producers* of knowledge normally *control* it, individually or (as Galbraith (1967) suggests in his account of the 'technostructure') collectively. Or, as a second step, that they determine the uses to which it is put. There is more than anecdotal evidence on this. As the military and economic importance of the sciences has grown, and the scale of output has increased in spectacular fashion, so the characteristic institutional form of scientific life has become the research institute or research division of a corporation. The basis of this is a planned, subdivided labour process; and the basis of the division of labour is objectives defined by the managers, generals and bureaucrats who provide the grants.

The other striking difficulty with the 'new class' theories is their characteristic assumption that possession of certain kinds of knowledge in itself defines a social class. What we have here is a clear example of the categorical type of theorising discussed in Chapter 6. It is no more adequate for analysing historical dynamics in this case than it has been in others. Konrád and Szelényi's position is more sophisticated than Gouldner's, as, rather than a formed category, they speak of a structural location around which a class is in process of formation. But even this takes the possession of certain kinds of knowledge as in itself constitutive of a social position and a social interest, which is surely putting the cart before the horse.

Behind this, again, is a reification contained in the very term 'the intellectuals'. We constitute the category by using the word, whether or not such a grouping has historically been constituted by actual social process. If we question this assumption, then much of the history appealed to by authors such as Gouldner appears as a pseudo–history, something like the history of left–handed people or the history of famous redheads.

I would want to argue, in fact, that while there is a seamless web of intellectual activity through history, the true history of the *intelligentsia*—using that word to mean a formed social group—is discontinuous. Different intelligentsias form, operate, and collapse in quite specific historical circumstances. To think about 'intellectuals' as if medieval priests begat enlightenment litterateurs, who begat industrial chemists, who begat revolutionary agitators and corporate planners, i.e. that they are all figures of the same kind, is utterly misleading. It may of course be useful to a particular intelligentsia to be able to claim such filiation as its own creation myth. Perhaps the most influential of such claims is the one implied in the term 'scientific socialism', by which marxists claimed filiation with the natural scientists.

It follows that we should beware of arguments that use one *type* of intellectual to determine the truth of others, as a touchstone tested the proportion of gold in an alloy. The classic alienated–intellectual literature did just this. Recent writing about the history of women writers and artists demonstrates, among other things, how totally misleading such an approach can be. We have to recognise that there are qualitatively different ways of doing intellectual work. More, the specific *relationships* among these different ways can be extremely important in understanding the structure of the cultural field and the politics of intellectual work, as I shall suggest further below.

The classic opposition between 'the intellectual' and 'society' is, then, a false opposition in several ways. But even a cliché–ridden falsehood may point to something important. It becomes apparent when we shift the focus from the derivative categories of 'intellectual' and 'intelligentsia' to the more basic category of *intellectual work*, considered as a type of social practice.

Intellectual work always involves a confrontation with the real. Even where the object is accurate reflection of reality, as in the descriptive moment of social research, there must be a shift of plane, a movement out–and–back, before reflection is achieved. This shift is a highly contingent achievement; and it needs some kind of practical basis and continuing support.

Some of the devices by which the gaps are created, the confrontations sparked, are familiar enough: solitude, drinking, walking in the bush, haunting Left Bank cafés, and others too numerous and embarrassing to mention. There is good reason why such things have become part of the comic stereotype of the intellectual. One bright idea isn't enough. There must be means of *sustaining* the dislocation, of repeating the internal shocks, if there is to be progress with problems of any depth. Especially if we want the work to confront, not just reality, but a reality constituted by a logic of social domination—as all interesting social science does.

This need not return us to the Archpoet as archetype. Rather, it helps make sense of Gramsci's very important observation that a good deal of intellectual work is done by people who aren't *socially* defined as intellectuals at all (1971: 8–9). It is often not a question of institutional support for intellectual dislocation. It is a question of struggle to achieve distance and dislocation within the routines of everyday life, a continuing effort to hold apart the bright edges of reality and reach through into the nothingness of the not–yet–formed, the not–yet–true. Either way, we need to make a closer examination of intellectual work and its circumstances.

Intellectual work

Gouldner elaborates on the category of intellectual by trying to spell out some of its content. Intellectuals, he suggests, have a common culture, the 'culture of careful and critical discourse'. This is institutionalised in the education system, and passed on as a form of privilege, a kind of cultural capital, to the rising generation of intellectuals. Under this rubric he is able to blend Bernstein's (1971) notion of elaborated codes, Bourdieu's notion of cultural capital (Bourdieu and Passeron 1977), and Habermas' (1971) notion of discursive redeemability, into American perspectives on higher education—quite a multinational achievement.

The prospect of such a synthesis is seductive, and the idea of a culture of critical discourse has commended itself widely. If it is sound, then it is cause for the profoundest pessimism, especially to those concerned with education. For it reverses the classic notion of schooling as the articulation of a common heritage (even if, *à la* Matthew Arnold (1869), this involved an attempt to refine it). In Gouldner's world education becomes, not only *de facto* but also in principle, a means of exclusion, of social closure. It is a way not only of separating the sheep from the goats but also of institutionalising and preserving goat–ness.

The facts of educational inequality to which Gouldner appeals are factual enough; they are, indeed, among the most thoroughly documented in modern sociology. How we should interpret them is another matter. It seems to me that there is a problem here, as with the Birmingham school discussed in chapter 12, with the concept of 'culture'. To put it simply, it is an exaggeration. The evidence doesn't come near justifying our thinking of intellectuals as bearers of a distinctive 'culture' that marks them off from other social groups. Consequently Gouldner's implications about the unity and the political directions of the 'new class', which hinge on this assumption, mostly fail.

What Gouldner has succeeded in doing, I would suggest, is gathering some useful starting–points for an analysis of intellectual work and its methods. 'Careful and critical discourse' is not so much a 'culture' as a *labour process*.

In writing this paper I am doing a job of work. Though it doesn't quite meet Bertrand Russell's splendid definition ('What is work? Work is of two kinds: first, altering the position of matter at or near the earth's surface relatively to other such matter; second, telling other people to do so.'—1935: 12), I am still pretty tired at the end of a day of it. It has taken me two days to get as far as this in writing the first draft. The job has its materials, its tools, its methods. At the most mundane level, if I am going to be writing at a desk for twelve hours in a day, it matters that I have a chair that won't give me backache, a pen that is comfortable in the hand, and a colour of ink that I like to look at. (Green.) I have never been able to compose on a typewriter, and envy those who can. My method of writing involves a lot of immediate rereading and rephrasing which I have found impossible to do on a machine.

At a more abstract level, the methods of this work include such things as testing generalisations against facts, eliminating inconsistencies, constructing inferences, comparing ideas with those in the literature. Gouldner's notions do help make sense of these. However this isn't all I am doing. I am also inventing, analogising, feeling shapes, guessing at connections between issues. I more often sense emotionally that an argument or line of thought is wrong than I discover error rationally. Another objection to the notion of a 'culture of critical discourse' is that it understates the role of intuition, imagination, and irrationality in intellectual production. Jokes, metaphors, likes and dislikes are as native to the trade as syllogisms, hypothesis–tests and refutations.

Of course writing is only one form of intellectual work, and the nature of the labour process varies from one kind to another. The vital thing is to see that it really is work; it is sheer mystification to talk about intellectuals and intellectual life without recognising that. It is remarkable how much discussion of academics, for instance, goes on without consideration of their daily labour. Perhaps this reflects a lingering prejudice, from the days when universities were even more markedly class institutions than they are now, that academics should somehow be above 'labour', that they inhabit a more ethereal world altogether. But the current development of industrial struggles within universities underlines how futile a prejudice that is. Academic activity is no more and no less than a specialised kind of intellectual work, with its own particular milieu, audiences, customs, contra-dictions—and possibilities.

A number of influential ideas about intellectuals become clearer, or at least more usable, when taken in the context of an intellectual labour process. When Habermas speaks of the discursive redeemability of claims, the point is initially epistemological: it is about the logical status of claims that can in principle be shown to be correct, given sufficient time to work through all the arguments and evidence. But there is something more, too: for this points directly to the social practices in which arguments actually are developed, challenged, and tested. Habermas' argument for freedom and equality as the conditions of undistorted evaluation implies precisely that the labour process involved, the work of evaluation, is structured by the power relations in which it occurs.

This has become one of the main themes in Foucault's recent writings (1977, 1980) about power and knowledge. He indeed pushes it further, stressing the way specific kinds of knowledge are generated within (and in response to the needs of) specific regimes of power, and come to be a resource for, perhaps even a form of, power. There can be no doubt that this is so. But if we take knowledge to be wholly internal to power (as some of the followers of Foucault seem to do), then we lose the ability to tell truth from lies. And that seems a very basic error for intellectuals to make, as well as a very dangerous strategic blunder.

I would suggest, rather, a relationship. The more immediately active power is in an intellectual labour process, and the more dominant interests shape the criteria of intellectual work and evaluate the products, then the more likely the product is to be composed of lies. This is not a trivial relationship. A great deal of the intellectual work done in our society does go into producing lies and misleading people. The advertising industry, the official propaganda agencies and the churches are merely the most conspicuous examples. Truth is not a necessary, or even an ideal, outcome of properly done intellectual work. A well–designed advertising campaign may be quite as much an intellectual achievement as a well–designed scientific experiment. Truth is merely one of the possibilities. Whether or not it is treated as a preferred outcome depends on the social context and organisation of the work.

We can make a similar point about the idea that intellectual work is, of its nature, universalising, that it attempts to articulate the general as against the particular. This is familiar in discussions of science, having been made a methodological rule by Popper (1965). Kant once wrote of education that it should prepare children not for the present, but for a better future condition of the human race, for the idea of humanity. And the search for expressions of the cosmic, the sublime, and the universal are stock ideas in romantic literature, music and criticism.

That there might be particular interests and practices underlying this is most clearly argued in recent feminist writing about science. This has documented the subordination of women's interests in the scientific power structure—most dramatically in the case of Rosalind Franklin and the analysis of DNA (Sayre, 1975). It has shown the way men's interests have structured scientific problems (e.g. research on contraception). Writers like Ehrenreich and English (1979) have shown how men's interests and perspectives have also shaped the applications of scientific knowledge to women's bodies and bodily processes in medicine. Further, there is an argument that the character of scientific discourse itself, its abstractness, its ban on emotion, its orientation to power over nature (experimental manipulation), grow out of masculine ways of viewing the world and are sustained by a patriarchal social order.

This last argument seems more true of a particular ideology of science (admittedly the dominant one) than of the realities of research. Alongside the textbook account of science (Pearson's *Grammar of Science*, Popper's *Logic of Scientific Discovery*) there has also been a less noticed account that has stressed intuition, practical experience and personal involvement (Polanyi's *Personal Knowledge*, Hudson's *The Cult of the Fact*). It is, in fact, only when we give full weight to these dimensions of intellectual work that the true importance of universalising arguments and representations can appear.

These do not in themselves define intellectual work. But their relation to intuitive and particular knowledge is vital in giving intellectual work *critical* potential, ability to subvert. A statement like 'People are born equal, and everywhere they are in chains' may strictly have no meaning, considered as a factual claim. But it works very effectively as an injunction to compare the real and the possible, and to start rattling the links of the real.

It is no accident that the patriarchal reaction against women's liberation has focussed, not on feminist accounts of women's experience, nor on the strategies of constructing women's culture, but on ridiculing the generalisable claim to equality. This is as true of the male–supremacist reaction in pornography and popular culture (e.g. the widely–distributed *Slave Girl of Gor* by John Norman) as it is of the work of anti–feminist theorists such as Theo Lang (*The Difference*

Between a Man and a Woman), Steven Goldberg (*The Inevitability of Patriarchy*), George Gilder (*Sexual Suicide*) and that ilk.

Seeing intellectual work as a kind of practice helps make sense of a general feature of the history of science, at least the human sciences in the west. Really important departures in thought (of the scale, say, to be regarded as paradigm shifts in the language of Kuhn, 1970) rarely, if ever, are a matter of an intellectual sitting down in the proverbial armchair, sending up clouds of smoke, and nutting out some deep problem. They are associated with new kinds of practical activity, which seem to give the theorist a different sort of lever on reality from those available to predecessors.

Marxism was in no sense an 'immense theoretical revolution' in the head of young Karl alone. It responded to a major change in practical politics, the emergence of organised mass working–class movements in industrialising Europe. The new intellectual work was principally an attempt to theorise that new practice. Even such vital abstract concepts as the labour theory of value are built directly on claims and perspectives of working–class activists that can be traced for a generation before *Capital* was written.

With Freud the connection with a new practice is even more obvious, as he was himself one of the inventors of modern psychiatric technique. Abstract statements of psychoanalytic theory tend to conceal what is very obvious from the whole corpus of his writing, that the elaboration of theory was intimately and extensively linked with the development of psychoanalytic method. The theory cannot really be understood without the case studies.

Finally, the most important change that is occurring in the social sciences at present—the recognition of the importance of gender relations, sexual power structure, and the construction of a theory of patriarchy—is so plainly linked to the political practice of women's liberation and gay liberation as to need no comment. It is entirely in accord with the view of intellectual work being suggested here that this departure in ideas should have to be accompanied by a continuing struggle about patriarchy within academic institutions and professional organisations. This seems to be more advanced in sociology and political science than in psychology or economics, but is nowhere ended, as witness Stacey's remarks (1982) on the current state of play in British sociology.

If a departure in practice is the lever with which the modern Archimedes shifts the intellectual world, it also has to be recognised that practice is a key to the ways intellectuals go wrong. I have already touched on the ways the practices of intellectual production can become embedded in systems of domination and participate in their logic. Even practices of disconnection can become rituals of eccentricity. History is littered with characters who cut themselves off in a private universe and persuaded themselves that they had discovered a key to the secrets of existence: some sinister and influential (de Sade), some amiable and ineffectual (Chidley: see Hornadge, 1971), some just nutty. Still, it is always hard to distinguish new insights from new idiocies. Apparent insanity may be the condition or the means of a major shift out of a received frame of thought. The habit of mind that balances one extreme position against another and settles for something in the middle shows a preference for comfort, not truth.

The circumstances of
intellectual work

Labour never occurs in a vacuum. There is usually an immediate institutional context, a communication network, a market of some sort. Likewise with intellectual labour.

To point to the institutional setting isn't to imply that the nature of the work is settled by the characteristics of the institution. There is a politics of institutional life; its outcomes are settled by struggle, not known from the start. To take the academic example again, Australian universities and CAEs are currently facing a campaign by the central government and big business to redefine their work on criteria of efficiency, defined in personnel–management terms, and of relevance to the needs of capital. The response to this pressure is complex. Some academics embrace it, and attempt to construct new empires in the spaces thus opened up. Others contest it as a barbarian invasion, though remaining vague about what academia should do instead. Some appeal to notions of academic freedom. Others note how such notions have served to protect the interests of older and established academic staff, at the expense of the untenured and junior staff. Pressure from students has ebbed in the last decade, but may develop again.

More dramatic is the struggle going on in the other main institutional base of Australian intellectual life, the mass media. In a sense this has been continuous since the late 1950s, when the construction of a commercial TV system transformed the great media empires. A turbulent, but continuing, process of centralisation of ownership and control; a displacement of traditional printing technology and weakening of printers' unions; a growing penetration of popular culture by the controllers and purchasers of electronic media (most dramatically shown by the virtually complete takeover of big sport by big advertisers in the last ten years—see Tatz, 1982, and Sandercock and Turner, 1982), are the most familiar episodes in the story. The outcomes are by no means all clear. Nevertheless it seems a reasonable conclusion that while the sophistication and penetration of journalists has grown markedly in the last generation, so has the ability of the owners and managers to monitor and control their work, and to penetrate the everyday life of the working class at large. The successful bid for control of an Australian communications satellite by a consortium of media capitalists (Kerry Packer to the fore) with an interest in networking, is the keystone of this development.

It is in the conditions of intellectual work, I think, that we have to seek the main reasons for the prominence of fashions and factions in intellectual life. Of course some turnover of ideas is technically necessary where argument is in any sense cumulative. A farmer–politician in the 1980s may pronounce pretty much the same set of ideas that his grandfather did around 1920, when the Country Parties were being formed, but a physicist or sociologist couldn't do it without being laughed out of the country. Beyond this, however, there seems to be a strong tendency among intellectuals to respond to fashions and sort themselves out into factions.

Not least those on the left. A sterling example is the dispute that recently arose among Australian Trotskyites (admittedly not the most pacific bunch) over the correct revolutionary line to take in relation to Packer cricket. Were the World Series Cricket players to be regarded as traitors to the proletariat, selling out to the nearest capitalist who waved a fistful of dollars; or as exploited workers who had finally stood up for themselves and gained a large wage rise by determined industrial action, an inspiration to us all? A more serious example, with larger consequences, was the curious popularity among Australian radical intellectuals of French structuralist marxism. This was enthusiastically endorsed in its most rigid and dogmatic form, and is now displaced (just as it was, perhaps, being bashed into useful shape) by an equally implausible fashion for Foucault-style discourse analysis. The baby of class analysis is duly thrown out with the bathwater of Althusserian dogmatism.

It is easy to see this kind of thing as an example of the dog–eat–dog political economy of a basically bourgeois intelligentsia. Just as there have to be periodic economic crises in which some capital is destroyed and the weaker capitalist driven to the wall, so, we may speculate, there have to be crises in intellectual life in which old cultural capital is destroyed, and successful entrepreneurs prove their fitness by being among the first to tool up with the new doctrines. For this purpose any kind of doctrine will do; the fantastic combination of Christianity and Maoism that gave rise to the 'nouvelle philosophie' in France, as described by Dews (1979), is only one of the most recent. From that point of view it is not surprising that in a period of economic depression, mass unemployment, and a hardening contest for state power, a sizeable fraction of Australian radical intellectuals are deep in contemplation of the nature of language and the structure of discourses.

But though that may be part of the story, the concept of 'cultural capital' is too fragile to stand up to very serious examination. And such a thesis doesn't account for the significant groups who don't get involved with succeeding fashions. It is notable that through a decade of vehement criticism of 'empiricism', good old conventional survey research has plodded along regardless, regularly training new graduate students, regularly turning out its crop of polls and attitude studies, regularly filling its journals. I've commented in Chapter 10 on the equal imperviousness to criticism shown by role researchers, once set moving in their grooves.

The point is that the institutional bases of intellectual work are themselves divided; and the practices that sustain the degree of distance I've suggested is essential are necessarily at odds with other routines. There is, then, an *unstable* practical base for intellectual work, which admits radically different outcomes from its contradictions, and makes fashion flip–flops possible. (The essence of fashion, surely, is that one is just as good as another; what counts is merely its currency.) The factionalism of intellectuals is the attempt to mobilise support for one out of a number of possible current resolutions of shared dilemmas. It is more striking among intellectuals than among Country Party politicians mainly because the interests that structure practices are so much more settled among the latter. If factionalism is a pathology of intellectual life, it is one that arises from its fundamental constitution.

The 'semi-professions'

The idea that the growth of the intelligentsia is reshaping the ruling class strikes me as very wide of the mark; but I don't think there can be any doubt that intellectual work and intellectual workers have been having a major effect in reshaping the working class. In *The New Working Class* Mallet argued that the conditions of production in high–technology (especially continuous–process) industry gave a key strategic role to groups of technically trained workers, who were making issues of worker control central to working–class politics. That was twenty years ago, and not all of Mallet's ideas have been borne out in the meantime. But it does seem as if the same kind of thing is now happening among another group of tertiary–trained workers. It is not in high–tech industries this time, but in occupations like teaching, welfare, and paramedical work.

Questions of control and authority are anyway built into these trades. Keeping order in the classroom and handling resistance is one of the major tasks teachers have to do. Welfare workers, like it or not, have to police the regulations under which welfare is distributed. Nurses, perhaps the oldest semi–profession, have an elaborate traditional authority pattern to administer between patients, doctors and nursing administrators. And it seems that in each of these cases the task has got more difficult in recent years. Put another way, there is a much more explicit politics of authority in these jobs, more contestation and debate about control and autonomy. And it seems that the questions of control built into the work have now spilt over into the employment relations in which it is done. There was for a long time great resistance to seeing the problems of these occupations as boss–and–worker industrial issues at all. The politicisation of relations with clients, more complete unionism, and much more active unionism, have now changed that quite drastically. (Connell *et al.*, 1982; Game and Pringle, 1983.)

The semi–professions—a vague and somewhat condescending name, but so far we lack a better—are now the largest group of intellectual workers in countries like Australia. Their training and equipping provides much of the daily bread for another group, the academics; and they provide a major part of the active audience for the work of yet others, journalists, writers, and artists of divers kinds. Their structural importance is obvious, and it is worth trying to get some grip on their relationship to knowledge and their place in the politics of knowledge.

Teaching, welfare work, and current forms of paramedical work are jobs that have practically been created in their modern form by a credentialling process, in which academic institutions have played a very active part. Just how active was borne in on me recently when sitting in a committee discussing courses at one of our institutions of higher learning. The most vigorous debate of the day occurred over what were the best kind of credentials to design for people who wanted to work in the field of 'Recreation'. That *some* scheme of credentialling (with its corollary, preference in employment over those who couldn't afford to get credentialled) was necessary, did not seem to be a doubt in the mind of anyone on the committee.

How much of the organised knowledge supposed to be conveyed in the training is then actually used on the job is a moot point. Most of the high school teachers I have spoken to had a singularly low opinion of the usefulness of their teacher–training, though rather more respect for their training in their teaching *subjects*. Even with such a technical business as engineering, as Bishop (1973) notes, there is reason to think the length of training has more to do with the status–politics and economics of credentialling than with what knowledge is actually used on the job. (But then, how much of what an academic was initially trained and tested for is ultimately used in that job? I am currently teaching, and researching, almost none of the subject–matter that I got my ticket for.)

It makes little sense to see the semi–professions as part–time intellectuals, to be understood on the model of the proper full–blown ones. They are groups of intellectual workers whose relationship to organised knowledge is of a different kind from that of academics and researchers. Perhaps better put, whose occupational knowledge is organised in a different way. To some extent they are consumers of research, but very selectively. Academics who assume a leader–follower relation in intellectual matters with such workers are likely to be in for a rude shock, if they wait around to hear the reactions. The endlessly–repeated criticism that the research isn't useful because it is 'academic', because the researcher doesn't know what it is really like on the job, is not obscurantism. It reflects genuine differences in the ways knowledge is organised and deployed.

Yet there is danger in a complacent acceptance of those differences. Teachers, welfare workers and others do use general ideas as well as their craft knowledges. That is to say they need the output of researchers and writers, and if they don't get good current ideas they will make do with bad old ones. Conversely researchers, especially in the social sciences, can make the most god–awful blunders if they ignore the logic of working knowledge in these occupations. The point is depressingly illustrated by much recent writing in the sociology of education.

Constructing relations among the different forms of knowledge is a necessary, though difficult, business. And it has to be recognised as a political process. Just to take one example: bringing the research knowledge about sexual and racial discrimination and labour market segmentation into relation with the practical knowledge embodied in promotion and appointment procedures is a political campaign in itself. It is a campaign currently being fought inside the NSW public service, sparked by the Equal Opportunity legislation (Ziller, 1980). It requires mobilisation, it has met resistance, and its eventual outcome is still far from clear.

As this example suggests, workers in semi–professions are commonly state employees. The ways they jump, the degree of autonomy they can establish, and what they do with it, are going to be very important in deciding what is the actual role of the state in the current economic trough. The closeness of welfare and health workers to the effects of the depression, and teachers to issues of hegemony, hardly need underlining. Politics is inescapable. So the time has come to take a deep breath and plunge into that most hackneyed, but also most central, theme in all modern discussions of intellectuals. I think there are some new dimensions.

Intellectuals' politics

The most striking political fact about intellectuals recently is what they have made a home for. Students, teachers, academics and other intellectual workers have provided a large part of the western resistance to the Vietnam war, of the environmental movement, and above all, of contemporary feminism.

Why? It would be nice to say it was because intellectuals are naturally progressive; but that isn't true, if we take sexual politics seriously. Though it was among younger radical intellectual women that second-wave feminism crystallised, it was the reactionary sexual politics of the men in the same movements that catalysed the reaction, as Rowbotham (1973) and Piercy (1970) record. If feminism has made more progress here than in other milieux, it is not without continuing and exhausting struggle.

Yet something did happen. There was a widespread politicisation, and on the whole a radicalisation, of western intellectuals in the 1960s. The civil rights movement and Vietnam war were the main occasions in the USA; but as the French student movement of 1968 showed (and indeed the Free Speech Movement at Berkeley in 1964) other occasions would do. Whatever the reasons, and they are certainly complex, there was a politicisation of a group among whom women were numerically in new strength (women's high school completion rates and higher education entrance rates were at this time rapidly approaching men's), while still excluded from power.

There is little difficulty in seeing why a feminist response should emerge, or more exactly strengthen (since feminism certainly did not disappear between the first and second 'waves'), in such circumstances. It is perhaps more important to understand why that response continued to make headway in this milieu when it didn't in many others, why the mobilisation here was 'sticky'.

On this, I would suggest that there are things about intellectual life and work that, if they don't actively produce feminism, at least weaken the defences of patriarchy. The drive for universality makes the claim to equality difficult to reject, once made. The special pleading involved in the defences of male supremacy is more or less transparent in a milieu where arguments are routinely tested for such things as special pleading. That is why Gilder, Goldberg and Co. haven't had very much credibility among intellectuals, however much men might *like* their arguments to be true. The defence of patriarchy in academia, therefore, has rested more on the plea of irrelevance (for instance, that there is no local injustice to be remedied because our university's selection procedures already allow well–qualified women in) than on the plea that inequality is justified (the main defence in popular literature), or on the attempt to ridicule reform (the main defence in journalism). Admittedly I have heard vigorous attempts to ridicule feminism among academics, too—usually among all–male groups of senior academics.

Finally, to the extent that resistance to feminism is bound up with the defence of hegemonic masculinity, male intellectuals have already sold the pass. Teaching, writing, playing instruments and so on are effeminate jobs, by general repute. ('Those who can, do; those who can't, teach.') They don't demand the confrontations with matter or with other men that manual work or management do. A more fragile masculinity could, in principle, lead to a more vehement reaction to threat. But on the whole the dynamics of masculinity are the reverse of that; it is hegemonic masculinity that is organised for struggle in the defence of male supremacy.

I don't mean to imply that the responses of intellectual men have been straightforward gain for women's liberation. The same milieu produced the curious phenomenon of the 'men's liberation movement', which started among radical men in the US about 1970. (For the following, see Carrigan, Connell and Lee, 1983). Interpreting women's liberation as a matter of women breaking out of their constraining sex–role, some concluded there was mileage in this for men too. They proceeded to set up men's consciousness–raising groups to help them confront their own sexism, get in touch with their own emotions, find the true self beneath the social shell. Within a few years of starting down this track, some men's liberationists were denying that there was anything special about the oppression of women; others were talking about ways to challenge 'discrimination against men', and how to enforce 'men's rights' against women through the courts. . . In short, what this turned into was a new liberal politics of heterosexual male supremacy, utterly at odds with the fragmentary 'men against sexism' groups and with gay liberation, let alone women's liberation.

This hardly scratches the surface of the sexual politics of intellectuals. The conditions of intellectuals' life and work have plainly also influenced the varieties of feminism that have emerged, a complicated problem in its own right. But it is perhaps enough to suggest the significance of the issue and the ways it is interwoven with other political threads, especially the tense and tangled relationship between intellectuals and the broader left.

That relationship is, I think, also implicated in the shift of fashion among radical intellectuals already noted. In a number of areas of radical thought there has been a turn in more or less the same direction within the last ten years. It was first signalled by the popularity of a linguistic version of psychoanalysis (via translations of Althusser's translation of Lacan's translation of Freud); then followed by the conversion of the theory of ideology into an analysis of discourses; a massive preoccupation with semiotics and its application to such enterprises as film criticism; a turn in feminist thought from analyses of practices of oppression and the mobilisation of resistance to discussions of language, discourse, speaking; and the sudden popularity of Foucault as a theorist rather than as a historian, and of the idea that discourse is itself power. (Foucault is a brilliant historian of ideas, an interesting historian of institutions, and a bad social theorist.)

I have mentioned the irony of such a fashion developing in the current political and economic circumstances. Perhaps there is a closer link. Its main practitioners have been the new left and feminists. For both groups the second half of the 1970s was a period of disillusion after the worldwide radical upsurge of 1965–75. In the second half of the 1970s it was increasingly clear that the masses weren't following. It was perhaps natural that a good many intellectuals should then discover that the masses weren't necessary, and that their own speciality—discourse—was at the heart of things.

Intellectuals' ability to talk to themselves is one of the conditions of intellectual work in general, one of the ways of distancing thought from the demands of immediate practice. But it also invites the intellectuals' primal political sin, which is talking only to themselves. The effect is not so much to radicalise or help other people as to exclude them, make them feel stupid and put down. Into the vacuum has stepped the eminently understandable simplicity of the new right, with its pseudo–radical messages of individual freedom and the oppressiveness of all state control.

Looking at the impasse reached by the women's movement, and the rightward drift in Labor politics, there are plainly a number of causes; but I do think one of them has been a default among radical intellectuals. There are a good many exceptions to this, of course, but there does seem to have been a quite widespread lack of concern with questions of mass relevance, questions of policy, mobilisation, everyday life.

This is particularly troubling because the very circumstances that have produced the current depression are also opening up new opportunities, directions for radical politics in which intellectuals would be centrally involved. The contracting labour market, and especially the sharply–contracting youth labour market, has placed new stress on credentials and redefined their significance. For twenty years or more a means by which working–class families could guarantee their shares of an expanding economic pie, the vastly expanded credentialling apparatus of secondary and tertiary education (TAFE and CAEs as well as universities) has suddenly changed its significance. It has rapidly become a means of defence, of exclusion, through which the heaviest costs of the depression are focussed on the least credentialled. Those without tickets have the highest rates of unemployment and the lowest wages.

This development is sharpening a contradiction that has long been present in education. For the business of credentialling—and that *is* the business of every teacher and academic in the system, whatever else they may do—is at odds with some basic features of intellectual work. Credentialling means that work has to be judged right or wrong, good or bad, 'A', 'B', or 'C', after a fixed period of time. To a psychometric mind, of course, that is merely a time–sample of the student's behaviour, and a more or less adequate indicator of the level of the trait (ability, attitude or whatever) being measured. Lots of teachers and academics do follow the logic of their institution so far, and come to believe that each student has a more or less fixed quantum of ability which they can infallibly detect. But so far as they believe that, they have abandoned intellectual method. When Habermas speaks of 'discursive redeemability', or Popper of refuting hypotheses, or Collingwood (1946) of the testing of evidence and inference, as keys to intellectual method, they are talking of processes that must go on until the job is done—until the statement is well and truly redeemed, the hypothesis properly refuted, the evidence fully tested. To cut this short by a time–limit is not just to cramp the process, it is to destroy its logic entirely. The process of credentialling fundamentally subverts what is supposedly being credentialled.

A second aspect of the contradiction has to do with the uses of credentials. Intellectual work is not necessarily radical, but it must always be subversive of authority in its own domain. There is nothing exotic about this, it is implicit in the very notion of intellectual *work*. If the answers to problems are settled by received authority, there is literally no intellectual work to be done. (There may be make–work, or a kind of brain–muscle–flexing, but there is not intellectual work. Intellectual work may of course need to manoeuvre around the question of authority by playing with the injunction to take it as given. Abelard's compendium of contradictions among the Fathers of the Church, *Sic et Non*, is the classic of a genre which is now flourishing again in the universities of Eastern Europe and among western marxists.) Now what teachers and academics are doing, in administering the credentialling system, is quite plainly constructing, operating and extending a new system of authority. We are shoring up a structure of power and privilege which is legitimated by our own claims to knowledge.

I've described these contradictions as they appear in my teaching, since that is how I came to be aware of them. I loathe the time when teaching turns into marking, and examiners' meetings loom out of the mist as the final goal of the academic year. It seems to be undoing everything I have tried to do in the courses up till then. But that isn't to suggest that university teaching is the main point where a politics of credentialling has significance. That point is, plainly enough, the semi—professions; and I think some of the turbulence now found there has to do with the contradictory character of the relationship to knowledge which they have to solve in their own practices.

Preaching what you hope to practice

When I wrote the final chapter of *Ruling Class, Ruling Culture* seven years ago, I thought that the main vulnerability of Australian capitalism was its structure of hegemony, and that intellectuals had a key part to play in contesting it. History hasn't been kind to that idea; the economy proceeded to collapse, while the hegemony of the ruling class held firm. I also thought, in a less articulate way, that intellectuals were in fact likely to challenge the prevailing power structure. On this point the verdict has been mixed. On the one hand the student movement has evaporated, the left has tied itself in knots, an intellectual right has flourished and won the ear of influential persons. On the other hand there are still a good number of radicals working in print and radio; and there are a few places in academia where, for the first time in Australian history, whole curricula have been built around radical perspectives in the social sciences.

What is clearer now is that, while there are preconditions of intellectual work that distance intellectuals from accepted realities and set them at odds with authority, there is nothing that guarantees the outcome will be *socially* radical. The point is ironically confirmed by the bizarre belief of new—right authors (see Ray, 1974, and Manne, 1982) that they are heroic outsiders battling a left—wing establishment. It seems the formulae of dissent are necessary even to the energetic defenders of inequality and the American Way...

Some large hopes died; or at least, their foliage had to be cut and dug in as compost for a different crop. The new husbandry requires steadier work and longer perspectives on time. Time (if we're granted it by Kremlin and Pentagon) to develop the positive side of practices that can be all too easily conceded to the opposition.

The circumstances of academic life, for instance, have led to many abuses, and are an immediate source of much that is abstruse, obscurantist, and irresponsible in radical theory. But that isn't to say that the idea of academic life, a retreat devoted to intellectual pursuits at the highest level, is a false one. What's wrong is that it is attached to social privilege, that it therefore has a corrupted notion of excellence as competitive achievement, and that it makes intellect itself a means of exclusion. Attach it rather to a programme of social equality, try to make it work in an inclusive, egalitarian way, and we have a powerful tool for the development and democratisation of culture.

Theoretical work is often useless; but it also has potentials, and high stakes. When we do get something right, it can illuminate a whole area of practice. It matters to progressive teachers whether theory tells them their puny efforts are doomed from the start, or helps them see the way towards changes that are actually in their power. It matters to activists in feminist campaigns what theory tells them about the nature of patriarchy, and what forces can be mobilised to shift it. It matters to activists in the labour movement whether theory tells them to go bald–headed for revolution, or that there are strategies that give practical gains now.

This is why I have been so much concerned, through the essays in this book, with the various ways social theorists—especially those of a progressive cast of mind—get things wrong. There is a whole ocean of error and a few islands of truth, and neither chart nor compass to go by. We build up the map by accumulating shipwrecks . . .

Of all the magnificent variety of ways to go wrong, the one that is most seductive for the left, and most destructive in the long run, is theoretical dogmatism. There is an endless temptation, when confronting power structures and trying to mobilise people who by definition tend to be powerless and poor, to seize on and solidify a dogma. It can be a genuine shield against cooptation, a means of guaranteeing at least a verbal militancy. It also can become a talisman, a magical guarantee that right will triumph in the end if only one keeps the faith and rejects all modifications and alternatives. That happened with marxism, and is one of the reasons why most serious socialist thought now goes on outside the marxist framework; I am afraid it is now happening with some kinds of feminism too.

The worst thing about theoretical dogmatism is the way it becomes a means of separation. Fashions, factions, and cliques are good fun in a way, can even be a sign of life. But they are also a main way in which academic radicals turn inwards and cut themselves off from the active relation with intellectual workers in other milieux, such as the semi–professions and journalism, that is a crucial testing–ground of their work. Perhaps more important, it serves the other way round as a mechanism of exclusion, defining the masses, at best, as brethren in error, and drawing a hard line around those who possess the true doctrine.

It has long seemed to me that dogmatic and exclusive theory is the kiss of death for a movement that claims to be democratic, radical, participatory. The essence of contemporary radicalisms is participation—mainly as a practice, but also as an idea. It was the notion of participatory democracy that defined the new left; a network of self–managing groups have constructed and sustained women's liberation; programmes of worker control have defined the growing edge of the labour movement. I learnt about it through campaigns for student participation in higher education in the 1960s, and most of all through the practical attempt to create a collectively–controlled learning process in the Free University in Sydney; it still seems to me what is vital in progressive education. There is no way an elitist practice of theory can serve such movements.

One of the crucial points about participation is that it uncompromisingly demands equality. Trying to define socialism a few years ago in the pamphlet *Socialism and Labor*, I listed 'social equality' and 'direct democracy' among the five key ideas. I'd now want to stress how close these ideas are when we get to the level of practice. Equality without a practice of participation remains a myth; participation without equality is endlessly vulnerable to corruption. The stresses this relation can produce are no doubt familiar to everyone who has tried to work democratically in a hierarchical institution, from a university to a paint shop.

To get a participatory intellectual life, then, demands a steady struggle against the inequalities of power and wealth that surround us. This essay has dwelt on what goes wrong among progressive intellectuals, but I don't for a moment suggest this is the main obstacle. It is inequality itself, the whole massive machinery by which some humans treat other humans as dirt, that stands in the way of a genuinely open and genuinely popular intellectual life.

In the long run, that must grow into something rich and strange. A really participatory culture has not yet existed. We have some idea of the kind of intellectual, artistic and moral ferment and flowering that occurs in periods of social upheaval, such as happened in Europe in 1915-1925 and in the advanced capitalist countries in 1965-1975. We don't have very much idea of what it would be like to live in a settled, unthreatened, and radically democratic society.

It isn't really possible, then, to plan intellectual work in anything but the limited and technical sense in which research institutes do. We never really know what approach is going to bear fruit. All we do know is that, while the conditions of intellectual work create the possibility of going very wrong, they also create the possibility of going very right. We do, sometimes, manage to understand something that had been misunderstood before.

That may sound a small ambition. I think it is a large one. The growth of understanding is one of the few forces that can be pitted against the global disaster that lunatic development and an even more lunatic arms race are storing up for us. It is also a means of contesting the plenitude of small disasters with which the structures of power and oppression fill our lives.

It seems most important to work on understanding the main structures of power, which I take to be world capitalism and world patriarchy. It matters that we get them the right way up in our minds; and that is what intellectuals are for. Overturning them in practice requires much greater social forces. In that business intellectuals will have a part. It will be a helpful one only so far as they are willing to listen and learn as well as plan and advise.

References

Poems

The full texts of the poems quoted can be found in the following sources.

Archpoet, 'Confessio' in H. Waddell ed. *Mediaeval Latin Lyrics* Harmondsworth: Penguin, 1952, pp.182–95
J. Donne, 'Elegie XIX: Going to Bed' in *Poetical Works* Oxford: Oxford University Press, 1933, pp.106–8
——'The second Anniversarie' *ibid*. pp.227–42
W.S. Rendra, 'Song of a Family Photograph' in *State of Emergency* Sydney: Wild and Woolley, 1980, pp.42–51
——'Song of the Condors' *ibid*. pp.58–61
W. Shakespeare, Jacques' speech from *As You Like It* Act II, Scene 7
W.B. Yeats, 'Byzantium' in *Collected Poems* 2nd edn London: Macmillan 1950, pp.280–81
——'Whence Had They Come?' *ibid*. p.332
——'The Circus Animals' Desertion' *ibid*. pp.391–92

General references

Abelard, P. (1978 [c.1115]) *Sic et Non* Chicago: University of Chicago Press
Althusser, L. (1969) *For Marx* London: Allen Lane
——(1971) *Lenin and Philosophy* London: New Left Books
——(1976) *Essays in Self-Criticism* London: New Left Books
Althusser, L. and Balibar, E. (1970) *Reading Capital* London: New Left Books
Amin, S. (1974) *Accumulation on a World Scale: A critique of the theory of underdevelopment* 2 vol, New York: Monthly Review Press
——(1980) *Class and Nation* New York: Monthly Review Press
Andreski, S. (1964) *The Elements of Comparative Sociology* London: Weidenfeld and Nicolson
Arnold, M. (1869) *Culture and Anarchy* Vol.5 in *Complete Prose Works* Ann Arbor: University of Michigan Press
Aronson, R. (1978) 'The individualist social theory of Jean-Paul Sartre' in New Left Review ed. *Western Marxism, a Critical Reader* London: Verso
Arrighi, G., Hopkins, T.K. and Wallerstein, I., (1982) 'Re-thinking the concepts of class and status-group in a world-system perspective', paper prepared for Fourth International Colloquium on the World-Economy, New Delhi.

Austin, J.L. (1961) *Philosophical Papers* Oxford: Clarendon Press

Babeuf, G. (1796) 'Manifesto of the equals' in J.H. Stewart (1951) *A Documentary Survey of the French Revolution* New York: Macmillan, pp.656–7

Bales, R.F. and Slater, P.E. (1955) 'Role differentiation in small decision–making groups' in T. Parsons and R.F. Bales *Family, Socialization and Interaction Process* Glencoe: Free Press, pp.259–306

Balibar, E. (1970) 'On the basic concepts of historical materialism' in L. Althusser and E. Balibar *Reading Capital* London: New Left Books, pp.199–308

Barrett, M. (1980) *Women's Oppression Today* London: Verso

Barrett, M. and McIntosh, M. (1979) 'Christine Delphy: Towards a materialist feminism?' *Feminist Review* 1, pp.95–106

Bauman, Z. (1969) 'Modern times, modern marxism' in P. Berger ed. *Marxism and Sociology* New York: Appleton–Century–Crofts, pp.1–17

Beauvoir, S. de (1972 [1949]) *The Second Sex* Harmondsworth: Penguin

Beechey, V. (1979) 'On patriarchy' *Feminist Review* 3, pp.66–82

Bem, D.J. and Allen, A. (1974) 'On predicting some of the people some of the time: the search for cross–situational consistencies in behavior' *Psychological Review* 81, pp.506–20

Berger, J. (1972) *Ways of Seeing* Harmondsworth: Penguin

Bernstein, B. (1971) *Class, Codes and Control* London: Routledge and Kegan Paul

Berry, D. (1974) *Central Ideas in Sociology* London: Constable

Biddle, B.J. and Thomas, E.J. (1966) *Role Theory: Concepts and research* New York: Wiley

Bishop, P. (1973) 'Values and legitimation in professionalism—the primacy of status' *Australian and New Zealand Journal of Sociology* 9, 3, pp.37–41

Blau, P.M. (1964) *Exchange and Power in Social Life* New York: Wiley

Blau, P.M. and Duncan, O.D. (1967) *The American Occupational Structure* New York: Wiley

Blume, F. (1950) *Two Centuries of Bach: An account of changing taste* London: Oxford University Press

——(1963) 'Outlines of a new picture of Bach' *Music and Letters* 44, pp.214–27

Boudon, R. (1974) *Education, Opportunity and Social Inequality* New York: Wiley

Bourdieu, P. (1977) *Outline of a Theory of Practice* Cambridge: Cambridge University Press

Bourdieu, P. and Passeron, J.C. (1977) *Reproduction in Education, Society and Culture* London: Sage

Bowlby, J. (1953) *Child Care and the Growth of Love* Harmondsworth: Penguin

Bowles, S. and Gintis, H. (1976) *Schooling in Capitalist America: Educational reform and the contradictions of economic life* London: Routledge and Kegan Paul

Braverman, H. (1974) *Labor and Monopoly Capital: The degradation of work in the twentieth century* New York: Monthly Review Press

Brim, O.G. (1960) 'Personality development as role–learning' in I. Iscoe and

H.W. Stevenson eds *Personality Development in Children* Austin: University of Texas Press, pp.127–59

——(1966) 'Socialization through the life cycle' in O.G. Brim and S. Wheeler *Socialization After Childhood* New York: Wiley, pp.1–49

Broom, L. and Jones, F.L. (1976) *Opportunity and Attainment in Australia* Canberra: Australian National University Press

Burgmann, M. (1980) 'Revolution and machismo' in E. Windschuttle ed. *Women, Class and History* Fontana [no place] pp.453–91

Callinicos, A. (1976) *Althusser's Marxism* London: Pluto

Campioni, M. (1976) 'Psychoanalysis and marxist feminism' *Working Papers in Sex, Science and Culture* 1, 2, pp.33–59

Carchedi, G. (1977) *On the Economic Identification of Social Classes* London: Routledge and Kegan Paul

Cardan, P. (1972) *The Meaning of Socialism* London: Solidarity Pamphlets

Carrell, N. (1967) *Bach the Borrower* London: Allen and Unwin

Carrigan, T., Connell, R.W., and Lee, J. (1983) Hard and Heavy Phenomena: The Sociology of Masculinity, unpublished paper

Carter, A. (1979) *The Sadeian Woman: An exercise in cultural history* London: Virago

Castles, S. and Kosack, G. (1973) *Immigrant Workers and Class Structure in Western Europe* London: Oxford University Press

Centre for Contemporary Cultural Studies—see also Clarke *et al.*, Hall and Jefferson; Willis

Centre for Contemporary Cultural Studies, Women's Studies Group (1978) *Women Take Issue* London: Hutchinson

Cheshire Cat, 'Gender rules O.K.?' *Humpty Dumpty* (Child Care Issue) 9, pp.21–3

Chesler, P. (1973) *Women and Madness* New York: Avon

Chiapusso, J. (1968) *Bach's World* Bloomington: Indiana University Press

Childe, V.G. (1954) *What Happened in History* rev. edn, Harmondsworth: Penguin

Chodorow, N. (1974) 'Family structure and feminine personality' in M. Rosaldo and L. Lamphere eds *Women, Culture, and Society* Stanford: Standford University Press, pp.43–66

Chomsky, N. (1957) *Syntactic Structures* The Hague: Mouton

——(1959) 'Review of B.F. Skinner "Verbal Behavior"' *Language* 35, pp.26–58

——(1965) *Aspects of the Theory of Syntax* Cambridge, Massachusetts: Massachusetts Institute of Technology Press

——(1976) *Reflections on Language* Fontana [no place]

Clarke, J., Critcher, C. and Johnson, R. eds (1979) *Working Class Culture* London: Hutchinson

Clarke, S. (1977) 'Marxism, sociology and Poulantzas' theory of the state' *Capital and Class* 2, pp.1–31

Claudin, F. (1975) *The Communist Movement: From Comintern to Cominform* Harmondsworth: Penguin

Cleaver, E. (1968) *Soul on Ice* New York: Dell

Collingwood, R.G. (1946) *The Idea of History* Oxford: Oxford University Press

Connell, R.W. (1978) *Socialism and Labor* Sydney: Labor Praxis Publications
Connell, R.W. and Irving, T.H. (1980) *Class Structure in Australian History* Melbourne: Longman Cheshire
Connell, R.W., Ashenden, D., Kessler, S. and Dowsett, G. (1982) *Making the Difference* Sydney: Allen and Unwin
Cooper, D. ed. (1968) *Dialectics of Liberation* Harmondsworth: Penguin
——(1971) *Death of the Family* London: Allen Lane
Coulson, M.A. (1972) 'Role: A redundant concept in sociology? Some educational considerations' in J.A. Jackson ed. *Role* Cambridge: Cambridge University Press, pp.107–28
Dahrendorf, R. (1959) *Class and Class Conflict in Industrial Society* rev. edn, Stanford: Stanford University Press
——(1973) *Homo Sociologicus* London: Routledge and Kegan Paul
David, H.T. and Mendel, A. eds (1966) *The Bach Reader* rev. edn, London: Dent
Davies, A. (1967) *Images of Class* Sydney: Sydney University Press
Davis, E.G. (1971) *The First Sex* New York: Putnam
Davis, K. and Moore, W.E. (1945) 'Some principles of stratification' *American Sociological Review* 10, 2, pp.242–9
Delphy, C. (1977) *The Main Enemy: A materialist analysis of women's oppression* London: Women's Research and Resources Centre
Desan, W. (1974) *The Marxism of Jean-Paul Sartre* Gloucester, Massachusetts: Peter Smith
Dews, P. (1979) 'The Nouvelle Philosophie and Foucault' *Economy and Society* 8, 2, pp.127–71
Dolgoff, S. ed. (1971) *Bakunin on Anarchy* New York: Knopf
Dos Santos, T. (1970) 'The concept of social classes' *Science and Society* 43, pp.166–93
Ehrenreich, B. (1977) 'Toward socialist feminism' *Heresies* 1, pp.4–7
Ehrenreich, B. and English, D. (1979) *For Her Own Good* London: Pluto
Eipper, C. (1980) The Bantry Bay Example: The Advance of Capitalism in County Cork, Ireland, Ph.D. thesis, Anthropology Department, Sydney University
Eisenstein, Z.R. (1979) *Capitalist Patriarchy and the Case for Socialist Feminism* New York: Monthly Review Press
Ellis, H. (1936 [1897]) *Sexual Inversion*, vol. 2 of *Studies in the Psychology of Sex* New York: Random House
Encel, S. (1970) *Equality and Authority* Melbourne: Longman Cheshire
Engels, F. (1970 [1884]) 'The origin of the family, private property and the state' in K. Marx and F. Engels *Selected Works* vol 3 Moscow: Progress Publishers
Evans, G. and Reeves, J. (1982) *Labor Essays 1982* Richmond, Victoria: Drummond
Fejtö, F. (1974) *A History of the People's Democracies* Harmondsworth: Penguin
Fenwick, P., Novitz, R. and Waghorne, M. (1977) 'Introduction to symposium on sex–roles and sexuality' *Australian and New Zealand Journal of Sociology* 13, pp.116–18

Firestone, S. (1972) *The Dialectic of Sex: The case for feminist revolution* London: Paladin

Ford, J. (1969) *Social Class and the Comprehensive School* London: Routledge and Kegan Paul

Foreman, A. (1977) *Femininity as Alienation: Women and the family in marxism and psychoanalysis* London: Pluto Press

Foster, J. (1974) *Class Struggle and the Industrial Revolution* London: Weidenfeld and Nicolson

Foucault, M. (1977) *Discipline and Punish* London: Allen Lane

——(1980) *Power–Knowledge* Brighton: Harvester

Franzway, S. and Lowe, J. (1978) 'Sex role theory, political cul-de-sac?' *Refractory Girl* 16, pp. 14–16.

Freud, S. (1899) 'The interpretation of dreams' *Standard Edition of the Complete Psychological Works* vols 4–5 London: Hogarth

——(1905a) 'Fragment of an analysis of a case of hysteria' *Standard Edition of the Complete Psychological Works* vol 7 London: Hogarth, pp.1–122

——(1905b) 'Three essays on the theory of sexuality' *Standard Edition of the Complete Psychological Works* vol 7 London: Hogarth, pp.123–243

——(1908) '"Civilized" sexual morality and modern nervous illness' *Standard Edition of the Complete Psychological Works* vol 9 London: Hogarth, pp.177–204.

——(1909a) 'Some general remarks on hysterical attacks' *Standard Edition of the Complete Psychological Works* vol 9 London: Hogarth, pp.229–34

——(1909b) 'Analysis of a phobia in a five–year–old boy' *Standard Edition of the Complete Psychological Works* vol 10 London: Hogarth, pp.1–149

——(1909c) 'Notes upon a case of obsessional neurosis' *Standard Edition of the Complete Psychological Works* vol 10 London: Hogarth, pp.151–249

——(1913) 'Totem and taboo' *Standard Edition of the Complete Psychological Works* vol 13 London: Hogarth, pp.1–161

——(1915a) 'Papers on metapsychology' *Standard Edition of the Complete Psychological Works* vol 14 London: Hogarth, pp.103–258

——(1915b) 'Thoughts for the times on war and death' *Standard Edition of the Complete Psychological Works* vol 14 London: Hogarth, pp.273–300

——(1918) 'From the history of an infantile neurosis' *Standard Edition of the Complete Psychological Works* vol 17 London: Hogarth, pp.1–122

——(1921) 'Group psychology and the analysis of the ego' *Standard Edition of the Complete Psychological Works* vol 18 London: Hogarth, pp.65–143

——(1927) 'The future of an illusion' *Standard Edition of the Complete Psychological Works* vol 21 London: Hogarth, pp.1–56

——(1930) 'Civilization and its discontents' *Standard Edition of the Complete Psychological Works* vol 21 London: Hogarth pp.57–145

Friedan, B. (1965) *The Feminine Mystique* Harmondsworth: Penguin

Fromm, E. (1942) *The Fear of Freedom* London: Routledge and Kegan Paul

Galbraith, J.K. (1967) *The New Industrial State* Boston: Houghton Mifflin

Gamarnikow, E. (1978) 'Sexual division of labour: The case of nursing' in A. Kuhn and A. Wolpe eds *Feminism and Materialism* London: Routledge and Kegan Paul, pp.96–123

Game, A. and Pringle, R. (1979) 'Sexuality and the suburban dream'

Australian and New Zealand Journal of Sociology 15, 2, pp.4–15

——(1983) *Gender at Work* Sydney: Allen and Unwin

Gardiner, M. ed. (1971) *The Wolf–Man, By the Wolf–Man* New York: Basic Books

Geiringer, K. (1967) *Johann Sebastian Bach: The culmination of an era* London: Allen and Unwin

Giddens, A. (1973) *The Class Structure of the Advanced Societies* London: Hutchinson

——(1976) *New Rules of Sociological Method* London: Hutchinson

——(1979) *Central Problems in Social Theory: Action, structure and contradiction in social analysis* London: Macmillan

Gilder G. (1975) *Sexual Suicide* New York: Bantam

Gimenez, M.E. (1978) 'Structuralist marxism on "the woman question"' *Science and Society* 42, 3, pp.301–23

Glasser, W. (1965) *Reality Therapy* New York: Harper

Goebbels, J. (1948) in L.P. Lochner ed. *The Goebbels Diaries* London: Hamilton

Goffman, E. (1971) *Relations in Public* New York: Basic Books

——(1972) *Encounters* Harmondsworth: Penguin

Goldberg, S. (1973) *The Inevitability of Patriarchy* New York: William Morrow

Goldman, E. (1972a) 'Marriage and love' *Red Emma Speaks* New York: Vintage, pp.158–67

——(1972b) 'The traffic in women' *Red Emma Speaks* New York: Vintage, pp.143–57

Goldmann, L. (1964) *The Hidden God* London: Routledge and Kegan Paul

Goldthorpe, J.H. and Hope, K. (1974) *The Social Grading of Occupations: A new approach and scale*, Oxford Studies in Social Mobility, London: Oxford University Press

Good, K. (1976) 'Settler colonialism: economic development and class formation' *Journal of Modern African Studies* 14, pp.597–620

——(1979) 'The class structure' in A. Amarshi, K. Good and R. Mortimer *Development and Dependency: The political economy of Papua New Guinea* Melbourne: Oxford University Press, pp.97–160

Gorz, A. (1967) *Strategy for Labor: A radical proposal* Boston: Beacon Press

Gouldner, A.W. (1971) *The Coming Crisis of Western Sociology* London: Heinemann

——(1979) *The Future of Intellectuals and the Rise of the New Class* New York: Seabury Press

Gramsci, A. (1971) 'The intellectuals' in *Selections from the Prison Notebooks* London: Lawrence and Wishart, pp.5–23

Greenbaum, J. (1976) 'Division of labor in the computer field' *Monthly Review* 28, 3, pp.40–55

Greer, G. (1971) *The Female Eunuch* London: Paladin

Gross, N., Mason, W.S. and McEachern, A.W. (1958) *Explorations in Role Analysis* New York: Wiley

Gutman, H.G. (1976) *Work, Culture and Society in Industrializing America* New York: Knopf

Habermas, J. (1971) *Toward a Rational Society* London: Heinemann
——(1976) *Legitimation Crisis* London: Heinemann
——(1979) *Communication and the Evolution of Society* London: Heinemann
Hall, S. and Jefferson, T. eds (1976) *Resistance Through Rituals: Youth subcultures in post-war Britain* London: Hutchinson and Centre for Contemporary Cultural Studies
Harris, K. (1982) *Teachers and Classes* London: Routledge and Kegan Paul
Hartley, R.E. (1964) 'A developmental view of female sex-role definition and identification' *Merrill-Palmer Quarterly* 10, pp.3–16
Hartmann, H.I. (1979) 'The unhappy marriage of marxism and feminism: Towards a more progressive union' *Capital and Class* 8, pp.1–33
Hartsock, N. (1979) 'Feminist theory and the development of revolutionary strategy' in Z.R. Eisenstein *Capitalist Patriarchy* New York: Monthly Review Press, pp.56–77
Harvey, D. (1975) *Social Justice and the City* Melbourne: Edward Arnold
Hindess, B. (1971) *The Decline of Working-class Politics* London: Paladin
Hindess, B. and Hirst, P.Q. (1975) *Pre-capitalist Modes of Production* London: Routledge and Kegan Paul
Hirst, P.Q. (1977) 'Economic classes and politics' in A. Hunt ed. *Class and Class Structure* London: Lawrence and Wishart, pp.125–54
Hoggart, R. (1958) *The Uses of Literacy* Harmondsworth: Penguin
Hornadge, B. (1971) *Chidley's Answer to the Sex Problem* Sydney: Review Publications
Hudson, L. (1972) *The Cult of the Fact* London: Cape
Hunt, A. ed. (1977a) *Class and Class Structure* London: Lawrence and Wishart
——(1977b) 'Theory and politics in the identification of the working class' in A. Hunt ed. *Class and Class Structure* London: Lawrence and Wishart, pp.81–111
Hunt, P. (1978) 'Cash-transactions and household tasks: Domestic behaviour in relation to industrial employment' *Sociological Review* 26, 3, pp.555–71
Ibsen, H. (1900 [1879]) *A Doll's House* London: Scott
'Il Manifesto' group (1972) 'Technicians and the capitalist division of labour' *Socialist Revolution* 9, pp.65–84
Industrial Workers of the World (1955) *Songs of the Workers* Chicago
Inkeles, A. and Levinson, D.J. (1969) 'National character: The study of modal personality and sociocultural systems' in G. Lindzey and E. Aronson eds *Handbook of Social Psychology* vol 4 2nd edn Reading, Massachusetts: Addison-Wesley, pp.418–506
Janeway, E. (1971) *Man's World, Woman's Place* New York: Dell
Jencks, C. ed. (1972) *Inequality* New York: Basic Books
Johnson, V. (1981) *The Last Resort* Ringwood: Penguin
Jones, E. (1954-7) *Sigmund Freud, Life and Work* vols 1, 2, 3 London: Hogarth
Jungk, R. (1979) *The Nuclear State* London: Calder
Kando, T.M. (1977) *Social Interaction* Saint Louis: Mosby
Kimmel, D.C. (1974) *Adulthood and Ageing* New York: Wiley
Keller, S. (1963) *Beyond the Ruling Class* New York: Random House
Kessler, S., Ashenden, D., Connell, R.W. and Dowsett, G. (1982) *Ockers*

and Discomaniacs Sydney: Inner City Education Centre
Kimmel, D.C. (1974) *Adulthood and Ageing* New York: Wiley
Kinsey, A.C. Pomeroy, W.B. and Martin, C.E. (1948) *Sexual Behavior in the Human Male* Philadelphia: Saunders
Klima, B. (1962) 'The first ground–plan of an upper palaeolithic loess settlement in middle Europe and its meaning' in R.J. Braidwood and G.R. Willey eds *Courses Toward Urban Life* Edinburgh: Edinburgh University Press, pp.193–210
Koestler, A. (1954) *The Invisible Writing* London: Collins
Kollontai, A.M. (1977) *Selected Writings* London: Allison and Busby
Komarovsky, M. (1973) 'Presidential address: Some problems in role analysis' *American Sociological Review* 38, pp.649–62
Konrád, G. and Szelényi, I. (1979) *The Intellectuals on the Road to Class Power* Brighton: Harvester
Korda, M. (1974) *Male Chauvinism: How it works at home and in the office* London: Hodder and Stoughton
Krafft–Ebing, R. von (1965 [1886]) *Psychopathia Sexualis* 12th edn New York: Paperback Library
Krauss, I. (1967) 'Some perspectives on social stratification and social class' *Sociological Review* 15, pp.129–140
Kropotkin, P. (1914) *Mutual Aid* Boston: Extending Horizons Books
Kuhn A. and Wolpe, A. (1978) *Feminism and Materialism: Women and modes of production* London: Routledge and Kegan Paul
Kuhn, T.S. (1970) *The Structure of Scientific Revolutions* 2nd edn Chicago: University of Chicago Press
Laclau, E. (1975) 'The specificity of the political: The Poulantzas–Miliband debate' *Economy and Society* 4, pp.87–110
Laing, R.D. (1960) *The Divided Self* London: Tavistock
——(1967) *The Politics of Experience* Harmondsworth: Penguin
Laing, R.D. and Cooper, D.G. (1964) *Reason and Violence* London: Tavistock
Lang, T. (1971) *The Difference Between a Man and a Woman* New York: John Day
Lazarsfeld, P.F., Berelson, B. and Gaudet, H. (1944) *The People's Choice* New York: Duell, Sloan and Pearce
Laplanche, J. and Pontalis, J.-B. (1973) *The Language of Psychoanalysis* New York: Norton
Lefebvre, H. (1946) *Introduction à la critique de la vie quotidienne* vol I Paris: l'Arche
——(1971) *Everyday Life in the Modern World* London: Allen Lane
——(1976) *The Survival of Capitalism: Reproduction of the relations of production* London: Allison and Busby
Lenski, G.E. (1966) *Power and Privilege* New York: McGraw–Hill
Light, D.J. and Keller, S. (1975) *Sociology* New York: Knopf
Linton, R. (1934) *The Study of Man* New York: Appleton–Century–Crofts
Lippert, J. (1977) 'Sexuality as consumption' in J. Snodgrass ed. *For Men Against Sexism* Albion: Times Change Press, pp.207–13
Lloyd, P. (1982) *A Third World Proletariat?* London: Allen and Unwin

Macciocchi, M.A. (1979) 'Female sexuality in fascist ideology' *Feminist Review* 1, pp.67–82

McDonough, R. and Harrison, R. (1978) 'Patriarchy and relations of production' in A. Kuhn and A. Wolpe *Feminism and Materialism* London: Routledge and Kegan Paul, pp.11–41

McIntosh, M. (1978) 'The state and the oppression of women' in A. Kuhn and A. Wolpe *Feminism and Materialism* London: Routledge and Kegan Paul, pp.254–89

McRobbie, A. (1978) 'Working–class girls and the culture of femininity' in Centre for Contemporary Cultural Studies, Women's Studies Group *Women Take Issue* London: Hutchinson, pp.96–108

Mallet, S. (1975) *The New Working Class* Nottingham: Spokesman Books

Manne, R. (1982) *The New Conservatism in Australia* Melbourne: Oxford University Press

Marcuse, H. (1955) *Eros and Civilisation* Boston: Beacon Press

——(1964) *One Dimensional Man* London: Routledge and Kegan Paul

——(1969) 'Repressive tolerance' in R.P. Woolf, B. Moore Jr and H. Marcuse *A Critique of Pure Tolerance* London: Cape

——(1972a) *An Essay on Liberation* Harmondsworth: Penguin

——(1972b) *Counterrevolution and Revolt* London: Allen Lane

Marx, K. (1852) 'The eighteenth Brumaire of Louis Bonaparte' reprinted in Marx–Engels *Selected Works* vol 1 Moscow: Progress Publishers

Marx, K. (1867–94) *Capital* vol 1, 2, 3, various edn (references therefore given by chapter)

Mead, G.H. (1934) in C.W. Morris ed. *Mind, Self and Society, from the Standpoint of a Social Behaviorist* Chicago: University of Chicago Press

Meillassoux, C. (1975) *Femmes, Greniers et Capitaux* Paris: Maspero

Merton, R.K. (1957) *Social Theory and Social Structure* rev. edn, Glencoe, Illinois: Free Press

Mill, J.S. (1912 [1869]) 'The subjection of women' in *Three Essays* World's Classics Series, London: Oxford University Press

Millett, K. (1972) *Sexual Politics* London: Abacus

Miner, J.B. (1971) *Management Theory* New York: Macmillan

Mitchell, J. (1971) *Woman's Estate* Harmondsworth: Penguin

——(1975) *Psychoanalysis and Feminism* New York: Vintage Books

Molyneux, M. (1979) 'Beyond the domestic labour debate' *New Left Review* 116, pp.3–27

Morris, B. (1971) 'Reflections on role analysis' *British Journal of Sociology* 22, pp.395–409

Nadel, S. (1957) *The Theory of Social Structure* Melbourne: Melbourne University Press

Negri, A. (1974) *Crisi dello Stato-piano: Comunismo e organizzazione rivoluzionaria* Milano: Feltrinelli

——(1977) *La forma stato. Per la critica dell'economia politica della Costituzione* Milano: Feltrinelli

——(1978) *Il dominio e il sabotaggio. Sul metodo marxista della trasformazione sociale* Milano: Feltrinelli

Norman, J. (1978) *Slave Girl of Gor* London: Universal

Oakley, A. (1972) *Sex, Gender and Society* London: Temple Smith

Osborn, R. (1937) *Freud and Marx, A Dialectical Study* London: Gollancz

Ossowski, S. (1963) *Class Structure in the Social Consciousness* London: Routledge and Kegan Paul

Owen, R. (1927 [1813]) *A New View of Society and Other Writings* London: Everyman

Paine, T. (1915 [1791]) *The Rights of Man* London: Dent

Parkin, F. (1972) *Class Inequality and Political Order* St Albans: Paladin

Parsons, T. (1951) *The Social System* Glencoe: Free Press

——(1954) 'A revised analytical approach to the theory of social stratification' in *Essays in Sociological Theory* Glencoe: Free Press, pp.386–439

Parsons, T., Bales, R.F. and Shils. E.A. eds (1953) *Working Papers in the Theory of Action* Glencoe: Free Press

Parsons, T. and Shils, E.A. eds (1951) *Toward a General Theory of Action* Cambridge, Massachusetts: Harvard University Press

Pearson, K. (1937) *The Grammar of Science* London: Dent

Pericot, L. (1962) 'The social life of Spanish palaeolithic hunters as shown by Levantine art' in S.L. Washburn ed. *Social Life of Early Man* London: Methuen pp.194–213

Pfohl, S.J. (1975) 'Social role analysis: The ethnomethodological critique' *Sociology and Social Research* 59, pp.243–66

Piaget, J. (1971a) *Biology and Knowledge* Edinburgh: Edinburgh University Press

——(1971b) *Structuralism* London: Routledge and Kegan Paul

Pickvance, G.C. ed. (1976a) *Urban Sociology* London: Tavistock

——(1976b) 'On the study of urban social movements' in G.C. Pickvance ed. *Urban Sociology* London: Tavistock, pp.198–218

Piercy, M. (1970) 'The Grand Coolie Damn' in R. Morgan ed. *Sisterhood is Powerful* New York: Vintage, pp.421–38

Plummer, K. ed. (1981) *The Making of the Modern Homosexual* London: Hutchinson

Plunkett, M. (1981) 'ASIO's annual report: Australian spooks trail unemployed and Chinese' *National Times* 28 June

Polanyi, M. (1958) *Personal Knowledge* London: Routledge and Kegan Paul

Popitz, H. (1972) 'The concept of social role as an element of sociological theory' in J.A. Jackson ed. *Role* Cambridge: Cambridge University Press, pp.11–39

Popper, K. (1965) *The Logic of Scientific Discovery* 2nd rev. edn New York: Harper

Poster, M. (1979) *Sartre's Marxism* London: Pluto

Poulantzas, N. (1969) 'The problem of the capitalist state' *New Left Review* 58, pp.67–78

——(1973) *Political Power and Social Classes* London: New Left Books and Sheen and Ward

——(1974) *Fascism and Dictatorship* London: New Left Books

——(1975) *Classes in Contemporary Capitalism* London: New Left Books

——(1977) 'The new petty bourgeoisie' in A. Hunt ed. *Class and Class Structure* London: Lawrence and Wishart, pp.113–24

Ram, K. (1981) The Indian Working Class: Critical Issues in the Study of Class Formation in the Third World, MA Hons thesis, Sociology, Macquarie University

Rapoport, R. and Rosow, I. (1966) 'An approach to family relationships and role performance' in Biddle and Thomas *Role Theory: Concepts and research* New York Wiley: pp.231-36

Ray, J.J. (1974) *Conservatism as Heresy* Sydney: Australia and New Zealand Books

Reich, W. (1949) *Character Analysis* New York: Farrar Strauss and Giroux

Reiche, R. (1970) *Sexuality and Class Struggle* London: New Left Books

Reik, T. (1948) *Listening with the Third Ear* New York: Farrar Strauss and Giroux

Reiter, R.R. (1977) 'The search for origins: Unravelling the strands of gender hierarchy' *Critique of Anthropology* 9/10, pp.5-24

Rieff, P. (1963) 'Introduction' in S. Freud *Dora* New York: Collier

Riesman, D. (1950) *The Lonely Crowd* New Haven: Yale University Press

Riesman, D. and Glazer, N. (1952) *Faces in the Crowd: Individual studies in character and politics* New Haven: Yale University Press

Ritchie, J., Villiger, J. and Duignan, P. (1977) 'Sex role differentiation in children: A preliminary investigation' *Australian and New Zealand Journal of Sociology* 13, pp.142-45

Rohde, S. (1979) *A Private View of L.S. Lowry* London: Collins

Rokossovsky, K.K. (1968) quoted in H.E. Salisbury (1971) ed. *Marshal Zhukov's Greatest Battles* London: Sphere, p194n

Rousseau, J.-J. (1968 [1762]) *The Social Contract* Harmondsworth: Penguin

Rowbotham, S. (1973) *Woman's Consciousness, Man's World* Harmondsworth: Penguin

Rowbotham, S., Segal, L. and Wainwright, H. (1979) *Beyond the Fragments* Newcastle: Newcastle Socialist Centre and Islington Community Press

Rowbotham, S. and Weeks, J. (1977) *Socialism and the New Life* London: Pluto

Rowland, R. (1977) 'Australian data on the attitude towards women scale: Norms, sex differences, reliability' *Australian Psychologist* 12, pp.327-31

Rubin, G. (1975) 'The traffic in women: Notes on the "political economy" of sex' in R.R. Reiter ed. *Toward an Anthropology of Women* New York: Monthly Review, pp.157-210

Runciman, W.G. (1968) 'Class, status and power?' in J.A. Jackson ed. *Social Stratification* London: Cambridge University Press, pp.25-61

Russell, B. (1935) *In Praise of Idleness* London: Allen and Unwin

Russell, G., Antill, J. and Cunningham, J. (1975) 'The measurement of masculinity, femininity and androgyny: A reply to Rowland' (1977) *Australian Psychologist* 13, pp.41-50

Ryan, M.P. (1979) 'Femininity and capitalism in antebellum America' in Z. Eisenstein *Capitalist Patriarchy* New York: Monthly Review Press, pp.151-68

Sade, Marquis de (1966 [1791]) *Justine ... and Other Writings* New York: Grove

——(1976 [1797]) *Juliette* New York: Grove Press

Sahlins, M. (1972) *Stone Age Economics* Chicago: Aldine–Atherton
Sampson, A. (1974) *The Sovereign State: The secret history of ITT* London: Coronet
Sandercock, L. and Turner, I. (1982) *Up Where, Cazaly?* Sydney: Granada
Sarbin, T.R. (1954) 'Role theory' in G. Lindzey ed. *Handbook of Social Psychology* vol. 1 Reading: Addison–Wesley pp.223–58
Sarbin, T.R. and Allen, V.L. (1968) 'Role theory' in G. Lindzey and E. Aronson eds *Handbook of Social Psychology* 2nd edn vol. 1 Reading: Addison–Wesley, pp.488–567
Sartre, J.–P. (1960) 'The room' in *Intimacy* London: Panther
——(1958) *Being and Nothingness* London: Methuen
——(1965) *Nausea* Harmondsworth: Penguin
——(1968) *Search for a Method* New York: Vintage Books
——(1971–72) *L'idiot de la famille* Paris: Gallimard
——(1976) *Critique of Dialectical Reason. I. Theory of Practical Ensembles* London: New Left Books
Sayre, A. (1975) *Rosalind Franklin and DNA* New York: Norton
Schlegel, A. ed. (1977) *Sexual Stratification* New York: Columbia University Press
Schweitzer, A. (1911) *J.S. Bach* London: Black
Sharp, R. (1980) *Knowledge, Ideology and the Politics of Schooling* London: Routledge and Kegan Paul
Sklar, H. ed. (1980) *Trilateralism* Boston: South End Press
Sorel, G. (1961 [1906]) *Reflections on Violence* New York: Collier
Stacey, M. (1982) 'Social sciences and the state: Fighting like a woman' *Sociology* 16, 3, pp.406–21
Stoller, R.J. (1968) *Sex and Gender: On the development of masculinity and femininity* vol. I London: Hogarth
——(1976) *Sex and Gender: The transsexual experiment* vol. II New York: Aronson
Stone, K. (1974) 'The origins of job structures in the steel industry' *Review of Radical Political Economics* 6, 2, pp.113–173
Stopes, M. (1933 [1918]) *Married Love* 21st edn London: Putnam
Stretton, H. (1976) *Capitalism, Socialism and the Environment* Cambridge: Cambridge University Press
Szasz, T. (1972) *The Myth of Mental Illness* London: Paladin
Tatz, C. (1982) 'The corruption of sport' *Current Affairs Bulletin* 59, 4, pp.4–16
Taylor, S. de B. (1971) *The Chorale Preludes of J.S. Bach* London: Hinrichsen Edition
Teilhard de Chardin, P. (1959) *The Phenomenon of Man* New York: Harper
Terray, E. (1972) *Marxism and 'Primitive' Societies* New York: Monthly Review
Thompson, E.P. (1968) *The Making of the English Working Class* 2nd edn Harmondsworth: Penguin
——(1978) *The Poverty of Theory, and Other Essays* London: Merlin
——(1980) 'Notes on exterminism, the last stage of civilization' *New Left Review* 121, pp.3–31

Tolson, A. (1977) *The Limits of Masculinity* London: Tavistock
Trainor, B. (1977) 'Epistemology, the state and welfare' *Arena* 47–48, pp.146–62
Tripp, C.A. (1977) *The Homosexual Matrix* London: Quartet
Urry, J. (1970) 'Role analysis and the sociological enterprise' *Sociological Review* 18, pp.351–64
Wachtel, H.M. (1980) 'A decade of international debt' *Theory and Society* 9, pp.504–18
Waddell, H. (1954) *The Wandering Scholars* 6th edn Harmondsworth: Penguin
Wallerstein, I. (1974) *The Modern World-System: Capitalist agriculture and the origins of the European world-economy in the sixteenth century* New York: Academic Press
——(1975) 'Class formation in the capitalist world-economy' *Politics and Society* 5, pp.367–75, reprinted in (1979) *The Capitalist World-Economy* Cambridge: Cambridge University Press, pp.222–30
——(1979) *The Capitalist World-Economy* Cambridge: Cambridge University Press and Editions de la Maison des Sciences de L'Homme
Weber, M. (1958) *From Max Weber* New York: Galaxy
Weeks, J. (1977) *Coming Out: Homosexual politics in Britain, from the nineteenth century to the present* London: Quartet
West, J. (1978) 'Women, sex and class' in A. Kuhn and A. Wolpe eds *Feminism and Materialism* London: Routledge and Kegan Paul
West, R. (1972) *River of Tears* London: Earth Island
Wheelwright, E.L. (1974) *Radical Political Economy* Sydney: Australia and New Zealand Book Company
Whyte, W.F. (1955) *Street Corner Society: The social structure of an Italian slum* enlarged edn Chicago: University of Chicago Press
Wilden, A. ed. (1968) *The Language of the Self* Baltimore: Johns Hopkins University Press
Williams, C. (1981) *Open Cut* Sydney: Allen and Unwin
Willis, P. (1977) *Learning to Labour: How working class kids get working class jobs* Farnborough: Saxon House
——(1978) *Profane Culture* London: Routledge and Kegan Paul
——(1981) 'Cultural production is different from cultural reproduction is different from social reproduction is different from reproduction' *Interchange* 12, 2–3, pp.48–67
Windschuttle, E. ed. (1980) *Women, Class and History* Fontana [no place]
Winship, J. (1978) 'A woman's world: *Woman*—an ideology of femininity' in Centre for Contemporary Cultural Studies, Women's Studies Group *Women Take Issue* London: Hutchinson, pp.133–54
Wollstonecraft, M. (1975 [1792] *Vindication of the Rights of Woman* Harmondsworth: Penguin
Wright, E.O. (1976) 'Class boundaries in advanced capitalist societies' *New Left Review* 98 pp.3–41
Wrong, D. (1961) 'The oversocialized conception of man in modern sociology' *American Sociological Review* 26, pp. 183–93
Young, K. (1978) 'Modes of appropriation and the sexual division of labour:

A case study from Oaxaca, Mexico' in A. Kuhn and A. Wolpe *Feminism and Materialism* London: Routledge and Kegan Paul, pp.124–54
Ziller, A. (1980) *Affirmative Action Handbook* Sydney: Review of New South Wales Government Administration

Name index

Johnson, V., 200
Jones, E., 4, 233
Joyce, J., 216
Jung, C.G., 5, 7
Jungk, R., 179

Kando, T.M., 192
Kant, I., 240
Keller, S., 88, 192
Kessler, S., ix, 17, 71, 245
Kimmel, D.C., 199
Kinsey, A.C., 77
Klima, B., 34
Koestler, A., 176
Kollontai, A.M., 48, 53
Komarovsky, M., 191
Konrád, G., 235
Korda, M., 31
Krafft-Ebing, R. von, 52
Krauss, I., 85
Kropotkin, P., 11
Kuhn, A., 35, 64
Kuhn, T.S., 241

Lacan, J., 3, 14, 27, 55, 151, 249
Laclau, E., 109, 116, 128
Laing, R.D., 13, 66, 159
Lang, T., 240
Laplanche, J., 60
Lazarsfeld, P.F., 83
Lee, J., 248
Lefebvre, H., 46, 142-54, 159, 185
Lenin, V.I., 94, 102-3, 106, 108, 110, 113, 118
Lenski, G.E., 87-8, 96
Lévi-Strauss, C., 55, 63, 89, 98, 109
Light, D.J., 192
Linton, R., 190, 195
Lippert, J., 173
Lowe, J., 192
Lowry, L.S., 30
Ludwig, D.K., 181
Luther, M., 209, 214, 217, 218, 220

McDonough, R., 35
McIntosh, M., 37, 47
McRobbie, A., 222, 225, 227
Macciocchi, M.A., 43
Mallet, S., 101, 115, 244
Manne, R., 251
Mao Tse-tung, 102
Marcuse, H., 3, 4, 11-12, 13, 46, 62, 73, 77, 129, 152, 157, 159-61, 175, 202, 206

Marx, K., 15, 92-7, 102-10 passim, 117, 126, 131, 134, 135, 163, 164, 165, 196, 233, 241
Maslow, A., 158
Mead, G.H., 11, 189
Meillassoux, C., 55
Merton, R.K., 127, 131
Mill, J.S., 51, 52, 54
Millett, K., 58
Miner, J.B., 192
Mitchell, J., 4, 12, 31, 40, 55, 56, 57, 63, 73, 148, 202
Molyneux, M., 35, 36, 63
Morris, B., 206
Morris, W., 142

Nadel, S.F., 191, 197-8
Negri, A., 185-6
Norman, J., 240

Oakley, A., 57
Osborn, R., 15
Ossowski, S., 91
Owen, R., 52

Paine, T., 48, 141
Parkin, F., 85
Parsons, T., 87, 106, 114, 131, 156, 191, 195, 197
Pearson, K., 240
Pericot, L., 34
Pfohl, S.J., 190, 196, 203
Piaget, J., 90, 98, 109, 150
Pickvance, G.C., 128, 132
Piercy, M., 247
Plummer, K., 76, 173
Plunkett, M., 179
Polanyi, M., 240
Popitz, H., 191
Popper, K., 240, 250
Poster, M., 67
Poulantzas, N., 91, 92, 99-101, 106, 108-136, 228
Pringle, R., 42, 61, 77, 245

Ram, K., 173, 184
Rapoport, R., 205
Ray, J.J., 251
Reagan, R., 176, 178
Reich, W., 73, 77, 142, 144, 152, 157, 159
Reiche, R., 48
Reik, T., 205
Reiter, R.R., 61

Subject index